"The race to be out with the first *serious* book on Jimmy Carter appears to have been won by Martin Schram."

—*New York* Magazine

Even though Jimmy Carter and his men were doing so many things right, the nomination might have gone elsewhere . . .

IF Udall's important phone call hadn't been 45 minutes too late

IF Jackson had seen Pennsylvania early on as his big confrontation with Carter, and had planned and organized and spent there accordingly

IF Hubert Humphrey had made a real run early, instead of just sitting on Capitol Hill assessing and reassessing and re-reassessing

IF the liberals had gotten behind one man from the start, rather than siphoning votes from one another

IF . . .
And it all might have been different. But it wasn't!

> "Skill and luck—they're both key parts of the political process. And in 1976 we had the best of both."
>
> —*Carter's aide, Pat Caddell*

Running for President

A Journal of the Carter Campaign

by Martin Schram

Based on reporting by Martin Schram, *Newsday*
Washington Bureau Chief, assisted by
Newsday Washington correspondents
Myron S. Waldman and Jean Heller

PUBLISHED BY POCKET BOOKS NEW YORK

RUNNING FOR PRESIDENT:
A Journal of the Carter Campaign

POCKET BOOK edition published October, 1976

Portions of this material originally appeared in *Newsday,*
the Long Island newspaper.

This original POCKET BOOK edition is printed from brand-new
plates made from newly set, clear, easy-to-read type.
POCKET BOOK editions are published by
POCKET BOOKS,
a division of Simon & Schuster, Inc.,
A GULF+WESTERN COMPANY
630 Fifth Avenue,
New York, N.Y. 10020.
Trademarks registered in the United States
and other countries.

FOR PAT
AND KENNETH AND DAVID

Acknowledgments

The story of Jimmy Carter's rise from semi-obscurity as an ex-governor of Georgia to the forefront of American politics is also, in part, the story of the many others who sought the Democratic Party's presidential nomination in 1976 and failed. How and why Jimmy Carter made it must be understood in the context of how and why Scoop Jackson and Mo Udall and Birch Bayh and George Wallace and Frank Church and Jerry Brown and all the rest did *not* make it. The story unfolded over many months, in events that occurred in many places across the country; and it could not have been covered fully by one person alone. Most of the major newspapers began covering the 1976 presidential campaign well before the first vote was counted in the caucuses in Iowa in January, and *Newsday* was no exception.

Newsday Washington correspondent Myron S. Waldman, one of the capital's most aggressive political reporters, is known not only for being savvy, but also for being well prepared. So it was that before leaving to report on the Iowa caucuses, he moved to fortify himself against the blizzards that often grip the heartland and discourage reporters from attempting farm-to-farm interviews. He stopped off at a discount warehouse in Washington, D.C. and bought a surplus World War II coat last worn by a British civil-disaster warden during the blitz. It was dark blue and double-breasted, with gold buttons each stamped with the royal crown; it fell to nearly floor length, was as thick as an Army-issue mattress, and cost thirty-nine dollars.

Acknowledgments

Thus prepared, Waldman went to the Midwest and covered the year's first political contest with his usual dedication, clarity, and attention to detail, undaunted by the fact that Iowa was experiencing a relatively mild and often snowless January. Throughout the campaign of 1976, Waldman kept aggressive and insightful watch over the efforts of a number of Democrats who sought the nomination that eventually went to Carter. His reporting contributions were invaluable to the making of this book.

Jean Heller is an award-winning investigative reporter who, over the years, has exposed inhuman syphilis experimentation on black men in Alabama and has recorded the dealings of major oil companies during America's energy crises. She reports on matters of national politics with equal skill. As a *Newsday* Washington correspondent, she spent most of the 1976 primary season covering one subject: the financing of the year's presidential campaigns. Time and again Heller was out in front in reporting on where the candidates were getting their funds from and in spotting money problems that eventually proved fatal to several of the candidates' campaigns. Her work was an important part of the reporting of this book.

David Laventhol, editor of *Newsday*, was instrumental in shaping the series on the campaign that originally appeared in *Newsday*. The long hours he spent reading and editing the series that became the basis for this book, and the advice he offered, were very much appreciated. Donald Forst, managing editor of *Newsday*, was responsible for seeing to it that the newspaper series could indeed be expanded into a book. His efforts and counsel were very welcome. I am also indebted to them both for the freedom they gave me to pursue this work.

Pat Golbitz, senior editor of Simon and Schuster's POCKET BOOKS division, was my editor on this project, and I am especially grateful for the many suggestions she made.

Jim Toedtman and Jim Klurfeld of *Newsday*'s Washington bureau helped me plug some last-minute holes.

I also want to thank Sharon Donnelly, who saw to it that *Newsday*'s Washington Bureau continued to function while I was immersed in this undertaking; Susan Drake and Catherine Wood, who helped research campaign facts; and Viola Banks, who typed the finished manuscript.

Acknowledgments

And finally, I want to thank the many staff members and advisors and associates of those who campaigned for the presidency—and the candidates themselves—for letting us all get a glimpse of what it was like to be running for President in 1976.

—MARTIN SCHRAM

Washington, D.C.
August 31, 1976

Contents

June 9/Plains

Jimmy Carter was wading through the people of Plains.

A hug here, a kiss there, a slap on the back, a handshake. It was 2:15 A.M. and the June 9 sky was black; yet several hundred people were acting as if it were midafternoon as they cheered and greeted the fifty-one-year-old hometown boy who had just finished his campaigning in the last of the primaries of 1976 with a big win in Ohio and second-place showings in New Jersey and California.

Suddenly someone pressed a piece of paper into Carter's palm. He glanced at the paper, mumbled apologies, then pushed through the crowd and headed for the old wooden train depot that had been painted white and converted into a campaign headquarters.

Inside, he glanced again at the paper. It was a telephone message slip.

CALLER: Gov. George Wallace.

MESSAGE: He has something to tell you.

There was a telephone number and a notation that the phone was beside Wallace's bed and that Carter should call regardless of the hour.

For a moment Carter was puzzled. He had already spoken to Wallace earlier in the day as part of a round of courtesy calls he had made to the other candidates. Inside the depot office, Carter went toward a telephone which, according to the note taped to it, was for his personal use. But a reporter was using the phone. Quietly Carter walked past the reporter and up a few steps to a row of telephones separated by shoulder-high wood partitions covered with gunnysacks. He entered the first makeshift booth on the left. His mother, seventy-seven-year-old Lillian Carter ("Don't call me Mrs. Carter . . . everyone calls me Miss Lillian"), followed him.

Carter dialed the number and the phone rang at Wallace's bedside. "He said he had been watching on television that night when I said I was proud to be a southerner," Carter recalled. "And then he said if I had no objection, he would endorse me the following day."

This was the moment when Carter knew at last—without a doubt—that the first ballot was his. He could not be stopped. He had talked so confidently for so long about how he knew he was going to win, but now it was not faith but fact. There would be no last hurrah in Madison Square Garden for George Wallace; he would be releasing his 171 convention delegates and pushing them to Carter instead.

Understandably, Carter told Wallace he had no objections.

The two men talked for a while longer. "He said that the only thing he wanted of me was that I do the best that I could to be a great President," Carter said. "He asked me if I would find the time to come to Alabama to see him. I said I certainly can. He said, 'Can you come tomorrow?' I said 'No, I can't come tomorrow; I have a press conference, got some responsibilities here, where I have to be.'

"So he said, 'Could you come sometime this week?' and I said, 'Yes, I would like to do that because I am going on vacation—Tuesday, if possible'—and I said that I would be there before Sunday night and I'd let my staff work it out at his convenience.

"And he said, 'I am very proud of what you have done and I look forward to seeing you.' "

(Later Carter reflected on George Wallace's closing line —that Wallace was *very proud* of what Jimmy Carter had done. After all, Wallace had been privately bitter, antagonistic, and even derisive toward the self-styled New South governor from Georgia who had beaten him in Florida and trounced him in North Carolina, thus ending forever his campaign dream. It was a dream not of winning the presidential nomination, but of being accepted and respected; a dream of being known North and South as something more than the man who had stood in the schoolhouse door. Carter had shattered this, yet now Wallace was saying he was *very proud* of Carter.

("I think he meant the success of my campaign," Carter later said, his normally soft conversation voice dropping to just a whisper. "The acceptance of a southerner in such a wide geographical area and the overwhelming victory in Ohio, the sure dominance in the number of delegates as compared to the other candidates. It was a very gracious statement he made. . . . Animosity had never been expressed by him or me personally whenever I had been with him. He and I had been very cordial in our greetings to one another, as I had been with the other candidates. There had never been any estrangement, animosity.")

Carter and his mother stepped out of the gunnysack enclosure. Carter, quietly ecstatic, sought out Rex Granum, the highest-ranking aide who had bothered to make the trip to Plains from Atlanta, where an official Carter victory party was being held. He told Granum to telephone the good news to Carter's three top advisers—Hamilton Jordan, Jody Powell, and Charles Kirbo—who had remained in Atlanta. But above all, Carter cautioned, do not tell the press. It was important that Wallace not be scooped on his own announcement.

While Carter was talking to Granum, his mother had moved on and was telling a few reporters that her son had just spoken with Wallace.

3:30 A.M. Granum telephones Jody Powell's room at the Hyatt Regency in Atlanta. Powell gropes for the phone from the disadvantage of a sound sleep; he fumbles to make a few notes, sees the futility of it all, figures he will take care of it in the morning, says he is happy, and hangs up the phone. Then he makes the call he hates to make: he phones the hotel operator and has his wake-up call moved earlier, to 7:00 A.M. He will have to confer early with Hamilton Jordan. Things have moved far faster than he or anyone else in the Carter campaign had anticipated.

The morning after—really later that same Wednesday morning—Carter awoke early and made a couple of quick decisions. First, he decided he ought to let the world know that he had the Democratic presidential nomination locked up. And second, he decided that it ought not to be George Wallace alone who had put him over the top. So Carter moved to round up other blocs of delegate support. It took only two phone calls to do it.

The first, in mid-morning, was to Chicago's mayor, Richard J. Daley, who controlled 86 Illinois delegates. The call was not unprecedented; Carter had kept in careful touch with Daley throughout the year, calling him regularly every ten days or so. Like courting the banker's chubby daughter, the wooing of Mayor Daley made sense even if it was not strictly an affair of the heart.

"I would say that I called him about every ten days or two weeks," Carter recalled. "You know, quite often we would call his office, at his suggestion and my commitment, and he would not be in and we would just leave word with the staff members that I had called. Sometimes later he would call me back. But I had done this with him and with Senator [Adlai] Stevenson [Daley's favorite son candidate] . . . just as a matter of courtesy, to let them know directly from me how the campaign was going and that I was not a high-pressure person. I never did ask them to do anything specific for me. I just let them know that I needed their support, friendship, and later on I hoped that I would have their endorsements."

Carter had thought for weeks that the Daley-controlled delegates would eventually be his. "Well, I have always thought—through my own analysis, not through any statement of his—that after I did so well in Illinois [winning the preference primary and delegates as well] he would be looking for someone, if there weren't obstacles in his effort, who could do well as the head of the ticket [Daley's Illinois Democratic ticket]. I had shown in my campaign my ability to get votes in his state. So that gave me a kind of a feeling of confidence—not of surety, but of confidence, although that is not something he had expressed to me. I kind of analyzed that myself."

As he dialed that call from Plains to Chicago on the morning of Wednesday, June 9, however, Carter had more reason to be confident than just his own analysis. The night before, Daley had told Chicago reporters that Carter deserved to win the nomination if he won Ohio big (which Carter had then proceeded to do). Now, on that Wednesday morning, the ex-Georgia governor gave the current Chicago mayor a kind of soft-touch hard sell.

"He had never made any definite commitments to me and he had told me earlier that he was not going to make any public commitment until much later," Carter said. "And when I called him Wednesday morning, I told him that I didn't want to put any pressure on him, that I didn't want him to think I would feel aggressive about it, but that I *particularly* would like to have his public statement of support that day."

He got it.

There remained one more call for Carter to make—to the Washington office of Senator Henry (Scoop) Jackson, a man whose presidential hopes Carter had dashed in the Pennsylvania primary, a man who had once attacked Carter bitterly early in the primary season but who had since warmed to Carter. A man who had 248 delegates pledged to him.

Carter had spoken to Jackson several times since the veteran Washington senator had dropped out of the campaign. Jackson, he knew, was leaning toward Carter but wanted to talk to his delegates first; he did not want to be embarrassed by having his own delegates spurn his choice. Carter asked for an endorsement.

"He said that he didn't want me to announce his endorsement," Carter recalled. "That he was going to wait until the following week to make that kind of a statement."

But Carter pressed—politely—for something stronger. Jackson finally agreed. "He told me that I could tell the news media that I had had a favorable conversation with him and that I was sure that I would have his support and the support of his delegates—if I didn't quote him on that. So I was very careful to honor that."

Wallace plus Daley plus Jackson. They would officially put Carter over the top, and now all he had to do was to make their commitments public. A group of national political reporters was waiting down by the depot, a few blocks from Carter's sprawling home nestled in the trees at 1 Woodland Drive. He wanted to tell them personally about the phone calls, but first he had to attend to one detail: the

5

selection of his press conference attire. Carter chose denim
—freshly pressed blue jeans and a matching jacket. A careful choice aimed at showing that he was no standard establishment candidate.

"The people kind of have an inclination to knock down
the frontrunner," Carter said later. "Whenever we'd project
ourselves as the underdog fighting the establishment . . .
fighting a valiant battle, we did all right. . . . I figured after
Wallace, Daley, and Jackson endorsed me, I'd better . . . so
I took off my clothes and put my blue jeans on. I generally
wear those around Plains, but that was one reason I did it."

January 19/Iowa

"The first time we went to Des Moines, we had a reception at a hotel," Carter recalled. "There were Jody and myself and the man and woman who arranged the reception —and I think that there were three other people. We had enough food there to feed, I guess, 200 folks. So everybody was embarrassed, and somebody finally suggested that 'Governor, why don't you walk down the street . . . and at least you can shake hands with the folks in the courthouse.' "

Jimmy Carter, who became the most sought-after man in the Democratic Party, began to smile as he noted that at least there had been no danger back in February 1975 of the dismal turnout's coming to the attention of the public. "Well," he said, "there weren't any newspeople there to cover the event.

"In a way, it taught us a lesson. I don't like to be a dormant candidate. I don't like to sit in a hotel and have people come to me. I like to go out and meet them.

"The biggest problem I had was not campaign technique, or that I was from the South, or that I had not been in Washington, or that I didn't have any money, that I didn't have a good campaign organization—the problem I had was substantiality of campaign efforts in the minds of the people. Nobody thought I should be taken seriously. And we couldn't take any shortcuts to resolving it except to do better than we were expected to do in two or three of the states.

"We decided early on New Hampshire and Florida; later, we saw that Iowa was a good chance. There are only about

35,000 Democrats there who participated in the 1972 caucuses. We just saw a good chance to build that up with a major media event."

The Iowa caucuses became a major media event. Viewed in terms of the number of participants, the caucuses were insignificant—small clusters of people meeting in Legion halls, living rooms, and basement rec rooms. People raising their hands for the candidates they favored in precinct caucuses that would be followed by conventions that eventually selected only 47 of the 3,008 delegates that would vote at Madison Square Garden in July.

But the Iowa caucuses, held on January 19, were Number 1—the first political happening of the election year. So they would be watched carefully and covered heavily by the news media. A good showing could create an initial image that might project a presidential candidate into the lead.

As it turned out, the Iowa caucuses provided a study in miniature of what was in store for the 1976 campaign for the Democratic presidential nomination. The essential factors that would loom so large elsewhere in the following months were present in the wintry campaign in Iowa.

There was Carter's success at personal, grass-roots campaigning; the skill of his advisers at molding an organization; the ability of the Carter people to pick the right moments to make the right moves. There was the example of how Carter formulated his answers to win widespread acceptance within the party, and even the example of the occasional verbal slip—Carter's comment that he favored a "national statute" to limit abortion.

And there also was the hesitation by some of the other candidates and the lack of foresight and breakdown of the organizations of others. All of these factors would become apparent time and again during the primary elections throughout the spring; and all were apparent in the Iowa campaign.

＊ ＊ ＊

Once, while driving between Ames and Marshalltown, Carter stopped to do a bit of person-to-person campaigning at Fred McClain's farm. McClain wasn't home. So Carter wrote a note, telling McClain that he was sorry he had missed him and that he had a "beautiful farm." He signed the note "Jimmy" and stuck it on McClain's front door.

🏴 🏴 🏴

Charles Hammer is a theoretical physicist at Iowa State University. He lives with his wife, Hazel, off-campus at Ames. He also is the Fifth Congressional District chairman and a liberal who worked hard for Eugene McCarthy and George McGovern. He briefly had met Carter and his wife, Rosalynn, and after watching Carter answer tough questions in a town called Atlantic, Hammer told a Carter staff member that the former Georgia governor had made a good impression. He also cautioned that Carter should drop his trademark line, "I will not tell a lie." Said Hammer, "That stuff sets him up."

A few days later, Hammer got a phone call. "This is Jimmy Carter," said the caller. "I'd like you to be on the state campaign committee." Hammer was frank. He said he wanted to examine Carter's positions in greater detail first. Carter suggested that Hammer call him back in two weeks and gave him a phone number, a date, and a time—4:00 P.M.

When Hammer called to announce he was joining the Carter campaign, he was surprised to discover that he was phoning the Carter home in Plains, Georgia, and was surprised that Mrs. Carter answered the phone herself.

"Hi, Charlie. How's Hazel?" Mrs. Carter asked.

Hammer, more surprised, told her he was going to be on Carter's state committee. They got to talking, and Rosalynn mentioned that at a reception back in Iowa Hazel Hammer had said that her brother had the same birthday as Rosalynn. Now, Rosalynn asked for the brother's name (Harry Mills) and his address (in Michigan). Even though there was no immediate need to win a friend in Michigan, Rosalynn wrote a note to Mills—only to discover she had lost his address So Rosalynn telephoned Hazel, got the address again, and mailed the letter.

🏴 🏴 🏴

Tim Kraft arrived in Des Moines in 1975 with a list of politically active Iowa Democrats in his hand. His assignment: to put together a Carter organization in the first caucus state. He had met Carter in 1974, when the Georgia governor had swung through New Mexico and Kraft was working on the successful gubernatorial campaign of Jerry Apodaca. Early in 1975, Kraft volunteered to work for Carter, and he was hired by Hamilton Jordan, Carter's campaign director.

At the time, polls showed that Carter had a national recognition factor that hovered around 2 percent. A standard organizing tactic in political campaigns is to get a big name to head the statewide campaign. But Carter was so unknown, Kraft and Jordan reasoned, that it could be dangerous to have the Iowa campaign headed by a local political figure. Carter could be perceived as a liberal if his chairman were a popular liberal, or a conservative if his chairman were conservative.

So Kraft set out to put together a twenty-person Iowa Carter for President Steering Committee that scattered across the state geographically and ideologically. Because this was a working committee, it in effect gave Carter a quick twenty field offices.

That was the core of the Carter organization: twenty people throughout the state, each recruiting volunteers to work for Carter. Probably the most influential member of the steering committee was Soapy Owens, a former state president of the United Auto Workers who carried the Carter campaign into union halls and meeting rooms at a time when Carter was not perceived as being a union man. Owens had been the subject of some of that special Carter wooing. Carter had called him. Rosalynn had called him. By the time Kraft stopped by Owens' house in Newton (a spur-of-the-moment decision; Kraft was just driving through the area), Owens was about ready to sign on. He told Kraft he was just heading out on a fishing trip, but would "get involved"—he didn't say how—when he got back. Kraft told Carter to give Owens one more call. Carter did, and two weeks later, on October 4, Owens gave a ringing twenty-minute endorsement of Carter before the UAW Community Action Program meeting of 200 union activists in Marshalltown.

When Carter aides began looking for a suitable event to launch Carter's entry into Iowa, they cast throughout the state in search of speaking invitations and came up with just one: a February 26, 1975, banquet in Le Mars (population 8,895), twenty-five miles north of Sioux City, honoring Marie Jahn, whose thirty-eight years as Plymouth County recorder was the longest term that any woman had served in public office in that state. Nearly blind, she was retiring. Carter's appearance at her banquet—eleven months before the January 19, 1976, caucuses—came on the first of twenty-one days that he was to spend campaigning in Iowa.

▬ ▬ ▬

There was a time, Carter's press secretary and confidant Jody Powell recalls, that various Iowa politicians—"people like Tom Whitney," the young state Democratic chairman —were offering Carter people some early advice: "Stay out. It's not Jimmy's kind of state."

One of the first things Carter did when he came into Iowa in February 1975 was to set up a breakfast meeting with state party chairman Whitney. The breakfast was set for the Savery Hotel in Des Moines, one of the older hostelries of that city. Whitney, not knowing Carter's penchant for punctuality and his impatience with those who do not share same, arrived for breakfast a half hour late.

They talked about what it would take to become President. Said Whitney: "He [Carter] said there was a real need in America for a candidate who would respond to the kind of doubts people have not only about government but about themselves and where they are going. The quality that was most important [according to Carter] was believability—not in terms of a single issue but in terms of human life."

Even then Carter seemed confident that he would win. "I did not believe he was self-deluding," Whitney said. Carter told Whitney to watch him on a local television program. Whitney did. "He was probably the best TV figure, excluding Ted Kennedy, since John Kennedy," Whitney said. "I realized that, in fact, he is an ideal TV candidate. A cool medium, a cool candidate. I wrote him a note and said I was very impressed."

Carter and Whitney met four more times after that. Whitney finally told Carter that although he would remain

11

officially neutral, he would be helpful. But it was not until Whitney sat next to Carter at the head table of a lengthy Iowa fundraiser that he became deeply impressed.

"We spent two hours talking about Christ," Whitney said. "For a moment we shared a concept and a thought process that we both believed is a fundamental need in our society. Which was the concept of love—love thy neighbor. We explored the 'I Am Third' process in which God is first, family and friends second, and I am third. This nation needs a totally loving President."

Whitney says that after Carter learned that a woman active in the Iowa Democratic Party had a son who was an alcoholic and who had been hospitalized as a result, he "made a telephone call to him in the hospital, relating in a very personal way his own witness to personal difficulties in his own life."

"That quality within him ought not to be viewed cynically," Whitney said. "He's got a lot of quality and style—a lot of style. Most people feel perhaps on occasion he tells them less than the whole truth. But they want to believe."

He also remembers another of Carter's personal touches. "He always sent handwritten notes. Initially, at least, he wrote them all himself. Who knows how many he's written? The most important thing is handwritten notes. He wrote them to anyone. He'd get all the names at the meetings he'd go to [Jody Powell usually followed his boss around, noting names and addresses of people Carter met at gatherings]. And he'd write them. They might all have been the same note, but you don't get that from your congressman or senators. It was just class."

The Carter campaign in Iowa was not without its problems. There was, for example, the trip Carter made into blizzard-swept Iowa on January 1, 1976, with his new personal aide, Greg Schneiders, who eventually grew in the job from being a sort of traveling administrative aide to being an adviser of influence as well. Schneiders started out by losing his trenchcoat in the Atlanta airport; the candidate started out by boarding the plane with a 103-degree fever. They stepped off the plane in Iowa and into a minus

45-degree wind-chill factor—"Me with no coat, him with some kind of bad intestinal bug," Schneiders recalled. "What a way to break into a job!"

And there was the more serious problem of Carter's statement on abortion.

He had been interviewed on the telephone by a priest who wrote for Catholic publications. Carter had stated that he personally opposed abortion, but that he also opposed the proposed antiabortion amendment to the U.S. Constitution. The resulting article quoted him on this. But the interviewer had pressed him, and Carter was also quoted as saying that he would support some sort of "national statute" that might, in some unspecified way, restrict abortion.

Carter's opponents charged that he intentionally was clouding his position on the controversial issue, that he was trying to find a position that would seem more popular with the right-to-life people than the other candidates'—all of whom opposed unequivocally an antiabortion amendment.

Carter's abortion problems were further fueled by Rowland Evans and Robert Novak, syndicated columnists who were throughout the campaign among the Georgian's harshest critics. The column talked about "a recent whispered conversation in the basement of the Holy Spirit Church" in Creston, Iowa. Carter had said in a question-and-answer session that he considered abortion "morally wrong" but would not support a constitutional antiabortion amendment. But Evans and Novak said that Carter later told a woman in a conversation—speaking "even more softly than usual," the columnists said—that "under circumstances I would" support a constitutional amendment along the lines of the abortion ban that had been passed in Georgia and was struck down by the U.S. Supreme Court.

Carter finally issued a statement to clarify his position, which, among other things, said: "The confusion in Iowa did not originate because of any change of position of my own. I've had a very consistent position on abortion for several years. I think that abortion is wrong. I don't think the government should do anything to encourage abortion. I believe that positive action should be taken in better education, better family-planning programs, the availability of contraceptive devices for those who believe in their use, better adoption procedures to minimize abortions.

"I do not favor the constitutional amendment that would

13

prohibit all abortions. I do not favor the constitutional amendment that would give the states local option."

With that, Carter attempted to put to rest the controversy on the abortion issue. But a larger, more ominous problem had been born. Comedian Pat Paulsen would describe it by telling audiences how officials had wanted to put Jimmy Carter on Mount Rushmore, "but they didn't have room for two faces."

The image would remain throughout the campaign.

They were lonely days, those early Iowa days. Carter had no press corps to watch him and at times no staff members to aid him. There were days when he would get up with the sun and hurry out to a small rural airstrip in the stillness of early morning to get a lift in a tiny private plane to another town for another day of handshakes and speech-making, another day of having to make the rounds, introducing himself to unfamiliar Iowans and telling them what he was doing there and what he was all about. "Hello. I'm Jimmy Carter. I'm running for President. I'd appreciate your support."

On occasion, he had the luxury of two staff members to assist him; and there were times when he was torn between his desire for staff companionship and his penchant for punctuality. One morning Carter and his two aides, Jody Powell and Greg Schneiders, arrived at the airstrip for an early departure. Carter and Schneiders boarded the plane, a small Beechcraft; the engines revved and the plane had begun to taxi down the runway when Schneiders reminded the governor that Powell was not on board. Schneiders had the pilot radio the terminal and learned that Powell was inside using a telephone. Seconds later Powell came racing out of the terminal; he ran down the runway, caught up with the idling plane, and climbed on board. Carter, who had been willing to take off without his press secretary, said: "Jody, you've got one friend on this airplane—and it ain't me."

Meanwhile, the other Democratic candidates also were trying to capture the Iowa caucuses. Morris Udall came in early. Birch Bayh came in late. Fred Harris, Sargent Shriver, and Henry Jackson had cranked up in between. But none was able to put together an organization as effective as Carter's. The Georgian's twenty-person steering committee was working well and providing a statewide network of field offices.

Take the case of Morris Udall. He was the first candidate to announce for the Presidency. He had gotten into Iowa early, invested heavily in the state in both campaign time and money, and—like Carter—had sought to build the sort of organization nationally and in Iowa that would give him a head start on the field and would carry him to the White House.

But the Udall campaign proved to be a classic example of how not to begin.

▆ ▆ ▆

Memorandum

To: Mo, Stewart [Morris and Stewart Udall]
From: Jack Quinn [Udall's national campaign manager]
December 9, 1975
Re: Areas of Immediate Concern

. . . We've got a reputation, frankly, as the sloppiest campaign in memory. No one knows who is in charge, who can make a quick decision that will stick.

. . . Moreover, we're genuinely in danger of splitting this campaign into warring factions—anyone who disagrees should give Mankiewicz a call and ask him what happened in 1972 to a campaign which was hopelessly split among headquarters and congressional staff. . . .

. . . I've had my role defined by Mo several times. Unfortunately, it needs to be done again. Ditto for Terry Bracy. Those roles **must** be clear and concrete. They cannot overlap. . . .

Budget

Of chief concern to me in this regard is the **process**. . . . I think that on a day to day basis we're a disaster.

Stewart calls [Stanley] Kurz. I call Kurz. Coyle calls Kurz. Terry calls Kurz. Jo Baer takes a staff member off the payroll and Stan decides on his own to pay her. This is insanity. . . .

       📰   📰   📰

In June 1975 one of Udall's Iowa co-chairpersons, Cliff Larsen, received a master list from the Democratic state committee of people who had attended Democratic caucuses. It was not a "clean" list; there was repetition of names due to people who attended caucuses at various levels (precinct, county, congressional districts). Larsen broke up the list and sent portions of it around the state to various politicians so it could be cleaned up, scrubbed of repetition.

Then on December 23, Ken Levine was dispatched to Iowa by the national Udall staff and he reported back that things were not well in Iowa. He discovered that 80 percent of that master list had disappeared. No one knew where it was. Twenty-four thousand Democratic households were at stake. They resurrected one of the old, "dirty" master lists, and set about trying to use it—repetition and all. "The list we got in June was in the same shape by Christmas," one Udall worker complained.

       📰   📰   📰

In Polk County, which includes Des Moines and which has 10.6 percent of the state Democratic vote, the Udall coordinator was a young man making his first venture into politics. When Ken Levine arrived from Washington on December 23, he found the young Udall coordinator hard at work, trying to call by himself every name on a list of every registered voter in the county—Democrat and Republican—to tell them to go to the caucuses and vote for Udall.

In one corner of the room, unused and gathering dust, was the Polk County list of active Democrats who had previously attended caucuses—the list of people who had shown they were active and interested and would most likely attend the caucuses this year.

Levine went back to Washington and told Udall to forget Iowa. Rick Stearns, who achieved political fame as the young mastermind of the McGovern delegate hunt in 1972, also scouted Iowa for Udall and told the candidate much the same. But others came back with higher hopes. Ken Bode, a Udall man, conferred with Iowa State Democratic Chairman Tom Whitney (who was a closet Carter supporter trying to remain publicly neutral). Whitney told Bode that Udall might be able to take the state with a big media blitz. And Bode recommended to Udall that he make the effort.

The effort was made, but the problems continued. There were those on the Udall staff who had devised the television spots and who liked them; but there were others who thought the spots were terrible. They consisted of a headshot of the candidate against a stark background, the candidate talking to the people at home—talking too fast, some thought.

Staff bickering continued. Norma Matthews, the other Udall co-chairperson in Iowa, set up an event for Sunday at 8:00 P.M. and no television stations showed up to cover; she set up a press conference at 7:30 A.M. Monday and the TV people again did not show. This made Ken Levine mad. Some felt Levine had taken to poor-mouthing Iowans. He eventually left the campaign—some said he was dismissed —after he shouted across a street at Norma Matthews, "You son-of-a-bitch!" Asked about this, Levine said: "I yelled at everybody in Iowa. They let that mailing list lie for six months. No one showed up for that 7:30 A.M. press conference." He said he left the campaign by mutual consent.

≣   ≣   ≣

While Udall and Carter had announced their candidacies and gotten an early jump in Iowa, Birch Bayh—an early favorite among a number of pols—was in Washington, thinking about whether he really would run. "He kept thinking and thinking about it," said Bill Wise, Bayh's press secretary. "I recall writing him a memo saying you've got to stop talking about it, thinking about it. Either do it or don't.

"He was out of town, I sent the memo to his home. He had made up his mind to do it just before he got the memo. Did he perceive Carter as a threat? Not really, not seriously. We saw Carter as perhaps knocking over Jackson, as a candidate of the right."

On October 22, Birch Bayh formally entered the race.

"We were aware of the early time he [Carter] was putting in," Wise said. "Our first target was Udall. We felt we had to blunt Udall. He was the more formidable of the candidates on the left. The quicker we could knock Udall out, the quicker we'd get Udall people in [Bayh's corner]. We thought our weakest area was the liberal activists. . . .

"We thought the early primaries would be a holding action. We misjudged what we had to do in order for it to be a holding action. We felt we had to get into Iowa. We felt that Udall was strong in New Hampshire, that he had the best organization. We felt we had to beat Udall in Iowa to stop him from having a head of steam into New Hampshire. . . . But when we got into Iowa, everyone was saying it was a Carter–Bayh race (not a Udall–Bayh race). Bayh himself started to say that. We began to get sucked in."

▬   ▬   ▬

While Udall was suffering from organizational unraveling, and while Bayh was having trouble getting it together in the first place (he never did), the Carter machine pulled off what all camps now concede was the major strategic move in the Iowa fight.

"That silly poll in Iowa" is the way Morris Udall referred to the move much later. He was sitting in his Capitol Hill office, reflecting on what might have been, and what actually was.

"People say it was a conservative year, an anti-Washington year," Udall said in an interview after the campaign. "But with just a few breaks I could have been sitting in [Carter's place] and the people would have said this was a liberal year. There were mechanical things, accidental things, failures of strategy. Carter had a brilliant strategy [running everywhere]." And yet, Udall said, it might not have worked without that "incredible flow of press starting with that silly poll in Iowa."

Udall was talking about a straw poll at a Jefferson–Jackson Day fundraising dinner held in Ames on October 25, 1975, and attended by 4,000 people.

The poll was taken by the *Des Moines Register,* which conducts straw polls at many statewide political events, according to city editor Lawrence Paul. People attending Republican Lincoln Day dinners and Democratic Jefferson–Jackson Day dinners had been polled in the past on a variety of topical questions. Logically, the question in the Ames poll would be about who people favored as President. The Carter camp had anticipated that logic.

"We figured that somebody'd take a straw poll or something like that," recalled Carter's press secretary, Jody Powell. "So it gave us a chance to do a little influencing—and also to test our organization. See if it worked. That sort of thing." It was, Powell said, Tim Kraft's idea.

"We turned on the usual paraphernalia of politics as theater," one Carter aide said. Kraft telephoned all twenty members of the Carter steering committee and they in turn worked in their districts to get people to the dinner. In the parking lot that night at Ames, a Carter brigade was hard at work. At the dinner, the steering committee's twenty members acted as floor whips, moving about the hall, persuading fellow diners to support Carter. The other candidates, meanwhile, were concentrating on winning over the audience with the rhetoric of their after-dinner speeches.

Carter won the straw poll with 23 percent of the total. No one else was even close. Hubert Humphrey, who was not even on the ballot, came second with 12; Bayh was third with 10; Shriver, Udall, and Harris were further back.

Many national political correspondents were in Ames for the big Democratic dinner—a good place to get an idea of how the first caucus state would go, they figured. They picked up the results from the Des Moines paper. Jody Powell called a couple of reporters to tip them—"on a background basis"—that the *Register* had a poll that was worth looking at.

The event produced a number of stories in the nation's major newspapers. The *New York Times* used the poll results as the basis for a story headlined: "Carter Appears to Hold a Solid Lead in Iowa as the Campaign's First Test Approaches." The straw poll was viewed as the first significant, solid evidence that Jimmy Carter had emerged from the group of semiluminaries running for the Democratic nomination.

And, in fact, the Jefferson–Jackson Day dinner poll was not just a set-up. Iowa was a caucus state—not a primary state—and caucuses are won by the candidate who is able to convince the greatest number of people to devote an evening to a political meeting where they will support him. The poll at the dinner showed that Carter had the organization that could indeed bring out large numbers of supporters.

While the Jefferson–Jackson dinner poll put the spotlight on Carter, it put the pressure on him as well. "That early straw vote had a downside," Hamilton Jordan recalled. "After that poll . . . we *had* to win Iowa."

That, in fact, is just the way the Udall people were trying to picture it. The business of presidential politics, like the business of seduction, is conducted as much with illusion as it is with reality. To be a winner, a candidate must not only perform as well as he can, but he must perform as people expect him to, as well. It is, of course, best to win. But falling short of that, the next best thing is for the loser to make it appear that the winner somehow fell short of his goal.

🏴 🏴 🏴

Confidential

To: Mo [Udall]
From: Jack Quinn
November 19, 1975
Re: Campaign Progress and Strategy (#1)

The Setting—The Competition, Press Perceptions
. . . Carter is, in my judgment, the only viable contender that you and Bayh have at this point in time. Add Jackson and Humphrey and you have the entire field. . . .

Carter looks good in Iowa. The J–J dinner poll did two things for him: (1) it lent credibility to his efforts nationwide, and (2) it raised the expectation of him in Iowa. Similarly, the Florida convention poll raises the expectation of him in that state and he foolishly predicted a Florida victory, in the traditional sense, over Wallace. I have been hyping his New Hampshire prospects as well and he is thought to be in reasonably good shape there.

The Carter effort has these goals: (1) an Iowa victory

or, at least, second place; (2) strength in New Hampshire (first place or a second to Udall or Bayh); (3) a "startling" victory over Wallace in Florida. . . . After Florida, he takes off and begins a slow drift to the right where he becomes an attractive alternative to Jackson for "God and Guns Democrats."

▬ ▬ ▬

On January 19, caucus night in Iowa, Jimmy Carter was in New York. He was there by design. He wanted to be handy to the three television network news show interviewers in the morning. Since he was there that night he also attended a fundraising affair put on by Alice Mason, a numerologist who made sure everybody contributed in multiples of "7." Then Carter returned to the Manhattan apartment of Howard Samuels, a veteran of Democratic candidacies in New York, to spend the night.

Carter was asleep by 10:30 P.M. At 3:00 A.M., his aide, Greg Schneiders, entered the bedroom and woke him, saying: "Jody's on the phone with the results from Iowa." Carter went downstairs clad only in jockey shorts (he never wears pajamas) and was told that the news was good. He thanked Jody and he thanked Tim Kraft, the New Mexico transplant who had organized the winter effort in Iowa. "Now I guess we won't have to send you to Alaska," Carter joked to Kraft.

Carter went right back to bed.

THE RESULTS: *Uncommitted, about 37 percent of the vote; Carter, 27 percent; Bayh, 13; Harris, 10; Udall, 5; Shriver, 3; Jackson, 1; others about 3 percent. Just 50,000 Iowans had gone to the caucuses. Fewer than 14,000 of them voted for Carter. In Oyster Bay, Long Island, that would not be enough votes to elect him to the Town Council. But in Iowa, it was more than any other candidate got. In the morning, he appeared on NBC's "Today" show, the CBS "Morning News," and ABC's "AM America." Jimmy Carter had popped out of the pack.*

—Carter's aide, Pat Caddell

February 24|New Hampshire

When Birch Bayh looks back at New Hampshire, he recalls the Sunday before election day, when he went to the Wayfarer Hotel outside Manchester to meet with his staff. He had gotten into the race late, but he was looking for a big finish, and so he asked his aides for a review of the plan for getting out the vote.

There was no plan.

"He couldn't believe it," recalled one man who was there. No Bayh delegates were scheduled to be at polling precincts. A frantic effort ensued. Aides went for the telephones; even Bayh began making calls. Some delegates eventually got to the polls, but not enough. Bayh finished third, well off the pace set by Jimmy Carter.

▨   ▨   ▨

When Mo Udall looks back at New Hampshire, he sees it in terms of days lost.

"I should have taken those eight days in Iowa and gone into New Hampshire," Udall said. He figured that he was picking up 1,000 votes a day near the end for every day he campaigned in New Hampshire. By that measure, Udall fell a little more than four days short in the state primary.

"It was all so close," he said. "If I had gone into New Hampshire [by ignoring Iowa] I would have won New Hampshire. Tiny little things."

▨   ▨   ▨

When Jimmy Carter looks back at New Hampshire, he sees it as a solid winter of work by family and staff. No major strategy moves, just hard work. "I would say we had far superior organizational structure to Udall and the rest in New Hampshire," he says.

"We kind of played it down—we never bragged about it—but it was there. We contacted 95 percent of the Democratic homes in New Hampshire. And it was a tedious person-to-person relationship. I went into just about all the shoe factories in New Hampshire and a lot of the Beano games. I guess if you went to the stores and restaurants and jewelry shops, coffee shops and barbershops and beauty parlors in New Hampshire and the media centers, at least it would be hard for you to find one of those places where one of my family hasn't been. Chip or Caron or Jack or Julie or Jeffrey or Annette or Sissy or Ruth or any of them."

Carter and Udall and Bayh have explanations for why New Hampshire turned out to be Jimmy Carter's state. But perhaps the biggest factor was a man who didn't run. Senator Henry Jackson's decision not to enter the race assured that the first primary contest of 1976 would be among a collection of liberals, all vying for the votes of the left, and Jimmy Carter, alone to court the center and right of this state's essentially conservative, working-class Democratic Party.

The decision was not reached with unanimity in the Jackson camp. At least one adviser made a strong case very early that this would amount to giving Carter a free pass—a victory that would very likely boost him into the frontrunner's spot early. But back in mid-1975, Jimmy Carter did not exactly look like a force to be feared, and this advice was rejected. Of greater consideration to the Jackson men at that time was that their candidate carried a loser image from his disastrous primary showings in 1972, and that he could not afford to start 1976 with a defeat.

Jackson might well not have been able to win in New Hampshire. But it is likely that he could have taken enough of the center and right votes to have permitted Udall to win. "I don't like to think about it," said Hamilton Jordan. "It's just one of those things. But Jackson and Jimmy sure

24

do draw from the same well, and that just might have been the difference."

🏴   🏴   🏴

One of Birch Bayh's biggest problems was his campaign image. In a year of anti-Washington slogans, in a year when Jimmy Carter was telling people "I'm a farmer . . . a father . . . a Christian . . ." Birch Bayh was saying—on television, on radio, on the stump—"I'm a politician." It didn't work.

The television screen is dominated by the face of Birch Bayh, handsome, polished, staring straight at the camera and speaking against a stark, bare backdrop.

"To listen to the other candidates, none of them are politicians. Even the ones who've held public office say they're not politicians. Well, I'm Birch Bayh—and I'm a politician. It took a good politician to stop Nixon's plan to pack the Supreme Court. And it's going to take a good politician to break up the big oil companies to get jobs for unemployed workers and hold food prices in line. The question isn't whether you're a politician, but what kind of politician you are. Because it takes a good politician to make a good President."

With this appeal Birch Bayh sought to lure the liberal and moderate vote away from Morris Udall. Udall's television spots, meanwhile, focused on one of the nonpoliticians—former Watergate Special Prosecutor Archibald Cox —who helped bring down the crowd of politicians who created the very crisis in leadership that had become a theme of every candidate's campaign.

Cox said in endorsing Udall: "Trust in government is not to be had for the asking, nor is it gained by the politics of image. It begins with the trust that those who govern repose in people. Only a man of character can restore that confidence. Only a man of openness and courage can bring us together." ("Bring Us Together," ironically, was an old Nixon campaign slogan.)

🏴   🏴   🏴

Back as early as 1972, Carter and Hamilton Jordan had looked to New Hampshire as the place where Carter would make his move. Later, Iowa emerged as an opportunity for an even earlier test. But all along, in the Carter master plan, it was New Hampshire first, then Florida. New Hampshire to make a national reputation, Florida to show that Carter could wrest the South from George Wallace.

For the Carter people, in their first venture into the world of presidential primaries, New Hampshire seemed in many ways ideal. It was, as Jordan wrote Carter in 1972, "a small state . . . independent and given to the kind of personal campaigning that you and your family are capable of waging."

At 11:00 A.M. on the first Sunday in 1976, a chartered airliner taxied to a stop at the Manchester airport, and out into the bitter chill of a New Hampshire winter day stepped an incongruous assortment of visitors. Ninety Georgians wearing wing tips and double-knits and wide white belts, there to spread the word about Jimmy Carter through the land of the original Yankees. They were mostly middle-aged and well-heeled; each had paid his own way to come up north and politick.

The Georgians, headed by Carter campaign political coordinator Landon Butler, were taken to lunch at a Manchester restaurant and were divided into nine teams of ten each. Each Georgian was assigned to a street route in Manchester and Nashua and each was given a "walk packet"—hand cards assembled in street-address order bearing the name and address of every registered Democrat in the area.

By 4:00 P.M., the Georgians were on the streets, knocking on doors, handing out literature, telling people about how they personally knew Jimmy Carter and could vouch for his record and capability. Ninety Georgians working the streets on one of the coldest days of the year. If a registered Democrat was not home, the Georgians would write a personal note and stick it in the door or mailbox. The Georgians went at it throughout the next week. Each night they would meet back at the Sheraton Wayfarer, in a special "boiler room" that had been set up to chart the progress of the various teams, engaging in a competition of sorts. By Thursday, the Georgians figured they had talked to 10,000 of the 20,000 registered Democrats on their lists and had left notes for the rest. They returned to the warmth of their Georgia homes and then sent handwritten, handaddressed, handstamped letters to each New Hampshire voter they had met who seemed at all favorable to Carter's candidacy. Six thousand letters were sent in all—personal messages including phrases such as "I liked your cute dog" or "I hope your boy is feeling better."

The Georgians-to-New Hampshire operation was the idea of Hamilton Jordan and the Carter campaign director figures it was the single most effective campaign effort of the year's first primary. "Those Georgians gave Jimmy a lead in New Hampshire that was never lost and was never jeopardized," he said.

Carter and Jordan looked to New Hampshire as a place where, as Jordan wrote in a 1972 memo to Carter, "sure winners have stumbled and dark horses like Eugene McCarthy and George McGovern have established themselves as serious contenders."

Established themselves as serious contenders. McCarthy and McGovern established themselves not by winning; just by doing better than expected. McCarthy finished with 47 percent in 1968 but many people still remember it as a win because he had taken on a President, Lyndon Johnson, and had done well. McGovern scored with 37 percent, second to Edmund Muskie's 47.8 percent, but the Muskie people had been talking about how much bigger they expected their win to be and so Muskie was perceived as having fallen below his own expectations.

So it was that all Carter wanted to do in New Hampshire was to *establish himself as a serious contender,* not necessarily win. Winning came because of the combination of Carter's good fortune (at having Jackson shun New Hampshire and Bayh fumble it) and Carter's good organization, planning, and effort. And things like the plasticized notebook folder with a cover done in a Formica-like imitation of wood and a title page that read: "Jimmy Carter Presidential Campaign—New Hampshire Campaign Manual." Inside there was a section devoted to "Grassroots Projects."

RUNNING FOR PRESIDENT

A how-to-do-it guide to voter checklists, door-to-door canvassing, telephone canvassing, yard signs and posters, absentee ballots, the crucial get-out-the-vote strategy, and an interesting innovation called "The Postcard Plan."

The Postcard Plan called for volunteers and supporters to go to their local Carter headquarters on Saturday, February 14, and "simultaneously write messages to every New Hampshire eligible primary voter they can think of." The postcards were supplied by the Carter campaign: green background with a black-and-white photo of Carter in his workshirt, leaning on a fence, apparently down home on the farm. The messages too were supplied by the Carter campaign on a sheet in the campaign manual:

SAMPLE POSTCARD MESSAGES

1. John, I met Jimmy Carter the other day at Yoken's. Jimmy makes sense. I hope all of us in the Portsmouth area will support him February 24.

2. Tim and Judy, Jimmy Carter did a great job straightening out government in Georgia. I think he could do the same thing in Washington. I hope you'll support him February 24.

3. Dear Bill, Jimmy Carter is really an honest guy who would be a great President. I hope you'll vote for him. Kathy and I will.

4. Mona, I'm going to vote for Jimmy Carter. He's a hard worker and does what he thinks is right. That's what we need in Washington.

5. Jim, Jimmy Carter is a businessman like us and has commonsense ideas about making Federal government efficient. We need someone down there who has run a government. Hope you'll vote for him.

6. Joe, I just met a guy who's running for President. Jimmy Carter. He's really different. He's one of us. Vote for him.

7. Georgia, Jimmy Carter had a great record on en-

vironment as Governor. He stood up to the Corps of Engineers as Governor. He'll do the same thing as President. I hope you'll vote for him February 24.

🏴   🏴   🏴

The night of Jimmy Carter's first primary election was a quiet, home-style family affair. Carter chose to spend the evening at the home of his Concord campaign chairman, rather than partake in the noise and commotion of the Carter headquarters setup at the frayed Carpenter Hotel. There was Carter; his wife; his sons, Chip, Jack, and Jeffrey; their wives; and three close staff members, Jody Powell, Greg Schneiders, and pollster Patrick Caddell. They passed sandwiches, watched TV, small-talked, and waited for the results.

THE RESULTS: *Carter, 29.4 percent; Udall 23.9 (4,301 votes behind); Bayh, 16.2; Harris, 11.4; Shriver, 8.7. While enroute to a victory celebration on the night of February 24, Carter saw one of his supporters, leaned toward the car window, and flashed a single "V" sign. When he sat back, his wife, Rosalynn, concerned about the Nixonian imagery of it all, said in a quiet voice: "Jimmy, please don't make that sign—and especially, please don't use both hands!"*

🏴   🏴   🏴

Election night in New Hampshire was a many-ringed circus. All of the major candidates were there except the Republican incumbent, President Gerald Ford, and their campaigns had set aside large ballrooms and meeting rooms in hotels and restaurants as places for supporters to gather and party and await the outcome. Political reporters worked the circuit, moving from ballroom to ballroom, interviewing the candidates and their advisers. To Stewart Udall, brother of and campaign manager for candidate Mo, the scene stood in vivid contrast to another New Hampshire primary election night sixteen years earlier.

"You know where John Kennedy was on New Hampshire night in 1960?" asked Stewart Udall (who eventually became President Kennedy's Secretary of the Interior). "He was home in Washington—at his house in Georgetown having a quiet dinner with Jackie, my wife and me, and the Ben Bradlees. No TV cameramen, nothing. Then at about 10:30 someone called and gave him the percentages and he had won and that was it."

⚐⚐⚐

Interlude: The Kennedy Look

There was something familiar about the man on the screen. The hair was full, thick—John Kennedy had hair like that. The dress was casual, sporty, with a blue shirt open at the neck—Kennedy's dress was sporty, often open-necked blues, in those scenes at the beach or sailing off Hyannis.

And there was the full, easy smile—"He still has that Kennedy smile," Carter's long-time media adviser, Gerald Rafshoon, had written back in 1972, in a memo about how the Georgian could mold a national image.

Jimmy Carter, on the screen, has the image of "cool" and the "blurred, shaggy texture" that Marshall McLuhan said was the best thing John F. Kennedy had going for him. It was Rafshoon who gave Carter his cool, his blur, and his shag.

Jerry Rafshoon had recognized Carter's resemblance to Kennedy when he started handling Carter's political media campaign in 1966. But he carefully avoided it—for a time. "I never wanted to capitalize on it," Rafshoon said. "I didn't think that it would exactly be a big selling point in Georgia. . . . I didn't go out of my way to try to do any Camelot camera angles. And no shots on the beach and no touch football. . . . I tried to avoid the smiling pictures."

Actually, Jimmy Carter is in many ways more reminiscent of Bobby Kennedy than John. He is of small stature like Bobby. He is soft-spoken—at times even mumbling in private conversation—and shy like Bobby. Rafshoon saw that resemblance, too, but didn't attempt to project it. "After all, Bobby Kennedy was not too popular down here."

30

Jimmy Carter was struggling way back in the field in 1966 in his first gubernatorial try when Rafshoon came across his broadcast advertising and figured he needed some help. The spot was a country-western jingle that kept prattling: ". . . And Jimmy Carter is his name . . . Jimmy Carter is his name."

Rafshoon's assistance was accepted. He took all the money Carter had left, about $70,000, and used it to show short television spots of Carter—not smiling, but, as Rafshoon recalled, "playing up his basic appeal of the quiet, sincere, competent, reasonable person."

Carter finished third, narrowly missing a runoff against former Governor Ellis Arnall and the eventual winner, Lester Maddox.

Jerry Rafshoon has been marketing Carter ever since. The head of a successful Atlanta advertising agency, Rafshoon seemed younger than his forty-two years as he moved about his office planning ad strategies in 1976, wearing an open shirt and blue jeans, at times sitting cross-legged atop a desk or table as he conducted a conference.

In 1976, in New Hampshire, Rafshoon's commercials got two-state exposure; the state's residents largely watch Boston television, and the Massachusetts primary was just a week after New Hampshire's. Carter spent $130,000 on TV advertising that served the two state primaries, and another $30,000 on ads over virtually every radio station in New Hampshire. (In later primaries, Rafshoon would purchase radio ads on black stations, country-western stations, and "easy listening" stations.)

The Carter spots concentrated on the candidate as a farmer and working man, talking about his life and family and asking voters to trust him. Many of the spots showed the smile that stirred memories of John Kennedy. They also included the lines: "I'll never tell a lie, I'll never avoid a controversial issue. . . . Watch television, listen to the radio. If I ever do any of those things, don't support me."

The lines played like someone had taped a "kick me" sign to the seat of Carter's pants. Carter's critics seized gleefully on the challenge and sought to unearth anti-Carter evidence. Eventually, documented reports showed that Carter, like most politicians, had at times at least misled and evaded. Later, he dropped the "I'll never tell a lie" portion of his standard stump and advertising litany.

March 2/Massachusetts

"We were the leader. Compared to big shots like Wallace and Jackson, Bentsen, Udall and Bayh, Sanford, I was ahead . . . the dam was broken . . . I was kind of a giant killer."

Jimmy Carter was up, up, up. Once he and his men had talked about a long and bloody war—thirty primaries and every one a battle. But the sudden victories in Iowa and New Hampshire had changed all that. Now they were talking about a quick kill. Their strategy was so right, their judgment so fine. They could do no wrong. The nomination just might be won in a couple of weeks. A "high-risk strategy," Hamilton Jordan called it.

The Carter master plan had always been to concentrate first on New Hampshire's February 24 primary to establish a national reputation and then on Florida's March 9 primary to take the South away from George Wallace. The Tuesday in between, Massachusetts' March 2 primary, had never been big in their plans. A couple of months before the Massachusetts election, in fact, the Carter staff—fortified by a private poll—had become downright negative about the Bay State primary. The survey by Patrick Caddell in December 1975 showed Sargent Shriver with 18 percent, Wallace with 13 to 14, Jackson with 10, Carter barely surfacing with 3, and 40 percent undecided.

But the post-New Hampshire euphoria led to a radical shift in sentiment among the Carter men. On New Hampshire's primary night, they gathered in the Carpenter Hotel in Manchester and decided to extend the media spots that had been showing in Boston during the final week of that primary.

The next day, Caddell's staff reinforced the optimism with a report on what he calls a quick "panelback," returning to interview people who had been polled in December. The sample was small, but Carter's progress seemed substantial. Their candidate was in the high twenties; Jackson and Udall were in the low teens.

Another poll, by a network, showed Carter with a 5- to 6-point lead. By now, as virtually every member of the Carter inner circle—including Carter—recalls, there was strong support for a major push in that final week in Massachusetts.

If Carter was going to be officially running in Massachusetts, his aides began to reason, then he should run all-out. Try for the quick kill in Massachusetts; then a Florida victory over Wallace would be just a mop-up. Carter would have scored a farm belt win (Iowa), a true Yankee win (New Hampshire), a northern industrial state win (Massachusetts), and a southern win (Florida).

"We had a real tough argument about Massachusetts— about whether to leave Florida and go into Massachusetts," Carter said. "There was a good argument for that. If we had won Massachusetts the week after New Hampshire— we weren't supposed to do anything, you hip?—it would have made Florida unnecessary. Of lesser importance.

"I must say that the mistake, if there was one made in Massachusetts, was my own. Because—I think this is accurate . . . Hamilton Jordan, the campaign manager, warned me to put more time in Massachusetts, and I was reluctant to do it in order to maintain a high commitment to Florida." But Caddell said in an interview: "I guess I'm the most guilty party for Massachusetts. I wanted Jimmy to go for the kill."

(Note: Unlike Carter and a number of other top Carter aides, Jordan said he does not remember that he was advocating that Carter spend more time in Massachusetts than Carter wound up spending. "If a mistake was made," Jordan said, "we all made it.")

The Carter camp decided to make a big investment in money—especially television ad money—but not in the candidate's time. Carter did not appear in Massachusetts in the last five days of the campaign.

▄▄ ▄▄ ▄▄

Greg Schneiders looks, at first glance, much like the strain of bright young men that seem to be pulled to candidates' sides to function as aides de camp. He is twenty-nine, clean-cut, dresses conservatively and still wears dark-rimmed glasses; he has the job that in the Nixon circumstances was Dwight Chapin's and in the Ford White House was filled by Terry Parker. He seems at first glance to be out of the same mold; capable and efficient, upwardly mobile, but verging on humorless. Right and wrong. Schneiders is a newcomer to politics—he ran a couple of ultra-in restaurants in Washington, D.C. (Wimpy's and The Georgetown Beef Company), and he is a capable and conscientious man. But he is also partial to mixing business with wit.

At the time of the Carter inner circle's great debate over Massachusetts, Schneiders gave Carter a memo of his own. "I realize that you are constitutionally unable to contemplate a planned defeat. . . ." the memo began. Carter read the first sentence, paused, looked at Schneiders and said: "That's right."

The memo went on to make the case that if Carter effectively decimated his opposition so early, an effective Stop Carter movement might then be organized—with plenty of time in which to operate. Thus, it said, Carter might have a more serious problem in the long run if he did win Massachusetts.

It was a prophetic memo, for it did reflect the tentative plans of some of those liberal politicians from Washington who mistrusted Carter. In the nighttimes of debate and drinking at the two bars of Boston's Parker House Hotel during the Massachusetts campaign, liberal operatives confided to a reporter that they had just such an idea. If Carter won in Massachusetts, they said, there would immediately be a major effort to urge organized labor to abandon Jackson and join with McGovern liberals in a new alliance behind Hubert Humphrey. If Carter lost Massachusetts, the liberals said, the movement would be made more difficult because it would then lack urgency.

Eventually, when Carter eliminated his opposition in

Pennsylvania, a Stop Carter movement did form. Frank Church and Jerry Brown came in and landed some sharp blows in the later rounds. Had Carter won in Massachusetts and gone on to take Wallace in Florida, it might have spurred still earlier Stop Carter efforts—and Carter might have had trouble holding on to win the fight.

🏴 🏴 🏴

One of the central factors of the Morris Udall campaign in Massachusetts was the endorsement of Archibald Cox, a professor who is widely known and respected in the liberal circles of New England for the way he stood up to Richard Nixon and forced the President to touch off his Saturday Night Massacre in order to continue his Watergate cover-up.

It was Stewart Udall, Mo's brother, who was responsible for wooing and finally winning the Cox endorsement, according to Terry Bracy, aide to candidate Udall.

Cox had served in the Kennedy administration too, Bracy recalled. "Stu Udall started talking to Ken Galbraith and Archie Cox in late 1974. Archibald Cox's first major speaking engagement after he was fired was a testimonial dinner for Mo in Arizona. Cox always had a special feeling about the Udalls. . . . We were wooing him over a matter of months. . . . Ken Galbraith told Stu to go right at Cox but to be careful, that Archie is sensitive." Finally, Cox agreed to endorse and campaign for Mo Udall, "after a number of long talks on an intellectual basis," Bracy said.

🏴 🏴 🏴

On Monday, February 23, the League of Women Voters held one of its forums for candidates. It was televised over the Public Broadcasting System network.

That evening somebody asked a question about tax reform (Carter had said that the present tax system is a disgrace). Specifically: Would his tax reforms include eliminating the income tax deduction for home mortgages?

Carter said that "would be among those I would like to do away with" as part of his sweeping tax-reform proposal. It was an uncharacteristic answer—uncharacteristic in that it was not carefully thought out and structured.

Carter left immediately after the show. As his car was pulling out, his aides Greg Schneiders and Jody Powell ran into the street and flagged down the driver. Powell told Carter through the window that he was getting some questions from reporters seeking details of the mortgage plan. Carter told him to say that it would be part of his overall, comprehensive tax-reform program and that it would be based on studies and cut the tax rate for the average taxpayer by 40 to 50 percent. The car pulled away.

"He was operating on about three cylinders on that answer," Powell said months later.

The Carter people were slow to assess the impact, but it was just the opening that Udall, Bayh, and Jackson had been seeking. Jackson hit the hardest. He charged that Carter's "proposal" would mean "American homeowners will have to pay $6 billion more in taxes." Jackson also said: "He'd better do some homework before he comes up with fuzzy ideas." Carter would wear that "fuzzy" label the rest of the campaign.

Newspapers began taking note of how all three Democratic candidates had suddenly ganged up to run against— and attack—Carter. "We were in trouble," Bayh's press secretary Bill Wise said months later. "We were looking for some way to break out of the pack of candidates who were all saying the same things . . . we had to take the risk. We had nothing to lose. Apparently the Jackson people came to the same conclusion. Udall also at the same time. People thought there was an organized cabal against Carter. There was nothing further from the truth. We all decided independently."

The Carter men were unable to decide whether it would be better to slash back at the combined attackers or take the high road and deal with it in a statesmanlike manner. Carter basically did neither.

Carter made one attempt to deal with the attacks during an appearance at Faneuil Hall, Boston's historic meeting place, and wound up sounding like Richard Nixon. There Carter was asked about the criticisms; he replied that he himself could bear them without damage but that the attacks "may hurt the country."

After that he went to campaign in Florida, doing his business as usual and basically ignoring the charges of his opponents.

In those days, the controversy didn't seem very important to the candidate and his advisers. They were still savoring New Hampshire. Carter predicted, "I'll finish ahead of Jackson and Wallace. . . . I won't be embarrassed." Jody Powell kept telling reporters that Carter would do "very well."

The Carter people remained convinced that their candidate would be able to sail through on the strength of his momentum, his media spots, and his cover stories in *Time* and *Newsweek*. What they got, instead, was their first lesson on what it means to have a "soft" support. People had been saying all along that Jimmy Carter's vote was "soft," but few in the Carter camp had a good idea of just how bad that can be for the candidate. They just weren't very concerned with details such as that.

"Soft vote," Jody Powell said by way of formulating a definition, "is the voters who don't care enough to come vote for you in the rain."

THE RESULTS: *It did not rain in Massachusetts on election day. It snowed. A near blizzard. "That abominable snowstorm," Carter later called it. Fifty-five percent of the eligible Democrats went to the polls, about the same percentage that voted in 1972. But not many of them were Carter's. For the first time he discovered how soft support can melt.*

Carter, the favored "frontrunner," finished fourth, with a bare 14.2 percent. Jackson won with 22.7 percent; Udall finished second with 18; and Wallace was third with 17.1

Scoop Jackson had relied heavily in Massachusetts on the get-out-the-vote abilities of a young political neophyte, Bob (Skinner) Donahue. And Donahue did not let the veteran senator down. His organization worked smoothly, getting Jackson voters to the polls despite the heavy snow and wind. The twenty-six-year-old Donahue said at one point that he had some 500 cars in the field on election day.

Donahue had also picked some key precincts for the Jackson people to watch on election night. The Jackson advisers gathered in the senator's hotel suite in Boston to watch the returns. The early key precincts were all Boston precincts. Wallace won them all, but Jackson came in a strong second, and the rest of the pack was far behind. Jackson and his advisers knew then that they had it won. They would win the election in the suburbs and outlying areas. But the impact of Wallace winning in Boston precincts stunned one in the Jackson crowd—Daniel Patrick Moynihan, a tall, gray-haired man of Harvard with a Hell's Kitchen background and a Brahmin air, an individualist who served both Kennedy and Nixon, and who has long been a puzzle to people who like to put ideological labels on all those who dabble in politics.

Moynihan couldn't get over it. "Look at what American liberalism has done!" he exclaimed at one point, according to a friend who was in the room. "It's pushed Boston so far that it's voting for George Wallace! John Kennedy's city! Bobby Kennedy's city!"

Soon the results were official, and the Jackson suite was, in the words of one adviser, "a slightly delirious place." The man who in 1972 was the symbol of the political loser was now a winner—victorious in his first test of 1976. There were backslaps and handshakes and hugs and cheers, and, in the midst of it all, Jackson, Moynihan, and writer/adviser Ben Wattenberg were trying to take a serious look at just what the election meant. They moved through the bustle of ecstatic well-wishers, found no corner satisfactory, and wound up talking politics in the senator's bathroom. There, with their voices amplified by the acoustical mix of plumbing and tile, they agreed on a basic point: the Jackson victory had, as they saw it, changed the landscape of American politics—actually it ratified a change that had already taken place. The electorate had recognized that the Vietnam War was over. Jackson was a hardliner, a hawk in this state that was the nesting place of doves. Yet his support of the Vietnam War effort had not been a damaging campaign issue. Neither were his get-tough positions on negotiations with the Soviets on arms, on Jewish emigration, or on detente in general.

Jackson and advisers had been well aware that the senator was probably the most unpopular with Soviet officials of the entire field of candidates. In fact, at one point during the bathroom conference that night, Wattenberg exclaimed: "How'd you like to be a fly on the wall in the Kremlin tomorrow?"

It was a heady time for Scoop Jackson and his men, and in that night of euphoria they concluded that the Massachusetts election marked the end of the New Politics era of the Democratic Party, the end of the era of liberal control that had spawned the candidacy of George McGovern. The party was moving his way, Jackson felt that night, and if it continued on that course, he believed he would be the Democratic nominee.

The coming months would show that Jackson was right on the first point but wrong on the second.

On Massachusetts primary night, Jimmy Carter was in Florida. He awaited the returns in a room on the top floor of his hotel, a room that carpenters were transforming into a restaurant, a room that was still bleak, with bare boards in place where plush, padded dining room booths would someday be. First the results came by phone and later by television.

Carter sat stunned.

Late in the night, he went to a telephone and called his public opinion analyst, Pat Caddell, who had remained at the Boston headquarters. As Caddell remembers it, the candidate's voice was pure ice. Carter simply asked, in slow, measured tones of controlled rage: *"What happened?"*

Caddell explained about the snowstorm and the soft vote and how people who favored Carter apparently had not felt so passionately about him that they wanted to go out in bad weather just to vote for him. Caddell also noted that at least Carter had done well among the black voters of Roxbury. Carter listened silently.

Later that night Greg Schneiders tried to cheer his boss by looking for some saving grace. "Well," Schneiders said, "if we didn't do well in Boston, we must have done well in some other section that we can emphasize to the press." Carter replied emptily: "With fourteen percent, we didn't carry much of anything." End conversation.

Looking back sometime later, Jody Powell candidly discussed his own mistakes: "Our expectations jumped considerably [after New Hampshire] and we conveyed these expectations to the press—repeatedly—which was a stupid thing to do. . . . I'd gotten myself in a mental set. I'd been shooting off my mouth when I should have been quiet. . . . Later, as a result, we became overly cautious."

Hamilton Jordan put it this way: "It's a lesson—every time we get cocky, we get knocked on our ass."

The Early Days

Archery, Georgia, is a state of mind—an undefined and unorganized community, Jimmy Carter calls it—on a road that stretches across the low flatlands between Savannah and Columbus, just outside Plains (population 683). There is no signpost saying where Archery begins or ends. People just know.

It was a place on a dirt road, during the Depression, where trains would stop if someone put a red leather flag in the switch. A place where two white families and about twenty-five black families lived. One of the white families was that of the section foreman of the Seaboard Railroad. The other was that of James Earl Carter. His oldest son was born on October 1, 1924. He was named James Earl Carter, Jr., but everyone has always called him Jimmy.

The Carter farm was a pleasant, basic place. The wooden clapboard house was heated by fireplaces and a wood-burning stove. Water was drawn by a hand pump. An outdoor privy stood in the back yard. Dogs, chickens, guinea fowl, ducks, and geese came and went as they pleased.

Jimmy Carter tells of the farm and his family and his early life in *Why Not the Best?*, his autobiography, which was published to coincide with his run for the Presidency. The publisher, Broadman Press, specializes in religious works. On the jacket it has included an advertisement for two of its other books: *Modern Stories of Inspiration,* described as "true stories of people who have heard God through the clouds and in the middle of the storm," and *Politics and Religion Can Mix!*

In his book, Carter portrayed his boyhood in Archery and Plains in romantic Faulknerian passages laced with humble beginnings and Poor South adversities. Among the most interesting portions of the book are the sections in which Carter talks about his father's feelings toward blacks. Carter recalls that when he was a child during the Depression, Archery society was built around a black leader, Bishop William Johnson, who represented five or six states in the African Methodist Episcopal Church. One of Johnson's sons, Alvan, was educated and lived in Boston. "He was the only black who habitually came to our front door," Carter writes.

> Whenever we heard that Alvan was back home for a visit, there was a slight nervousness around our house. We would wait in some combination of anticipation and trepidation until we finally heard the knock on our front door. My daddy would leave and pretend it wasn't happening while my mother received Alvan in the front living room to discuss his educational progress and his experiences in New England for this was one of the accepted proprieties of the segregated South which Alvan violated. Even when Bishop Johnson came to see my father, he would park in front of the store and send one of his drivers to the back door to inform my daddy that he would like to see him, and Daddy would go out to meet the Bishop in the yard.

Earl Carter was a community leader: one of the early directors of the Rural Electrification Administration's local program in the Plains area, a member of the Sumter County School Board, and—one year before he died of cancer in 1953—he was elected to the state legislature. He ran a diversified farm and had a small store next to his house where he sold overalls, work shoes, sugar, salt, flour, meal, Octagon soap, tobacco, snuff, rat traps, and products off the Carter farm: syrup, side meat, lard, cured hams, loops of stuffed sausage, and wool blankets.

He was a respected man in his community, respected by both blacks and whites. In his book, Carter tells about how one of the prize possessions of Archery was the Carter family's battery-operated radio. He writes:

All our black neighbors came to see Daddy when the second Joe Louis–Max Schmeling fight was to take place. There was intense interest, and they asked if they could listen to the fight. We propped the radio up in the open window of our house, and we and our visitors sat and stood under a large mulberry tree nearby.

There were heavy racial overtones encompassing the fight, with Joe Louis given a good chance to become the new black heavyweight champion of the world. He had lost in his first boxing encounter with Schmeling, but in this return match Louis almost killed his opponent in the first round.

My father was deeply disappointed in the outcome.

There was no sound from anyone in the yard, except a polite, 'Thank you, Mister Earl,' offered to my father.

Then, our several dozen visitors filed across the dirt road, across the railroad track, and quietly entered a house about a hundred yards away out in the field. At that point, pandemonium broke loose inside that house, as our black neighbors shouted and yelled in celebration of the Louis victory. But all the curious, accepted proprieties of a racially segregated society had been carefully observed.

Earl Carter was a deeply conservative man, a product of his place and his time. He was a rural, Deep South man who never finished high school and never questioned the propriety of racial segregation. Jimmy Carter portrayed well his father's racial insensitivities in his book, and he later had times when he seemed uneasy about the picture he had painted of the man who he maintained was both his father and his "best friend." In June, for example, after he had the nomination locked up, Carter got into a rambling chat with reporters on board his airplane, beginning by trying to explain George Wallace and winding up talking about his father instead.

Jimmy Carter had been asked if he viewed Wallace as "evil" or "ugly." Carter shook his head.

"No, you have to remember that the Congress of the United States, the Supreme Court, the governors of I guess every state in the country all accepted racial segregation. The

Supreme Court ruling was separate but equal. Congress didn't pass the Voting Rights Act. There was no one-man, one-vote rule until just a short while ago. So Wallace is the last remaining public official on the scene who was part of that nationwide attitude.

"I don't know what would have happened had I been governor back in 1960, or 1955, whenever it was, I don't know. But I was lucky enough to come along after the crisis took place in the South. When I was trying to exemplify as a church member, and so forth, equality of the races, in a fairly timid way compared to what I could have done, that was just the embryonic stage of my political life. It was an accepted thing. Very fine governors like Ernest Vandiver of Georgia accepted the inequities that were in existence.

"So Wallace is anachronistic in that he's come over into this modern age. But it's not quite fair to say that he was malevolent or that he was ugly. And I think he capitalized on the racial issue by standing in the schoolhouse door. I don't know if he had any visions of what might proceed from that. My guess is that he did it at that time for Alabama consumption. I would guess that subsequent to that he thought about running for President. As you know, when he first ran for President, it was in a very tentative way. He only entered three primaries. I think he was surprised at the acceptance he got there [in Maryland, Wisconsin, and Indiana]. . . . He didn't have to mention race anymore. There's no doubt that he used the race issue."

A reporter interrupted to say that Carter is viewed as a better man than Wallace. But Carter, already victorious, was in a mood to be charitable.

"That's a mistake. It's easy for people to look back on the war in Vietnam and say, 'That's a terrible war, we never should have been there.' It's easy for people to look back on the South and the rest of the nation and say, 'We should never have had racial discrimination and blacks should always have been able to vote.'

"Somebody came out the other day and talked to my mother and asked her, 'How does it feel to have been married to a racist?' Well, you know, if my daddy was still living, he would be part of the modern, enlightened consciousness between black and white people. He died in 1953. Even the black people who lived at home never thought about, you know, equality and riding in the front of the bus and going to the same school as whites.

"It's not right to stigmatize people into generic groups or as individuals because of the times they lived in and when they got their reputation and shaped their political image."

Jimmy was the oldest of the Carter children. Gloria was born about two years later. Ruth was born when Jimmy was five and his only brother, Billy, when Jimmy was thirteen.

"Ruth was always his [Earl Carter's] favorite child," Jimmy told reporters during that same lengthy, free-flowing airplane conversation. "Gloria was much more rebellious against Daddy than Ruth was. Ruth was just her father's little girl. . . . I don't know, I can't explain it psychological-ly . . . Gloria always had a mind of her own; I'll say that. . . . [But] I think Ruth was Daddy's favorite, and it was kind of an accepted thing. I didn't feel any jealousy over it. Gloria and I were almost of equal age and we were competitors with each other."

Carter's mother, Lillian, recalled that, in fact, it was Gloria who was the leader of the Carter children as they were growing up on the farm outside Plains. "Gloria tended to be more aggressive," she said. "She was bigger than he [Jimmy] was—he was of small stature and she was larger from the time she was five. She was more or less the leader of my children. . . . He teased them and pulled their hair, but they usually got along just fine. Once she hit him with a monkey wrench and he shot her in the behind with a BB gun."

Jimmy had been a very sick baby. "Until he was two years old, he had colitis, and he almost died," his mother recalled. "It was so prevalent. He had diarrhea and would be constantly passing blood. He was in and out of the hospital, and we tried to do everything we could for him, changing one diaper after another, and there was always so much blood. A country doctor from Montesula—he told me what to do. He told me to make a saturated solution of corn starch for Jimmy, and that worked. But it was a terrible time."

His mother likes to tell how Jimmy worked diligently at his farm chores. "Jimmy never complained about doing his chores," she said. "I remember when he was older, his friends used to drive up to the house and ask him to go with them. But he used to just smile and wave and do his never let him stay out in the field in the middle —he's so fair, he blistered easily."

early boyhood, until he was about fourteen or fifteen, virtually all of Carter's playmates were black. "That's all I played with," he said. "We used to wrestle, fight, fish, swim, and have footraces and play baseball. There was never any deference shown me at all because I was white." In his book, Carter writes of his black boyhood friends:

> We hunted, fished, explored, worked and slept together. We ground sugar cane, plowed mules, pruned watermelons, dug and bedded sweet potatoes, mopped cotton, stacked peanuts, cut stovewood, pumped water, fixed fences, fed chickens, picked velvet beans, and hauled cotton to the gin together.
>
> In addition to the many chores, we also found time to spend the night on the banks of Choctawhatchee and Kinchafoonee creeks, catching and cooking catfish and eels when the water was rising from heavy rains.
>
> "We ran, swam, rode horses, drove wagons and floated on rafts together. We misbehaved together and shared the same punishments. We built and lived in the same tree houses and played cards and ate at the same table.
>
> But we never went to the same church or school. Our social life and our church life were strictly separate. We did not sit together on the two-car diesel train that could be flagged down in Archery. There was a scrupulous compliance with these unwritten and unspoken rules. I never heard them questioned. Not then.

As a youth in Plains and as a young adult as well, Carter felt uncomfortable about the racial segregation that was a fact of life in the South. But he kept his disquietude largely low key. "Jimmy was never really critical [about segregation]," Rosalynn said once. "He just quietly let people know what he thought. He never had any hot arguments or debates on it."

Eventually, as an adult, Carter did take a stand against

the racist elements in his home town, and later, as governor of Georgia, he won the support of blacks for such emotional, symbolic acts as ordering that a portrait of Martin Luther King, Jr., be placed in the state capitol. His stand on the race issue has angered a good many of his fellow Georgians; indeed, not even all the members of his family shared his view. One who did, though, was his mother.

"Yes, he got that from me," Lillian Carter, Jimmy's mother, once told Helen Dewar of the *Washington Post*. "I've always been like that. My father was never a racist, and I grew up trying to be compassionate and kind to everyone. . . . I've stood alone in Plains, Jimmy and I have stood alone."

As Earl Carter was a traditional southern conservative, a segregationist as a matter of course and principle, Lillian Carter was a liberal, uncommon and even a maverick in the rural Deep South way of life. She was the daughter of a rural postmaster in south Georgia, one of eight children. She graduated from high school, received a nursing degree at Grady Hospital in Atlanta, and then promptly married Earl Carter and settled into a life alongside the Seaboard railway tracks outside Archery.

Rosalynn Carter, who was a friend of Ruth's long before she married Ruth's brother Jimmy, always considered Lillian Carter to be outspoken on matters of racial segregation, even when she was without allies among the white population of Plains. "I remember that Jimmy's mother was always a baseball fan," she said. "And when Jackie Robinson joined the Dodgers she went around telling everyone 'I'm for the Dodgers—because they're the team with Jackie Robinson,' and everyone would be shocked. You can imagine how that went over in Plains. Even now she likes the Atlanta Braves, but the Dodgers are still her team."

Lillian Carter says she didn't really become outspoken about race relations until the civil rights movement took hold in the South in the late 1950s and early 1960s. "When my husband was alive and the children were growing up," she said, "there was no such thing as segregation and integration. There were things for the blacks and things for the whites. That's all. My husband never joined anything against blacks, and you should know that everything I did as a nurse (caring for blacks) was done with my husband's consent. . . . My liberalism came much later, during the civil rights movement. I was for the blacks, who have been so mistreated. And that's when word got out that I was so liberal—and I was. It wasn't a frightening time—I was never afraid of anything in my life, except snakes, and that was a different period."

When she began to speak out in favor of equal treatment of blacks in the South, Lillian Carter says that it was made very clear to her that her views were resented by others in the community. "People would throw oranges and banana peels at my car," she said. "There were many things I wanted to say publicly. But I did not."

There was always in Lillian Carter a strong strain of independence. When Earl died in 1953, she set out to remake her life. She was a housemother to a fraternity on the Auburn University campus. She started up a small nursing home in Blakely, Georgia. And then in 1966, she was watching television one night when an ad for the Peace Corps came on the screen. "Age is no barrier." So at age sixty-eight, she sent away for information, and soon after she announced to her sons that she was volunteering for service in the Peace Corps. She would request assignment in either Africa or India.

Lillian Carter went to the University of Chicago to study the Marathi dialect as preparation for teaching nutrition to the people of India. Then the Peace Corps got word that family-planning aid was needed in India. So Mrs. Carter went back to school to learn Hindi so she could be of service in that program.

Vikhroli is a small town near Bombay. Lillian Carter did family-planning work there and eventually was transferred to a clinic there to make use of her nursing skills.

Years later, as she looked back on it, Lillian Carter spoke of the personal frustrations, doubts, and suffering she endured as she tried to go about her Peace Corps work in India. In her interview with Dewar of the *Washington Post*, she said, "India was killing me. I just couldn't bear it. I couldn't touch the dirt, the blood, the lice, the leprosy. I hadn't the strength to bear the horrible cruelty and indifference." So Mrs. Carter said she went up on a hillside and prayed. "And Christ let something come into me, and I knew I could do anything. I could wipe up blood . . . and blood had always appalled me, and I could touch leprosy without running to scrub my hands raw. I could stay in India."

Lillian Carter was more than seventy years old when she returned to Georgia from her service in the Peace Corps. She had worked herself into a weakened state, losing thirty pounds while in India. She was so debilitated that her children insisted in using a wheelchair to transport her from the plane to a waiting car. Within a short time, though, she regained enough strength to set out on the lecture circuit, telling organizations about the Peace Corps and its work.

During Carter's campaign for the Presidency, his mother, then seventy-seven, assumed two diverse roles: she looked after Carter's youngest daughter, eight-year-old Amy, while her parents were off politicking; and she moved energetically about the business of being an available and quotable Carter figure for reporters who had suddenly become fascinated with the fact of a Deep South country boy who was taking on the whole of the Democratic Party and winning. She developed a good number of favorite lines.

"Don't call me Mrs. Carter—that's Jimmy's wife," she would admonish good-naturedly. "Everyone calls me Miss Lillian."

Also: "Everybody in Plains either loves me or owes me."

Also: "Jimmy says he'll never tell a lie. Well, I lie all the time. I have to—to balance the family ticket."

And: "Sure I'm for helping the elderly. I'm going to be old myself someday."

She is a small but solid-looking woman with striking white hair, a face etched with the lines of her years, and blue eyes that sparkle with life every time she gets off one of her favorite lines and sees that it is well received. Once, when dining with several reporters, she accepted a drink of their wine, but allowed as how she was just a little disappointed that they did not have anything more substantial to offer. "You probably shouldn't put this in the paper," she said. "Some of my friends don't know I take a toddy now and then."

Carter's uncle, Tom Gordy, his mother's youngest brother, was an enlisted man in the navy and he was fond of sending Jimmy postcards from each of his port stops. From the time he was in grammar school, Carter looked forward to attending the U.S. Naval Academy at Annapolis. As a youth, he wrote the academy and, without telling them his true age, requested a listing of their entrance requirements. He said later that he virtually memorized the catalogue word for word.

"I had ridiculous and secret fears that I would not meet the requirements," Carter later wrote in his book. "Some of the physical requirements listed in the catalogue gave me deep concern."

Childhood fears. They are so real at the time and yet so often they are quite the opposite of what is to become adult reality. So it was with Carter, who thought his problem was his teeth. " 'Malocclusion of teeth' was my biggest theoretical problem," wrote the man whose teeth and grin were to become more of a political trademark than his views on any of the issues of his day. "When I ate fruit, the knowledge that my teeth did not perfectly meet interfered with my enjoying the flavor.

"There was another requirement which caused me to worry, one called 'retention of urine.' I was always ashamed to ask whether that last clinging drop would block my entire naval career!"

As he has frequently announced in his campaign speeches, Jimmy Carter became the first member of his father's family to graduate from high school. In a revealing passage in his autobiography, Carter says that his father had supported Congressman Stephan Pace in each of his campaigns in the hopes of securing an Annapolis appointment for Jimmy. Had the Carters been New Yorkers, this would have come off like standard Sammy Glick; it is, in fact, the sort of long-term cunning and determined calculation that was passed from father to son in the Carters of Georgia and which became very much part of Jimmy Carter's way of operating. In 1942, Jimmy Carter got his Annapolis nomination.

Soon after his arrival at the naval academy, Carter—stubborn and proud of being a Georgian—set out to make it clear to his upperclassmen that there is one song that is most unsuitable for dinner music: "Marching Through Georgia." He succeeded in proving to his classmates mostly that he was well reared. The incident occurred during the standard, ritual mealtime hazing at the academy.

"We were plebes," recalled Robert Lee Scott, who was Carter's roommate for two years. "And at the dinner table one day Jimmy was ordered by an upperclassman to sing 'Marching Through Georgia.' Well, Jimmy absolutely refused—he flat refused to do it. And so Jimmy got belted pretty good on the rear end with a bread platter—I mean knocked quite a ways. But he held true. He didn't sing it."

Scott, who then lived in Arizona but now coincidentally lives just outside Atlanta, recalls Carter as a "private kind of guy. . . . He didn't need to be very studious because he was intelligent enough." Midshipman Carter did not date much, Scott said. One of their most memorable times, he said, was when Carter of Georgia and Scott of Arizona decided to see the big city. "We took a weekend in New York City," Scott said. "It's not that anything special happened. We just took in the sights. But for us it was really something."

Carter writes in his autobiography of how interested he was in classical music and how he and his roommate would spend their money on records and listen to them for hours. He drops names like Tristan and Isolde, and Liebestod. According to Scott, Carter's interest in the classics was acquired. "He was only slightly interested in music [at first]," Scott said. "I had been interested in classical music and got him interested in it. We chipped in on a record player and records, and he really got taken by it. When we were ready to graduate, we finally had to decide who would get the records and it turned out that he finally bought my half."

Carter graduated 59th out of 820 in his class of 1947—a class which was graduated in 1946, incidentally, after being rushed through the academy in three years in hopes of catching up with World War II. Carter set out to build a career in the navy. Eventually, he was picked to participate in the nuclear submarine program headed by Admiral Hyman Rickover, whom he frequently mentions as a person he admires.

He tells the story in his book of the time that he and a friend ran into his sister Ruth and a friend; they wound up double-dating at the movies—Jimmy's friend and Ruth, Jimmy and the other girl, Rosalynn Smith. At home that night, Carter says he told his mother about the date with the Smith girl. Mrs. Carter asked her son if he liked Rosalynn. "She's the girl I want to marry," Carter says he replied. He is unabashed in reporting this Andy Hardy dialogue to the world in his autobiography.

Jimmy liked Rosalynn and Rosalynn liked Jimmy and it was not long before they were married. But it took years for Rosalynn to realize that her husband had gradually come to give her a shorthand name: "Rosie." In fact, she says, she had gone through more than two decades of marriage before somebody asked her whether she liked it when Jimmy called her by the nickname. "I said he never does call me that," Rosalynn Carter recalls. "And I really believed that. I'd just never noticed it. And then one day just a short time later, we were at home and Jimmy called to me, 'Rosie, get the telephone.' . . . So he does call me Rosie sometimes after all. I don't particularly like it."

After they were married, Rosalynn accompanied her husband on tours to Hawaii; San Diego, California; New London, Connecticut; and Schenectady, New York. Then, after the death of his father, Carter reports that he and Rosalynn had their first real fight. He wanted to quit the navy and live in Plains; she preferred a life of wider horizons, free from the family influences back home. Carter won, and back in Plains he set about building a family seed peanut business.

■   ■   ■

While Jimmy Carter was busy building a peanut farming business, his cousin Hugh was busy making a killing on worms.

BIG MONEY IN FISHWORMS

Dear Sir:

Billions of fishworms needed yearly and not ½ enough people are raising them to supply this huge demand! . . .

You can make profit fast. . . . Our simple, detailed instructions show you how to raise and sell worms. . . . **Hurry, this is your big opportunity to make money fast.**

Yours Sincerely,
Hugh A. Carter
Plains, Georgia

PRICE LIST

Carter's Pure Bred Hybrid Red Wigglers

(Perfected After 20 Years of Breeding Experience)
1,000—$8.95. . . . 5,000—$42.50. . . . 100,000—$800.00

FISHBAIT LITERATURE
By
Hugh A. Carter, world's largest worm grower

"18 Secrets of Successful Worm Raising." "What to Feed and How to Feed the Hybrid Red Wiggler." "Over 300 Questions and Answers on Worm Raising."

Eventually Hugh Carter began to diversify. He went into crickets as well. "Raising the Gray Cricket and How to Raise and Sell the Hybrid Redworm." But worms were bigger than ever, and Carter had to subcontract his cricket business. Actually, it wasn't just the worms that took up so much of Hugh Carter's time. It was the worms and the politicians. For Hugh Carter took his cousin's seat in the Georgia State Senate when Jimmy made his first run for governor in 1966. And he then ran Jimmy's second—successful—race for governor in 1970. "I finally had to job my crickets," he said. "I just don't have time for them anymore."

▰   ▰   ▰

In Plains, Carter served as a member of the Sumter County school board. "It seems hard to believe now," he writes in his book, "but I was actually a member of the county school board for several months before it dawned on me that white children rode buses to their schools and black students still walked to theirs! I don't believe any black parent or teacher ever pointed out this quite obvious difference."

At about this time, the White Citizens' Council movement was springing up throughout the South as a way of trying to fight off integration. Carter refused to join the local Council—he refused when several influential Plains men told him that he was the only white man in the area who had not joined, and he refused when they later returned with some of Carter's customers warning that his business could suffer if he did not join. The ensuing boycott was small and short-lived.

Carter was a deacon at his Baptist church in Plains, a small and segregated institution. He failed to attend one meeting at which the eleven other deacons and the pastor voted unanimously to propose to the entire congregation that blacks be physically barred from the building if they attempted to attend worship services. When the matter was brought before the full congregation later, Carter urged that blacks be permitted to enter the church if they wished. Of the 200 people at the meeting, about 50 voted. Of these, Carter writes, only six voted to open the services to all who wished to worship: Carter, his mother, his wife, his two sons, and one other member of the congregation.

Jimmy Carter paid his politicking dues. He began his public service with quasi-political jobs: state president of the Certified Seed Organization, Lions' Club district governor, local planning commission chairman, Georgia Planning Association president, and member of the county library board, hospital authority, and school board.

In 1962 Carter ran for the Georgia State Senate. On primary election day at one polling place, in Georgetown, which is on the Chattahoochee River, Carter came upon some irregularities—for example, his opponent's literature being on the voting table and the election supervisor suggesting that this was the man to vote for and then watching the ballots being marked and occasionally reaching into the box to see how the votes went on ballots he couldn't see. Eventually, about 300 people had voted, Carter says, and there were 433 names in the ballot box and 126 of them had voted alphabetically and at times ballots had been folded together in clusters of four or eight when they were dropped into the ballot box.

If Carter's version is accurate, it was not only ballot-box

stuffing but a clumsy job of it. Carter lost the election by a few votes. He challenged the election and after a lengthy and flip-flopping series of rulings, he was eventually elected. His successful challenge was due in large measure to the work of an Atlanta attorney, Charles Kirbo, who had been hired to handle the Carter case, and an assisting attorney, Warren Fortsom.

Kirbo and Carter grew to be quite close, and a sort of father–son relationship developed between the attorney and his young politician/client. Eventually Kirbo became well known as Carter's closest adviser and confidant. Fortsom too achieved fame of sorts; he was from Americus, which is the nearest big town to Plains, and was a prominent citizen, being county attorney and a member of the school board and the Rotary Club and a church director and an ex-Marine; but after recommending in the mid-1960s that a biracial committee be set up to ease tension in the town, he and his family were harassed by crank phone calls and ostracized by their townsfolk, and he was superceded as county attorney by a specially appointed "assistant attorney." Eventually Fortsom and his family were effectively forced out of town and they moved to Atlanta. All because he had dared to be moderate enough to call for a biracial committee.

In 1966, Carter ran for governor. He passed up what he felt was a sure shot at a congressional vacancy to go for the state's top job. And he fell short. He came in third, behind Former Governor Ellis Arnall and fried chicken segregationist Lester Maddox, just missing the runoff. Maddox had become famous purely because he had run a segregated fried chicken restaurant in Atlanta and he had made the ax handle his symbol—an instrument for driving blacks out of his restaurant. Maddox represented a colossal insult not just to blacks but to all of mankind. Maddox won the runoff and became Georgia's next governor, and the people of that state were saddled with a Cro-Magnon image of their own making.

One notable thing about Jimmy Carter is that he is stubborn. Also, determined and hard-driving. Having been defeated once for governor he made up his mind that he would not rest until he became governor. He began his 1970 gubernatorial campaign almost as soon as the 1966 balloting ended. It was as if his 1966 campaign had never stopped. He went right on stumping the state and shaking hands. Maddox was barred by law from running again. This time, Carter's opponent was of a different stripe— former Governor Carl Sanders, a lawyer and a moderate who had been a generally popular political figure in Georgia and had a good following among the blacks. Sanders was the overwhelming early favorite; people paid little attention to the chronic campaigner from Plains.

With Sanders well ensconced with the moderate left, Carter moved after the right. He painted Sanders as a figure of the Atlanta country club set and labeled him "Cufflinks Carl." He portrayed his opponent as a big-spender liberal, and here he had some good fortune. It seems that a button manufacturer, in an effort to cut costs, had recycled some old Hubert Humphrey buttons by just putting a new finish on top of the old and turning them into Sanders buttons. But some nervous scratcher in the Carter camp absently peeled off the Sanders surface one day and gleefully discovered Humphrey. "Scratch a Sanders and get a Humphrey" became a quickie campaign jingle that did Sanders no good in Georgia. Carter also encouraged the segregationist elements by saying that he hoped to have the Wallace vote on election day (which was true, he would later explain, because he hoped to have votes of *all* people, liberals and conservatives, blacks and whites).

It was not a gentlemanly campaign. Pro-Carter forces distributed in redneck areas an Atlanta newspaper photo showing Sanders getting doused with champagne by two black Atlanta Hawks basketball players in a victory celebration. Carter denied personal involvement in the circulation of the photo.

Carter won.

On January 12, 1971, Carter, who was a product of a segregated society and who had been elected in part by successfully courting the Wallace vote, stood in the state capitol building and declared in an eight-minute inaugural address: "I say to you quite frankly that the time for racial discrimination is over. No poor, rural, weak, or black person should ever have to bear the additional burden of being deprived of the opportunity of an education, a job, or simple justice. . . ."

Carter's speech attracted national publicity and later, when *Time* did its cover story on the new breed of politicians who are governors of the New South, Carter was on the magazine's cover.

Running for President

The drive that made Jimmy Carter the choice of the 1976 Democratic National Convention began during the 1972 Democratic National Convention in Miami Beach. Advisers Hamilton Jordan and Gerald Rafshoon sought to have Carter considered for Vice President and found that they had trouble in just getting to see George McGovern's advisers.

"Boy, were we ever naive!" Jordan recalls.

The two men hoped to convince McGovern's advisers that the South Dakota liberal would fare better with a southerner—Carter—on the ticket. So they went to the Doral Beach Hotel and asked to see Patrick Caddell, then McGovern's pollster (now Carter's), because they had a poll supporting their position.

"A bullshit poll," Rafshoon later admitted. It was a poll that had been taken for a U.S. Senate race in Georgia. A question had been asked about how McGovern would do against Nixon and another asked how McGovern would do if Carter were his running mate. Obviously McGovern did much better in Georgia with the governor of Georgia on the ticket.

Jordan and Rafshoon were kept waiting one floor below the Doral floor that served as the McGovern convention headquarters for staff members, including Caddell. Almost an hour had passed when another McGovern aide, Alan Baron, saw the two Carter men waiting and asked: "What are you guys doing?"

"Waiting to see Pat Caddell," Rafshoon replied. Baron

offered to help out. He led the two Carter emissaries up a back stairwell to Caddell's floor and guided them past the guards and into the right room. (It is one of the delicious ironies of politics that Baron later played a role in the Carter story of 1976, as well—only this time he became one of the key figures in a last-gasp Stop Carter movement.)

Once in the room, Jordan and Rafshoon laid out their case and Caddell listened politely. "He said things like, uh huh, . . . oh, wow,' and said, 'I'm going to think about recommending a southerner.' And he thanked us for stopping by," Jordan says.

Eight minutes after they had been ushered in to see Caddell, the Carter men were on their way out, chagrined. They had seen Carter as one of the major figures of the party, *the* leading southern moderate. The McGovern people obviously had not.

"I thought people were going to fall all over Jimmy at the convention," Jordan said later. "But he was just one of thirty or forty guys there."

That night, Jordan and Rafshoon talked a bit about how Carter's national image needed improving. The conversation progressed in succeeding days to how Carter was just as qualified as any of the presidential aspirants. "We got to thinking, 'Hell, if we work at it for four years, we just might be able to take any of these guys,' " said Rafshoon.

Other Carter advisers talked about it, too. They included Peter Bourne, a psychiatrist who had set up a drug rehabilitation program for Carter in Georgia. On July 25, 1972, Bourne wrote a memo to Carter, suggesting for the first time that he run for President.

Meetings followed, usually in the Atlanta apartment of Hamilton Jordan. After one such session, Jordan, Rafshoon, and Atlanta businessman Landon Butler went to the governor's mansion. Carter greeted them, wearing blue jeans and a T-shirt, the clothes he often favored during his off-duty hours. Jordan spoke for the group and outlined their view that a southern alternative to George Wallace could make it in 1976. They figured then that Florida Governor Reubin Askew was better known outside the south than Carter—"if Jimmy was one percent toward his goal, then Askew was fifteen," said Jordan. But the men urged Carter to run.

"Yeah, I've thought about it," Carter replied, after hearing his advisers' arguments. He, too, had been figuring that he was as capable as any of the better-known politicians he had met—many of them men who had come to Atlanta seeking his help in their own presidential efforts. "During 1971 and 1972, I met Richard Nixon, Spiro Agnew, George McGovern, Henry Jackson, Hubert Humphrey, Ed Muskie, George Wallace, Ronald Reagan, Nelson Rockefeller, and other presidential hopefuls, and I lost my feeling of awe about Presidents," he writes in his book.

As the meeting at the mansion drew to a close, Jordan recalls that Carter gave them some simple instructions: "It's an enormous undertaking. We've got to work at it. Think about it. And we've got to keep our mouths shut."

The meeting with Carter led to the preparation of a couple of documents. One was a memo from Rafshoon to Jordan on how Carter should go about getting himself a national image. The memo showed that Rafshoon had spotted the Carter attribute that four years later was to become the Carter trademark—the smile. Specifically, Rafshoon noted, it was a "Kennedy smile," an image Rafshoon had shunned in past campaigns in Georgia but now planned to exploit nationally.

The Rafshoon Memo

1972.

As for a national image . . . I believe that despite the accusations of back-sliding by the liberal press, that Jimmy's image in national circles and in the media has not changed much since inauguration. He is still the man who said the time for racial discrimination is over. . . . He still has a Kennedy smile. . . . **What he does not have is much depth to his image. He is not as well known as many other big-name politicians in the U.S. and is not known for the heavyweight ideas and programs that he is capable of articulating.**

63

Getting this across should be the No. 1 priority now.
The first phase of any Carter campaign should be to
formulate a heavyweight program and project a heavyweight image, all at the same time, trying to infect other
southern states and other regions with the Jimmy Carter
"good guy" brand of populism. It will take more than the
hand-shaking and the projection of "I understand the
problems of the average man" image to put Carter over.
**This is still his greatest asset and it must be projected
but he will also have to convince press, public and politicians that he knows how to run a government (he has
a record to prove this). . . .** He knows about the problems
of the cities . . . the races . . . the economy . . . and the
problems of the world, national defense, foreign affairs.

Timing

1973 will be a very quiet year on the political front
but there are a lot of preparatory things that can be done.
This is the phase when Jimmy's accomplishments in
Georgia—such as reorganization, control, ecology, and
the upgrading of positions for blacks—can be heralded
nationally. I see 1973 as the year in which Carter is projected as the heaviest of the governors in accomplishments
and the year in which the rest of the country gets a good
look at him as a governor. It's really his last chance for
this because in 1974 we will have mid-term elections and
he needs to shift gears then for another phase of his
publicity.

In general, I see the publicity phases as follows:

Phase I 1973: Projection of the Carter record and
knowledge.

Phase II 1974: Carter as a leader in the Democratic
Party and someone involved in bringing it back.

Phase III 1975: Carter as a heavyweight thinker, leader
in the party (denote in Phases One and Two) who has
some ideas for running the country and is going around
the country talking about them and who may have presidential ambitions.

Phase IV 1976: Carter—a presidential candidate.

Each of these phases runs into the succeeding phase
and is an integral part of the overall buildup. They all
cannot be accomplished at the same time but they all must

be accomplished at the time allotted in order to evolve
into the next phase. Phase I must be accomplished early
enough to make the others work.

🏳 🏳 🏳

The second important document was written by Hamilton Jordan (he pronounces it "Jurd'n"), who had been a
Carter man ever since he heard Carter speak back in 1966
—when Carter was running for governor the first time
and Jordan was a twenty-one-year-old youth working at a
summer job spraying mosquitoes. Jordan had been impressed enough to sign on with Carter, trying to line up
the youth vote. Eventually, Jordan would wind up as Carter's 1976 presidential campaign manager, a stocky and
athletic type who had learned to be tough and exacting
on some occasions and beguiling and charming on others.

In 1972, at the age of twenty-seven, Hamilton Jordan
drafted the master plan that would ultimately carry Jimmy
Carter to the Democratic presidential nomination. Jordan
dated his memo to Carter November 4, 1972—just a day
before Richard Nixon's landslide victory over George Mc-
Govern. The Jordan memo turned out, all in all, to be a
remarkably accurate assessment of a political situation that
would exist four years later.

It talked about how "the New Hampshire and Florida
primaries provide a unique opportunity for you to demonstrate your abilities at an early stage of the campaign"—
Carter eventually won both and was on his way.

It talked of Carter's need to select a large industrial traditionally Democratic state where he would have to ultimately confront his opponents and suggested Pennsylvania
and Ohio—Carter eventually scored his biggest victory in
Pennsylvania, and he scored a victory in Ohio that was so
smashing it touched off a wave of endorsements that guar-
anteed him the nomination.

The memo also talked of how Carter must develop expertise in foreign affairs and suggested he make trade
mission trips to South America, Europe, the Mideast, and
Japan—and Carter did.

It urged him to write a book—he did.

It talked of how he would have to work to woo and

win the leaders of the media world, the "eastern liberal news establishment"—he tried.

It talked about how "compatible and comfortable" he appeared to be with Senator Henry (Scoop) Jackson, but warned him not to continue to praise Jackson in his speeches because Jackson could turn out to be one of his 1976 opponents. Jordan assumed, though, that Senator Edward Kennedy would run and that he would be the early favorite to win the nomination.

For all its accuracy, the Jordan memo began, surprisingly, with an error. Jordan said that a serious effort by George Wallace in 1976 *would* preempt Carter's candidacy. (The copy of the memo now in Jordan's file shows "would" crossed out and "could" inked in its place, along with a penned notation: "I have changed my mind about this. 9-10-74 H.J.") Throughout the memo, Jordan seemed to view Carter as a basically conservative southerner who could be an alternative to Wallace. Jordan also was critical of Edmund Muskie's 1972 efforts to enter all the primaries, and he praised George McGovern's strategy of carefully picking his primary battlefields; later, of course, Carter and Jordan would agree that Carter indeed ought to enter all of the primaries.

The Jordan Memo

November 4, 1972.

. . . The New Hampshire and Florida primaries provide a unique opportunity for you to demonstrate your abilities and strengths as a candidate at an early stage in the campaign. As you know, New Hampshire's primary traditionally has been a place where sure winners have stumbled and the dark horses like Eugene McCarthy and George McGovern have established themselves as serious contenders. New Hampshire is a small state which is rural and independent and given to the kind of personal campaign that you and your family are capable of waging. It only voted about 84,644 people in the primary this year, and I believe that your farmer-businessman-military-religious-conservative background would be well received there. It is not too early to begin to make some contacts with people there, learn something about the state, and be looking for an appropriate opportunity to make a major speech or address there.

Florida, as it follows the New Hampshire primary, affords an excellent opportunity to build on a good showing. It is not too early to begin thinking of people who should be contacted in Florida. . . .

. . . I could go on and on, but the point that I would like here is that we need to begin thinking **now** about party rules vis-à-vis primary states and your own effort. It is here where the nomination will be won or lost.

Establishing a national image

. . . I believe that Rafshoon's comments and overview are excellent. In keeping with his strategy and sense of timing, it is necessary that we begin immediately to generate favorable stories and comments in the national press. Stories in the **New York Times** and **Washington Post** do not just happen, but have to be carefully planned and planted.

I would hope that we could relate the accomplishments of your administration to the theme that revitalized state government is the key to solving many of the problems in this country today as has been demonstrated in Georgia by Gov. Jimmy Carter. The thrust of your national press effort should be that state government is working in Georgia and is solving the problems in meeting the needs of ordinary citizens. By emphasizing this theme and making your own political plans a secondary consideration, I believe you would have the forum and excuse you need to appear on television talk shows, write articles for national publications and serve as an obvious example that revitalized state government is where the action and the interest are.

. . . A particular problem facing the Democratic Party is that its preoccuppation with senators has resulted in many of its members having already been unsuccessful candidates for national office—Humphrey, Jackson, Hughes, Harris, Bayh, Muskie, Eagleton and McGovern being the most obvious.

For all these reasons, we have reached the time when

a governor who can demonstrate an understanding and ability in foreign affairs and domestic issues can be seriously considered for the presidency. . . .

. . . A lot of the research and leg work that needs to be done in the next year or so could be attributed to a possible race for the U.S. Senate. We could involve more people with less risk using this as an excuse for briefings and position papers on foreign affairs and domestic issues.

The years in between

. . . I believe that you should attempt to develop the image of a highly successful and concerned former governor of Georgia and peanut farmer living in a small rural town, speaking out on the pertinent issues of the day. Once your name begins to be mentioned in the national press, you will not lack for invitations and opportunities to speak in major groups and conventions. . . .

If you are in general agreement with Rafshoon's thinking, we should begin immediately to (1) generate favorable stories in the national press on the accomplishments of your administration, (2) develop and/or maintain a close personal relationship with the principal national columnists and reporters, and (3) take full advantage of every legitimate opportunity for national exposure as long as it is couched in terms of what you have accomplished in Georgia.

We should compile a listing of regional and national political editors and columnists who you know or need to know. You can find ample excuse for contacting them—writing them a note, complimenting them on an article or column and asking that they come to see you when convenient. Some people like Tom Wicker or Mrs. Katherine Graham are significant enough to spend an evening or a leisurely weekend with. . . .

Like it or not, there exists in fact an eastern liberal news establishment which has tremendous influence in this country all out of proportion to its actual audience. The views of this small group of opinion-makers in the papers they represent are noted and imitated by other columnists and newspapers throughout the country and the world. Their recognition and acceptance of your candidacy as a viable force with some chance of success could establish you as a serious contender worthy of the financial support of major party contributors. They could have an equally adverse effect, dismissing your effort as being regional or an attempt to secure the second spot on the ticket.

Fortunately, a disproportionate number of these opinion-makers are southerners by birth and tradition and . . . subconsciously desire to see the South move beyond the George Wallace area and assert itself as a region. . . . It is my contention that they would be fascinated by the prospect of your candidacy and would treat it seriously through the first several primaries.

In keeping with these recommendations, we should begin to: (1) Foster relationships with political columnists that you know. Establish relationships with those you don't know.

(2) Utilize Don Carter's [a cousin, and publisher of the Lexington, Kentucky, **Herald**] contacts to create situations where you can get to know key people. For example, let Don Carter invite Tom Wicker and Max [Frankel] to spend a weekend visiting with both of you on Cumberland Island.

(3) Generate stories in national . . . trade magazines on particular accomplishments. . . .

(4) Hire a professional, first-class speechwriter, researcher. When you go out of state you need to have something of substance to say. The same applies when you address national conventions in Atlanta. This is and should be a full-time position.

(5) Review and read portions of the **New York Times, Washington Post, Wall Street [Journal]** and other national selections every day. Despite its liberal orientation and bias, the **New York Times** is the best paper in the country and possibly the world. One cannot keep track of national politics or international affairs by simply reading the **Atlanta Constitution, Time** and **Newsweek.**

(6) Learn to speak from your prepared text. I have heard Jody and Rafshoon both say that this is your only shortcoming as a candidate and that this skill can be easily developed through practice.

(7) Schedule appearances on network talk shows, the focus being "Making State Government Work" or some tangible accomplishment of your administration.

(8) Write a book or column on some pertinent issue or

topic with the focus on how a problem was confronted by your administration. . . .

Staff needs

Schedule of tasks for the next six months

Description of Task	Target Date
1. Read **N.Y. Times** and **Washington Post** daily	Immediately and continuing
2. Hire professional speechwriter who can devote full time to research in preparation of speeches on pertinent issues of the day.	Jan. 1, 1973
3. Log up on your schedule beyond March 1, sufficient time for briefings, meetings and out-of-state speeches and trips.	Immediately
4. Devise plans to insure better follow-up on speeches to national groups and conventions, to include letters to key persons and acquisition of lists of convention participants.	Immediately
5. Begin to develop national files for special emphasis on primary states.	Immediately
6. Visit Sen. Kennedy and get to know him. He may tell you unequivocably that he is going to run. Such a meeting will give you some idea as to how you should proceed.	Jan. 1, 1973
7. Meet with Sen. [Henry] Jackson to determine if he has plans of his own. If not, seek his support and advice.	Jan. 1, 1973

Description of Task	Target Date

8. Make courtesy call on Gov. Wallace. If this is impossible, call him and seek his advice on national Democratic chairman.　　Jan. 1, 1973

9. Meet with Dean Rusk. Ask him to assume responsibility for educating you on foreign affairs and to develop a continuing program which would include regular briefings, a reading list and the establishment of a formal task force. Ask that he submit program outline to you in six weeks.　　Jan. 1, 1973

10. Meet with Don Carter. Ask him to develop a list of national editors and columnists you should know. Ask him to assume responsibility for liaison work with national press and be responsible for developing a realistic program that will permit you to spend some time with each of these. Ask that he submit listing and program in four weeks.　　Jan. 1, 1973

11. Ask Philip Alston to prepare listing of potential financial contributors who can be involved in an early stage and can be trusted. Schedule time with each of these.　　Dec. 1, 1973

12. Meet with Morris Dees. Try to involve him in your effort. His national fundraising expertise as well as his ability to make a sizeable contribution is needed.　　Jan. 1, 1973

13. Hire full-time persons to coordinate various aspects of early campaign.　　Jan. 1, 1973

71

Description of Task	Target Date

14. Begin to look for person with good reputation and contacts in Washington who can plan major role and campaign. Try to identify this person by target date. — June 1, 1973

15. Schedule weekend meeting for Advisory Committee. Outline to them their role in your effort. — March 1, 1973

16. Identify persons who can assume responsibility for developing a continuing program on education on pertinent domestic issues of the day to parallel Dean Rusk's activities in foreign affairs. Stu Eizenstat is a possibility. — March 1, 1973

17. Decide if you're interested in pursuing the chairmanship of the National Governors' Conference. If so, you will need to talk with Mandel about this soon. — Before Dec. 3, 1972

18. Select someone to devise complete budget for next two years. Mr. Kirbo should be involved. — Jan. 1, 1973

19. Assign someone responsible for accumulating data on national campaign cost with projection on media expense, polling and primary state campaign. Jerry Rafshoon would be a possibility. — March 1, 1973

▆ ▆ ▆

When Democratic National Chairman Robert Strauss came to Atlanta to give a speech on March 5, 1973, he dropped by the governor's mansion to talk with Jimmy Carter. Charles Kirbo was there, too—he was an old friend of Strauss. As they sat on the porch having a drink, it was not surprising that the talk was of politics.

As they recall it now, Strauss thinks it was Carter who brought up the idea and Carter and Kirbo think it was Strauss. At any rate, by the time dinner was ready, the plan was that Jimmy Carter, who would be going out of office in 1974, would serve that year as the chairman of the Democratic 1974 congressional campaign committee, a generally routine and thankless job.

Strauss may have been mildly pleased with the arrangement; the Carter people were tickled to death. The Rafshoon plan was on schedule: *"Phase II 1974: Carter as a leader in the Democratic Party and someone involved in bringing it back."*

Carter traveled around the country on the assignment, making friends. In Rochester, New York, he helped Democrat Midge Costanza in her unsuccessful effort to unseat Republican Congressman Barber Conable. Two years later, she was Carter's earliest New York supporter and served as co-chairperson of his state campaign.

In Palo Alto, California, while helping a congressional candidate, Carter dropped in on an environmental meeting aimed at saving the Stanislaus River. There he got up and said a few words, and by the time he sat down he had himself some key supporters for his still unlaunched Carter for President effort. Rodney Kennedy-Minott, a history professor and veteran political organizer in the area, had been impressed by Carter, his environmentalist outlook, and his willingness to attack the Army Corps of Engineers and the federal bureaucracy. Kennedy-Minott wrote Carter and volunteered to help him if he ever ran for President. Kennedy-Minott later served as his California co-chairperson.

In Washington, Carter worked with Bill Dodds, political director of the United Auto Workers, and Mike Miller, political director of the Communications Workers. It was the Georgian's first chance to get a good feel for the union leaders who are so important to any Democrat who wants to win in the northern industrial states. And it was their first chance to get to know him. Two years later, Carter received the endorsement of UAW President Leonard Woodcock.

Where Carter went, Jody Powell went too, keeping a

notebook with the name, address, and phone number of every person that Carter met. On several occasions, Powell, Hamilton Jordan, and another Carter aide, Frank Moore, traveled apart from Carter to conduct campaign workshops around the country—and each time they broadened their list of national political contacts.

Carter and his aides did not receive a salary from the party. But their travel expenses—$6,000 to $10,000, Jordan estimates—were paid by the Democratic National Committee. Whenever possible, Carter and his aides stayed as houseguests of the Democrats they were meeting —not really to save money, but because, as one Carter man observed, "It helped to build the close personal relationships—the family-type relationships—that are so important when you are later asking people to give of themselves and bust their humps for you."

Robert Keefe, executive director of the Democratic National Committee—and later the director of Scoop Jackson's campaign—approved the hiring of Jordan as executive director of the campaign committee. Keefe soon knew that Carter actually was running for President while he was heading the Democratic campaign committee. "Early on, some people left some things around that they should not have left," Keefe said. "I found them on my table." Keefe passed the intelligence information to Strauss. But neither Strauss nor Keefe did anything about it. "Carter was paying his own freight," Keefe said. "He was working like a bastard for the committee. It was not like he was milking it. . . . He did it in very good taste. . . ."

After the November 1974 congressional elections, Carter visited Capitol Hill and walked into the impressive office of the House Majority Leader to meet briefly with its occupant, Representative Thomas (Tip) O'Neill (D–Mass.). "I'm going to be the next President," Carter said to O'Neill, according to the recollection of the large, white-haired, classic old pol who has long believed that no presidential year is complete if there is not a Kennedy in the race. "I know you're supporting Teddy Kennedy, but he's not going to run. [Kennedy had officially taken himself out of the race in September, citing personal reasons.] Hubert Humphrey will make a lot of noise, but in the end he won't run either. Jackson won't get off the ground. The man I've been running against—Mondale—just announced he's withdrawing."

Tip O'Neill, who looks like he was appointed to the role of House Majority Leader by Central Casting, had seen enough bright-eyed politicians come and go that he was not impressed by the softly drawled hard sell of this guy from Georgia, whom he really did not know. "Tip just did not take him seriously," reports one close associate of O'Neill's.

Walter F. (Fritz) Mondale, a senator from Minnesota, had spent a year sampling his chances to win the Democratic presidential nomination; he had traveled widely and tried to spark some political enthusiasm. He found none. On November 21, 1974, Mondale announced that he was withdrawing from the contest. "Basically, I found I did not have the overwhelming desire to be President which is essential for the kind of campaign that is required," Mondale said then. (Later, when he was being chosen by Carter to be his vice-presidential running mate, Mondale would say that it was not that he did not have the stomach for the tough campaign; rather, he said, he just had campaigned hard and had found he was not making any progress. Mondale had hovered around 3 and 4 percent in the polls in 1974. But it is worth noting that this is higher than Jimmy Carter wâs—in fact, Carter was not even ranked at the time, he was so unknown.) The *Washington Post* devoted considerable space to the Mondale withdrawal, playing the story on page one. The next-to-last paragraph of the Mondale story said that Robert Keefe was resigning as executive director of the Democratic National Committee to head the Jackson campaign. And the last paragraph of the story said that Governor Jimmy Carter of Georgia planned to announce officially on December 12 that he would be running for President.

December 12, 1974, Atlanta. Jimmy Carter stood before more than 2,000 well-wishers, including Apollo 11 astronaut Edwin (Buzz) Aldrin. Live television carried Carter's words to his fellow Georgians:

"As of this time here, in the state that I love, surrounded by friends of mine from all over the nation—in

*fact even from the moon—I want to announce that I am
a candidate for the Presidency of the United States."*

🏳 🏳 🏳

For all his memos, for all his planning, for all his ma-
neuvering, Jimmy Carter still had two basic problems when
he set out in 1975 on his presidential campaign. Not many
people knew who he was. And not many cared.

In Philadelphia, Carter scheduled a press conference in
a downtown hotel and nobody showed up except the candidate and his press secretary, Jody Powell. "We soon
learned that things had to be pre-existing events for him
to get any coverage in many cities," Powell recalled.
"Either that, or else we had to finagle." Later Powell got
Carter onto a television talk show in Des Moines by agree-
ing to talk about subjects other than politics. He told
viewers about Plains, Georgia, and a recipe for cooking
fish.

JIMMY CARTER'S CATFISH RECIPE. Ingredients: catfish
(or bass); Heinz 57 Sauce; Bisquick or pancake mix; corn
oil.

Method: Cut fish into strips like French fries. Marinate
fish in Heinz 57 Sauce for several hours. Coat fish with
dry Bisquick or pancake mix. Fry in oil. May be served
hot or cold.

🏳 🏳 🏳

So it went on the campaign trail in 1975 for the gallop-
ing gourmet who in 1976 would become the Democratic
Party's presidential nominee. In each state, Carter and his
aides set about trying to establish some sort of organization,
building as often as possible on contacts Carter had made
in the past—including some from his work as the party's
1974 campaign chairman. Carter stuck to a schedule that
eventually took him to forty-six states and the District of
Columbia in 1975. But that is not to say things steadily
improved for the Georgian as he set about the business of
getting nationally known.

"By midsummer," Carter's press secretary and traveling
aide Jody Powell recalls, "in every state we'd go into,

some of Jimmy's supporters would pull me aside and say 'When are you going to get him on "Meet the Press" or "Face the Nation"?'

"They knew they were working hard in their area, but they had no idea—and saw no evidence—that we had anything going on anywhere else. They each thought they were the only ones working for Jimmy in the whole country, and you could tell clearly from the way they said things to me that their concern was that if Carter only had a press secretary who was worth a damn, he'd have been on 'Meet the Press' and 'Face the Nation' and 'Issues and Answers' already. Well, that just might have been true. But in those times, I was doing a better job of going around and lowering people's expectations than Jerry Brown ever thought of doing."

In those days, Powell was Carter's constant traveling companion, his personal aide, driver, spokesman, and issues expert combined. In 1968, as a political science graduate student at Emory University, Powell had written a paper disputing the theory that a Wallace-type third party would inherit the southern vote. In 1969, he wrote to Carter and told him about the paper and volunteered to help in the coming gubernatorial campaign. Powell had earlier been dismissed from the Air Force Academy for cheating, a fact he frankly admits. He told Carter about that black moment in his past; Carter told him to forget it. As Powell frequently drove Carter throughout the state, the two had many lengthy discussions of strategy and issues. Powell, who was thirty-two during the 1976 run for the Presidency, had emerged as a man of mature judgment and candid, self-effacing style who functioned as press secretary and whose counsel on strategy, issues, and public relations had the attention and respect of Carter.

Back in 1975, there wasn't much Powell could do about getting Carter frequent prestigious bookings like "Face the Nation" or "Meet the Press," but he did come up with a way of letting the Carter workers around the country know that at least they were not alone. The Carter campaign began sending out a nationwide newsletter, carrying clips from newspapers in every area Carter visited. Thus the Carter workers could see that at least their man was getting good local press coverage.

In 1975 Carter was doing more than just worrying about local press coverage. One glaring weakness in the presidential candidacy of the ex-Georgia governor was that he had no experience in foreign affairs—certainly nothing that could be compared favorably with the many men of Washington who had their eye on the White House. That was one reason why he seized on an opportunity in May to go to Japan as a member of a trilateral commission composed of North American, European, and Japanese representatives of government and the academic communities, as Jordan's 1972 memo had advised.

The commission effort was funded by the Rockefeller Foundation and its broad purpose was to bring together persons from the three geographic areas to discuss a variety of global matters. "We knew this was no opportunity for us—or anyone else—to get much media attention," said Jody Powell. "But we figured it was of good long-term benefit."

(As governor, Carter had traveled to Central and South America in 1971 to talk up business and investment opportunities in Georgia—including the sale of Lockheed aircraft. In 1973 he traveled to Europe on another state industry and trade mission; and he made a side trip over to the Middle East, where he arranged to meet with officials including Golda Meir, a meeting that he was not at all reticent to mention during his presidential campaigning before Jewish audiences three years later.)

While in Japan, Carter met with the then-current Prime Minister Tanaka, the future prime minister (Miki), and the past prime minister (Sato). And with his eye on future relationships, he also contacted various American reporters based in Tokyo at the time and arranged to meet with them for drinks and conversation. Some of the reporters wondered at the time what the sense was of spending time talking with a former governor of Georgia, but to Carter it was just part of the "long-term benefits" he has always looked for. (A couple of the reporters have since made their way back to prestigious jobs with major newspapers back home.)

"We didn't expect any story out of that get-together and I don't think anyone filed a line of copy on it," Jody Powell said. "But the thinking was that if you do things

like that wherever you go, eventually you get so you're
not a stranger to everyone."

■ ■ ■

In mid-1975, Morris Udall's legislative assistant, Terry
Bracy, received a telephone call from a man who said
he was, as Bracy recalls, "the just-dismissed desk coordinator for the Northeast for Jimmy Carter." The man
said he worked out of Atlanta. And he told Bracy that
he had taken some files with him when he left—including
media files and "basic Carter strategy, Carter contacts."

The man offered the Udall official a dirty tricks proposi-
tion of sorts.

"I asked him what he had," Bracy said. The caller gave
him a rundown. "I was really disturbed," Bracy said.
"This really bothered me." Bracy thought for a brief
moment about the political career of Donald Segretti.
Then he told the caller to "go fuck yourself" and hung
up.

Bracy promptly called Hamilton Jordan, Carter's campaign manager, who was based in Atlanta. As Bracy remembers it, "I said to him, 'We have got a problem. One
of your former guys has your stuff on the bidding block.' "

Jordan suggested that Bracy "go public" about the telephone call and the offer. "I said, 'Ham, I'm not dying
to go public.' " Instead, Bracy gave Jordan the name of
the ex-Carter man who had called him.

Jordan appreciated the way Bracy dealt with the matter. "Those Udall people were very decent and honorable
in the way they handled it," Jordan said. "They acted
truly first class."

Jordan called the young man in Arizona, where he
lived. "I called the kid and told him I knew he'd left here
mad. I told him I'd heard some rumors that he'd been
saying some things about files—I just said rumors; I
wanted to protect Bracy. I told him I'd looked over my files
and there were some things missing and that I'd hoped it
wasn't true what I'd heard but that if anything surfaced,
we'd have to take quick legal action.

"I was just bluffing him out of it. . . . I really didn't
know what was missing or anything. But we never heard
anything about it after that."

It was about a month and a half before Bracy mentioned the incident to Udall. There was no need to tell him in advance of rejecting the offer of stolen files, Bracy said. "That's what he would have expected," Bracy said. "Yes, we got tough and nasty in Michigan and in Ohio, but we stuck to the rules. I don't know of any dirty tricks. . . ."

There were tricks played in the campaign, but they were within the accepted rules of politics. On one presidential forum night in Louisville, Sylvia Chaplin, a Udall advance woman, discovered before the session that the podium to which the microphone was attached was far too short for her 6-foot, 5-inch boss.

Ms. Chaplin bought four reams of paper, each six inches thick, and placed a ream under each corner of the lectern. Then she did her work by decorating the new bottom with red, white, and blue bunting. That night, Udall stood tall as he spoke, looking straight at the audience. The other candidates had to stare at the ceiling to make themselves heard.

While Jimmy Carter was spending 1975 trying to get national recognition, six of his rivals, all philosophical allies, were trying to eliminate each other. Morris Udall, Birch Bayh, Sargent Shriver, Fred Harris, Milton Shapp, and Terry Sanford were six liberals in a race where they felt there was room for only one.

In September the liberals converged on Minneapolis to contest for the support of 1,500 liberal activists of the Midwest. Each addressed the meeting. The contender who drew the greatest applause was Harris, who could stir any crowd with his angry shouts against the way Washington ran things within the United States and overseas. Diplomacy was being conducted in secret. Harris thundered, and at home "the issue is privilege."

It was a long day of rhetoric and Bayh was the last speaker. He was the best known of the hopefuls and on that day the least impressive. In his opening remarks he did not talk of issues; instead, he spoke of his record in the Senate. To those familiar with his work on Capitol Hill, he responded to questions with less ability than he had shown in Washington.

This was just one of a string of unimpressive campaign performances by Bayh. His inability to attract a large following early in the primary year surprised many Democratic politicians, including a number of his opponents for the nomination. Among these were Jimmy Carter and his advisers, who believed all along that Bayh would be stronger than he proved to be.

Although it was Harris who received the applause, it was Udall who apparently won the support. The *Washington Post* conducted a straw poll at the Minneapolis meeting, found that Udall was a strong favorite, and said so in a big front-page story. He was the first choice of over half the audience at the meeting.

One of the most expensive investments of time and money by the liberal candidates was their effort to win the backing of the New York group known as the New Democratic Coalition. The endorsement of the NDC would "isolate the others from liberal support," Birch Bayh declared. And liberal support was viewed as the key to winning the New York primary.

"Our first target was Udall," Bayh's press secretary, Bill Wise, recalled. "We felt we had to blunt Udall. He was the more formidable of the candidates on the left. The quicker we could knock Udall out, the quicker we'd get Udall people in [Bayh's camp]. We thought our weakest area was the liberal activists. That's why we spent so much time and effort with the New Democratic Coalition. The NDC was significant. It makes it so much easier to get on the ballot in New York. We put in a helluva lot of early time, money, and effort to make that point."

One of Udall's top advisers also recalled the NDC campaign. "The time, concern, and energy we spent on the New Democratic Coalition was, I think, an outrage. An outrage because I was led to believe that was where it was at. We had to prevent Birch Bayh from getting that NDC nomination."

Udall adviser Ken Bode worked out a system in which he had the Udall delegates and the Harris delegates in constant communication at the NDC convention December 6, united in a common goal: Stop Bayh.

Sixty percent of the delegates were needed in order to win the support of the NDC. Bayh was stopped just short. "Two months from now," New York Assemblyman William Hoyt of Buffalo had said in making an endorsement appeal for Bayh, "the only name you're going to hear upstate is Birch Bayh." By the time of the New York primary, however, Bayh's name was not heard anywhere. He had already been knocked out of the race.

In October 1975 Broadman Press, publishers of religious books, came out with the first printing of Carter's combination autobiography and campaign book. Its title, *Why Not the Best?*, seemed to work two ways: it seemed to reflect the Georgian's self-assured nature as he went about trying to convince people that he was the best candidate of the field and that he was going to win the presidential nomination even if they did not think so (his book might just as well have been titled, "I'm the Best, You're O.K."); but as Carter saw it, the title was not immodest; it merely reflected the message he carried away from his job interview with Admiral Hyman Rickover when he was applying for the nuclear submarine program. (Rickover had asked Carter if he had always done his best at the naval academy and Carter had said no, not always, and Rickover had paused and finally responded: "Why not?")

Carter's book reflected a theme that became a central trait of his campaign. It offered something for everyone. It begins by quoting Reinhold Neibuhr and Bob Dylan and Dylan Thomas. It talks of his days of fishing and fighting and getting whipped by his father for misbehaving and goes right into quotes of Sören Kierkegaard and Paul Tillich; it tells of his passion for Tristan and Isolde and talks of the music of the Liebestod and the next sentence is, "I became an expert on the recognition of the world's ships and planes during that time [at the U.S. naval academy]."

Something for everyone.

■   ■   ■

A symbolic moment at the California State Democratic Convention, held early in 1975 in Sacramento: Mo Udall, after repeated attempts to meet privately with Governor

Edmund G. (Jerry) Brown, finally was told to come by at night. "We lope over from the hotel at about 11:15 P.M.," Udall aide Terry Bracy recalls. "We were thinking, 'There's no apparent purpose to this. What fool would stay up to do this?'" Just as we were walking into the governor's office, we meet Jimmy Carter walking out. Always one step ahead."

▬   ▬   ▬

In early December 1975 a Carter supporter in New York called the Carter Headquarters in Atlanta to report a bit of Manhattan cocktail-circuit gossip. There had been a cocktail party at the Automation House and someone who is in the magazine business said that *Harper's* Magazine had signed Steven Brill to write a piece about Carter —"and he's going to do a number on us."

In early January 1976 a person supporting Birch Bayh in New York contacted a person running as a Carter delegate in New York to pass on a warning. There is going to be a piece coming out in *Harper's* that will be just devastating to Carter—"so you better stay away from him."

At a reception a few weeks later in Washington given by the Energy Action Committee, Alan Baron told some people about a *Harper's* piece by Brill that did so much damage to Carter. He said he had an advance copy of it and people could take a look at it if they wanted.

Jody Powell called *Harper's* editor Lewis Lapham to see a copy. They were receiving queries about the article, and there were apparently advance copies of the article around. Could the Carter people have a copy too? Lapham eventually agreed and Carter got his first look at what *Harper's* would be printing in its March edition.

It was titled "Jimmy Carter's Pathetic Lies." By Steven Brill.

There were many hard swipes at Carter in the lengthy *Harper's* piece. But there was nothing in the piece that was as devastating a shot as the title itself. Had the article been called simply "The Jimmy Carter Story" it could have pulled off its anti-Carter attack with a touch of class. As it turned out, the title alone created an aura of a cheap shot. In fact, the Brill piece contained some elements that were well reported and some that were not. The article dealt in large measure with Carter's political career in Georgia—controversies about his earlier campaigns and his stewardship of the state in his years as governor.

Because he received an early copy of the *Harper's* piece, Powell was able to prepare a lengthy point-by-point rebuttal to the article by Brill. Some of Powell's points were in fact refutations; others were just responses. The Powell document proved indeed effective as a political tool; it took the edge off the Brill attack. The *Boston Globe,* for example, wound up running excerpts from the Brill piece and excerpts from the Powell responses on the same day.

Postscript: One of Jody Powell's rebuttals concerned a letter quoted in the article. Brill said it had been sent by Carter to a woman, Mrs. Lena Mae Dempsey, who had written him complaining about his endorsement of Jackson instead of Wallace at the 1972 Democratic convention.

Dear Mrs. Dempsey:

I have never had anything but the highest praise for Governor Wallace. My support for Senator Jackson was based upon a personal request from our late Senator Richard Russell shortly before his death. I think you will find that Senator Jackson, Governor Wallace and I are in close agreement in most issues.

Let me ask you to consider one other factor before I close. There are times when two men working toward the same end can accomplish more if they are not completely tied together. I think you will find that Governor Wallace understands this.

Please let me know when I can be of service to you or your children in Atlanta. I hope I have been able to give you a slightly better impression of me.

Sincerely,
Jimmy Carter

Brill was right. The letter did exist and it was sent. But Powell responded:

The letter to Mrs. Dempsey was written by a staffer, never seen by Gov. Carter, and did not accu-

rately express his views. Several hundred letters each
day often were answered from the Governor's office
by staffers; inevitably, a few of these staff responses
were not exactly what the Governor would have
written. Had the writer of the article asked, he would
have been told of the three-letter-initial code used to
identify staff letters.

The unfortunate choice of words by one staffer in
one letter is hardly a test of the national leadership
ability or the personal integrity of the Governor. . . .

Powell too was right. It was "the unfortunate choice of
words by one staffer." What his response did not go on
to say, however—but which Powell acknowledged without
hesitation when asked—was that the "staffer" who wrote
the letter had been Powell himself.

The Carter master plan for winning the nomination
would have been useless without money to make it work.
On December 12, 1974—the day he announced his candidacy—Carter began his fundraising with letters asking
some 30,000 Georgia friends and associates to contribute
to his campaign. Another letter was sent to about 500,000
other people culled from lists of Democratic National
Committee telethon contributors and McGovern campaign
contributors. That was the first large-scale Carter fundraising drive.

Up to that time, the Carter money effort had been made
strictly in Georgia. In August 1974 twenty-seven people
were invited to a pool party at the home of Bill Schwartz,
an Atlanta real estate man and friend of Carter's. "We
were really grubbing," recalled Frank Moore, a Carter
finance coordinator. "About half of them were Jimmy's
friends and the other half could afford to give." The
affair raised $40,000. By the end of 1975, Carter had
raised $850,000.

In 1975 Morris Dees, who had been successful in mass-
mailing fundraising efforts for McGovern and who had
helped set up similar systems for several of the 1976
Democratic candidates, officially signed on with Carter.

In December 1975 Dees proposed a "double-up" effort, in which all people who had given Carter $100 or more—some 1,800 people—would be asked to match their previous contributions. "The idea got a lot of horse laughs around here because the campaign had twisted people's arms to get them to pay $100 in the first place," Dees said.

The double-up letter, sent out over Carter's signature, was pitched to the Florida primary and his hopes of defeating Wallace.

Mr. John Doe
100 Main Street
Atlanta, Georgia   30303

Dear Mr. Doe:

We have done what seemed impossible.

I have emerged early as the Democratic candidate who has broken from the pack. . . .

The hour of decision is at hand.

Whether we can maintain our winning momentum until the early primaries and defeat Wallace in Florida on March 9th depends on you.

A bumper crop of peanuts, I learned years ago, is not made at harvest time but in early spring when you prepare a good seed bed. When I beat Wallace in Florida, the nomination will be within reach. To do this, I need $500,000 by December 26 to tie up prime TV time, buy billboards, and reach Florida voters.

We have wisely spent all the funds raised this year. Many of my key staff members are now going without pay to release new funds raised to be used for media advances.

To be very frank, our campaign's success may well depend on raising the Florida media funds prior to December 26th.

It is not easy to ask your help once more when I know how generous you have already been.

But history has always been made not by the multitudes but by the determined and courageous few. The $xxxxx you have already given is helping write a new chapter for America.

I believe so strongly that our government can be

decent, truthful, fair, compassionate and efficient
and I need your help so urgently that I am going to
ask you and each donor to make a personal sacrifice.

Please send me another $xxxxx in the enclosed
stamped envelope. I'm asking each donor to "double-
up" at this critically important time. I know the
financial strain this may create with the holiday season at hand. But I pray you will answer our urgent
need even if you have to borrow the funds.

Just think how shocked my opponents will be to
learn we doubled our total contributions in just two
weeks. Not only will this show unprecedented loyalty
and faith from my friends but it will make political
history.

Will you reach out your hand to me, once again?
Rosalynn and I will do our best to never disappoint
you.

Sincerely,
Jimmy Carter

P.S.—On December 26th I hope to announce to the
    press the success of our 'Double-up for Carter'
    drive. Please rush your check.

The plea brought in $225,000. And after that Carter
wrote to his donors every month, asking them to give
again. He raised more than $1 million using this technique.

Beat Wallace in Florida. That was the message of Carter's double-up letter and that, in fact, was the foundation
of the original Carter master plan. Carter had to win in
Florida to show that he could take the South from George
Wallace; he had to show that he alone could restore the
solid South to the Democratic Party in November. Only
then could Carter prove that he could be a winner nationwide.

Carter had started out sticking to his original plan—
doing better than he expected, in fact. He won in Iowa
and he won in New Hampshire. The plan called for him
to ride this bandwagon momentum straight to a victory in
Florida over Wallace. But on the way, Carter had let himself get sidetracked; he had tried for a win in Massachusetts
on March 2, and he had built up expectations for his showing there. And he had been crushed. He had been buried

by opponents, including the two men he now had to face in Florida, Jackson and Wallace. His momentum was gone. He had shifted his sights and he was paying a price. He had sabotaged his own bandwagon. Perhaps, he feared, irreparably.

March 9/Florida

A minor difference of opinion exists among the members of the Carter staff. Some say that when Jimmy Carter is angry the veins in his temples throb. Others insist that when he is angry it is his jaw muscles that throb.

Carter's temples and jaw muscles throbbed through much of the week that separated the Massachusetts and Florida primaries. They throbbed on airport tarmacs when Carter stood in the hot sun with microphones being shoved in his face as soon as he stepped off his plane. They throbbed in crowded motel meeting rooms as he held his question-and-answer sessions. They throbbed at a fish fry that turned into a press conference in Green Cove Springs.

"I'll be glad to repeat myself again—or else you can play your tape back to yourself," Carter snapped at a reporter who sought to question him.

On another occasion: "Do you want to stop talking so I can give you my answer or do you want to go ahead and ask a second question as well?"

When he wasn't snapping at the press, Carter was launching harshly worded attacks against Scoop Jackson. And even against George Wallace.

"He was off balance after Massachusetts," Hamilton Jordan said much later.

"The campaign was less sure of itself at that point than at any other time," recalled Greg Schneiders. "Massachusetts was the first sign that we were fallible."

"He was kind of at loose ends then," said Jody Powell.

"It was a case of not having cleaned it up and talked out in advance where we were headed."

Of the attacks on Wallace, Powell said: "We'd realized all along that doing it didn't cut with the voters. Frankly, even he knew that it wasn't the thing to do."

▄▄ ▄▄ ▄▄

Jerry Rafshoon was in a phone booth in the Washington National Airport on the day after the Massachusetts election, working his way through five dollars in dimes while waiting for his plane, when his secretary at the office told him that Jimmy Carter had been calling. Carter was at Cape Canaveral being briefed on missiles; he couldn't come to the phone right then. Rafshoon left the number of the telephone booth he was using and waited for Carter to call back. A woman entered the booth.

"Can you use another phone?" Rafshoon asked.

"Why?" asked the woman.

"Jimmy Carter is trying to call me," Rafshoon replied.

"So what?" said the woman, depositing her dime.

Carter finally got through to Rafshoon. He wanted to make a new rush TV spot for the Florida campaign—a spot countering Jackson's efforts to play up the Carter home mortgage snafu. Carter wanted to tape the spot that night.

Gerald Rafshoon Advertising, Inc., went to work and finally located a small, private studio on the outskirts of Jacksonville that could be used that evening. Rafshoon made his way to Jacksonville and he and Carter went to the studio. Rafshoon's script for the TV spot opened with something like: "One of the candidates has been talking against my position on tax reform." Carter wanted to blast Jackson by name. But he eventually agreed that there was no need to give Jackson the free publicity. The rushed spot was put on the air in Florida the following day.

In press conferences and interviews that week, Carter's attack on Jackson centered around Jackson's ad in the *Boston Globe* which proclaimed in large letters: "I AM AGAINST BUSING." Said Carter: "Senator Jackson ran a campaign centered around the busing issue . . . an emotional issue . . . one that has racial or racist connotations. To build a campaign on an issue . . . that has already created disharmony, and sometimes even bloodshed, is to me the wrong approach to politics. I wouldn't do it. But Senator Jackson did. It's legal. I don't think he is a racist. I think he recognized an emotional issue and capitalized on it."

Carter's attack on Wallace was broad-based: "Governor Wallace's position on the race issue is well known. And part of his support probably comes from the race issue—I don't think there's much doubt about that. . . . But Wallace's support also comes from a wide range of voters and beliefs—partly because they think he's going to clean up the federal bureaucracy. It's obvious he can't do it. He hasn't done it in Alabama. Part of it is because they think he's going to give the poor people a better break from taxation. Obviously he can't do it. He hasn't done it in Alabama—that's the most regressive tax structure in the nation, in Alabama. Part of his support is because he wants the federal courts to be out of the administration of government. Obviously Alabama is a horrible example, because for all practical purposes, the federal courts are running many important elements in the Alabama government. . . ."

    ▰   ▰   ▰

Massachusetts. The spectre of that snowstorm election verdict hung heavily over the Carter caravan as it crisscrossed sweltering Florida early in that final week.

Massachusetts. It was now very much a part of Florida, the Carter men feared. In Tallahassee at a businessmen's lunch, Carter received telephoned word that his campaign phone survey had shown his positive rating slipping and his negative rating climbing. There seemed to be a correlation between those statistics and the fact that Carter headquarters in Florida were receiving more and more phone calls from people wanting to know just what Carter was going to do with their tax deduction on home mortgage interest. Massachusetts. That damn Massachusetts.

But tucked into the bitter lessons of Massachusetts was the first indication of what proved to be a pleasant discovery to many of the Carter men. "It was the great surprise of '76 for us," Carter's pollster, Patrick Caddell, said later. "We got the black vote in Massachusetts. We never

91

dreamed we would, but we got it. Roxbury went for Jimmy. That was the one good thing about Massachusetts."

This pointed up what was to become the truly phenomenal thing about the Carter campaign: the candidate was able to attract large numbers of people from a wide range of disparate backgrounds, interests, and beliefs. Rednecks and blacks, McGovern liberals and hardline hawks, labor leaders and corporation executives, people who wear denim because it's good to work in and people who wear denim because it's good to party in.

Massachusetts, it turned out, gave the Carter people a good healthy scare. But it proved to be not as significant in Florida as several other factors. Chiefly, the liberals seeking the nomination had challenged Carter in the other states, but to a man they had bypassed Florida. They feared that Florida would be Wallace country once again, just as it had been in 1968 and 1972. As they were to do throughout the 1976 campaign, the liberals fought this year's battles on the basis of the past years' wars. Many Democrats feared in the beginning that Wallace would be a large and unpleasant problem for all the party in 1976, that he would do well outside the South in this year when people were so turned off by politics as usual. So they were content to let Carter have a clean shot at Wallace in Florida. After all, if the unknown Georgian should pull an upset win, they reasoned, he would be easy to pick off later.

      ▆   ▆   ▆

SCENE: Vero Beach, at the high school gym. The stage is bedecked in red, white, and blue, but in the crowd some people waiting for the candidate are pointing up at the eerie piece of furniture that sits on the stage front and center. "Look, he's got to set behind that little bulletproof thing now," a man in a straw Wallace boater says to his wife. "Poor fella. Look what it's like for him now." Wallace is wheeled in and is placed behind the lectern that is strangely small, with short wooden (lead-reinforced) walls and bulletproof glass that separate the candidate from the crowd.

Empty seats predominate, but Wallace pretends not to

notice. The people applaud his lines enthusiastically but the hoots, shouts, and rebel yells of old are largely missing.

    ▤   ▤   ▤

George Wallace 1976 was not George Wallace 1972 . . . or 1968 . . . or 1964. His people talked about Franklin D. Roosevelt, who was crippled yet a leader and unifier. But George Wallace had never been a national leader—certainly not a national unifier. His South had moved on from those early days of racial confrontation; blacks now starred on Alabama football teams and rednecks cheered them. His anti-Washington theme—lambasting the pointy-heads and the bureaucrats with briefcases full of peanut butter sandwiches—was no longer just his. Anti-Washington had become the gospel of Campaign '76, sung frequently with more sophisticated lyrics by a full choir of candidates—liberal, moderate, and conservative. (On the Republican side, even the President of the United States, Gerald Ford, would try his hand at running against the federal government.) It just might be that this could not have been the year of even a healthy George Wallace. But the fact that he was crippled could not be overlooked. FDR campaigned and won before the days of the ubiquitous video eye; newspapers then did not dwell on pictures of Roosevelt being lifted, doll-like, from his auto to his wheelchair; and certainly there were never reports of a time when his handlers dropped the dignified Roosevelt. Roosevelt grew to be the national leader and unifier; Wallace grew to be a national curiosity. People came to his rallies and their attention was riveted not on the man and his message, but on things like the midget-sized bulletproof lectern—just high enough to protect a candidate in a wheelchair from being wasted once and for all, eerie with its bulletproof glass rising from a base at less than waist high. It is cruel but true: you can't win votes sitting in the schoolhouse door. George Wallace would not be a major factor in the campaign of 1976; but the liberals, always fighting the last war, would not realize that until they read it in the newspapers.

    ▤   ▤   ▤

RUNNING FOR PRESIDENT

SCENE: Temple Emanu-El is a symbol of Hebraic strength on Miami Beach and on March 7 its chapel looks like Shea Stadium on cap day. A capacity crowd fills the huge downstairs seating area and there is standing room only in the semicircular upper deck. It is a pep rally populated by people of years, wrinkled and bent yet tanned and alert. They are cheering and hollering for the hometown hero, Scoop Jackson, and he is turning them on with his pledges of support for Israel and tough talk against the Soviets. Interestingly, the Temple Emanu-El crowd cheers just as lustily for a towering, florid-faced Irishman who was recently signed by the Jackson team after playing for both the Boston Kennedys and the Washington Nixons. Daniel Patrick Moynihan, the world's tallest leprechaun, had won himself a new constituency months earlier by sounding a hardline as America's ambassador to the United Nations, and now as designated hitter for the Jackson team Moynihan is being greeted as though he were Moshe Dayan. He loves it.

Jackson was running statewide, but he was focusing really on locking up the heavily Jewish areas of Miami Beach and North Miami Beach, looking to carry the South Florida Gold Coast districts and at least come out of Florida with a sizeable number of delegates. The Jackson people did not really expect to carry the state. But they did expect to carry Miami Beach. To this end, they had set up a squad of condominium commandos trained to mobilize, at the drop of a leaflet, the thousands of retired people who live in the tall New Yorkish apartment buildings that have overrun the once beautiful beachfront like ugly barnacles that have gotten the best of a once sleek ship. Susan Weiner, a twenty-six-year-old Jackson volunteer, has put together a most effective condominium organization, complete with condo captains, and lists of condominium people needing rides to the polls; eventually they ensure Jackson a good South Florida vote.

Carter strategists, meanwhile, did not want to concede even Miami Beach to Jackson. The Carter effort was headed by a Lutheran minister, Roger Volker, who hoped to be able to convince the Jewish voters that only Carter had a chance of beating George Wallace, who was the man who they really did not like. He hoped to convince them not to throw away a vote on Jackson, but to vote for

Carter instead. And after all, if the Miami Beach Jews went wild over Daniel Patrick Moynihan, perhaps Carter had a chance with them too.

🏴　🏴　🏴

SCENE: On the same weekend that Jackson and Moynihan are working Temple Emanu-El, Jimmy Carter goes to Yeshiva. He dons a yarmulke at the Jewish center school in the south end of Miami Beach, but it does not help. He only looks like "Jimmy," chief of the Mouseketeers. His audience has some elderly people, some middle-aged people, and a lot of children who are fidgety and noisy and bored; later most of the adults say they came not because they are Carter supporters but just because they were curious. Jimmy Carter, still in yarmulke, tells them all about his trip to Israel and how he talked with Golda Meir and how he toured the country in a car that he emphasizes was made available to him by Mrs. Meir. His words about Israel are about as strong as those of Scoop Jackson, but somehow, with this constituency, Jimmy Carter does not make it. He comes off like grits at a seder.

🏴　🏴　🏴

It was traveling Georgians, not transplanted Yankees, who provided the big boost for Carter's Florida campaign. First there was family: Rosalynn campaigned for weeks throughout the state; others in the Carter clan did too. And then there were busloads of Georgians, traveling across the border to carry the Carter campaign to even the smallest areas of northern Florida.

"I could depend on 1,000 Georgians in Florida," Carter recalled months later. "And they were almost like my family. And if they went to a barber shop and said, 'I know Jimmy Carter—he was our governor and he reorganized the government and he reformed our prison system, so forth, would you vote for him?' Very often that barber would say, 'Yeah, I'll vote for him,' and say, 'I met Chip, you know, six months ago. I remember Chip.' He's easy to remember." That personal investment of time—Carter's time, his family's time, his friends' time—was too large to be wiped out by something that happened in faraway Massachusetts.

　　🏴　　🏴　　🏴

SCENE: In the shade of trees heavy with gray moss, on the steps of a farmland courthouse at Brooksville, the local bank president is saying a few words about "the next President of the United States." Up to the microphones comes Jimmy Carter, smiling shyly. "My folks have all been farmers," he begins, and he tells them all about Plains and raising peanuts. "I'm the first member of my daddy's family to finish high school. . . . Something's gone wrong with the government in Washington— we feel like outsiders. . . . Now I don't want any of you to vote for me this year unless you want the federal government reorganized. . . . I'm campaigning hard and I don't intend to lose; I believe you're looking at the next President of the country. . . . What this country needs most of all is a government that is as good and honest and decent and truthful and fair and compassionate—and *filled with love*—as the American people are."

There is a knot of about 200 people clustered under the trees listening to the campaigner who is talking their language. They are applauding at all the right places and then some. They are Wallaceites and moderates, town folk and farmers who have come in for supplies and even just to hear the speech; those in the cluster are all whites; but a small number of blacks are hanging around the fringes of the crowd. "I'd like to see him elected," Cecil Bishop, a retired citrus grower, is saying. "Liked Wallace, but he can't win. This one can win. And we need a man from the South." By now Jimmy Carter is making his way across the lawn toward the street. A heavy-set white woman pushes forward and then when she is within reach of the candidate she gets shy about being there. Carter reaches out and pulls her toward him and gives her a hug and a kiss. "Oh, Lord bless you, Jimmy," she gushes. "I'll be praying for you." Carter walks over and does a round of handshaking in the Snacks 'n' Stuff Restaurant. A black woman who is eating there reaches out to receive a handshake and suddenly recoils in embarrassment; she wipes the grease of fried chicken off the hand and then extends it again. The candidate is appreciative and she is thrilled, beaming and saying incredulously, "How *about* that?" As Carter is crossing the street to his motorcade car, a Cadillac with ego plates reading "FDC" drives by and slows. "Hello, Jimmy! Good luck!" the man behind the wheel says, and he drives off.

Wallaceites, blacks, people who drive pickups and people who drive Cadillacs. Jimmy Carter is scoring well with them all in Florida. He is pictured by many as the liberal in the three-man race (Milton Shapp is in the race too, but he is making no headway at all); yet Carter is also drawing strong support among conservatives. A good part of his ability to attract voters of varied philosophies was due to the careful, deliberate way Carter constructed his position statements on many controversial issues. It was apparent that Carter had concluded that strident positions on issues are unlikely to win much support for a candidate, but they sure can make him some vociferous enemies among those who feel strongly—and oppositely— from him on any given issue. The Carter appeal was to faith and trust. So he decided to trim a bit, tacking first to the left and then to the right, a wily navy veteran trying most of all to sail through the sea of emotion-triggering issues without striking any perilous mines.

"Sure, Jimmy has worked out answers on controversial issues so as not to anger people," Jody Powell said later. "Why not try to find a solution—a way of getting it done—so as not to piss off a lot of people and create more problems than we started with?" Powell is asked about Carter's way of handling questions on amnesty for Vietnam draft dodgers. "His answer on amnesty," Powell replied, "is a classic example of how to say something and not piss off people."

Carter on amnesty. It is not an answer; it is an art form—carefully constructed so as to diffuse the emotions of the subject and come up with something for everyone. The shorthand of it is that he starts out by saying he is against amnesty, but he winds up saying he is for pardon. And he tells interviewers, when asked, that he thinks there is a difference, even though Webster defines "amnesty" as a "general pardon."

This shorthand explanation does not do Carter justice. His answer actually works like this:

"I'm not in favor of amnesty. . . . In my county, where I'm from, we don't have a dentist or a doctor or a pharmacist. There's a lot of ignorance there. But when boys were drafted, they didn't know where Sweden was. They went and fought and died. Others came back. . . ." He goes on to talk about how when he came home from the navy he was a hero to his townspeople, just for having gone; but when his son came back from Vietnam he was not treated as a hero at all; people were not proud of where he had been and what he had done. The divisions of Vietnam still run deep.

"So when I become President," he goes on, "although I do not want a blanket amnesty, I will issue a blanket pardon to those people [who dodged the draft]. . . . Amnesty is saying what you did was right. . . . A pardon says it was wrong but you are forgiven. . . . It is time to get the Vietnam War over in our country."

So, too, Carter staked out a position on the air force's controversial new B-1 bomber that was somewhere in between those of the B-1 backers and the B-1 opponents. "I oppose production of the B-1 bomber at this time. I believe that research and development should continue. The decision on the production of this weapon system should be made by our next administration." (Which, Carter says, would be *his* administration; so Carter thus left unclear just what he as President would do about the B-1.)

And on welfare reform, Carter would sometimes stress that he would cut off payments to all those who were able to work but would not; and other times (frequently before black crowds), he would emphasize that "Ninety percent of the people on welfare cannot work and ought to be treated with love and compassion by the government."

While Carter was amassing broad-based support from many diverse groups, he seemed to have genuine problems winning any sizeable expression of support from one special group: his fellow governors. The people who had presided over their states at the time Carter presided over his, who met with him and talked with him as equals during the various governors' conferences, were not fond of him.

Some of the other governors said privately they resented the way Carter wound up getting the major share of the publicity at their regional and even national governors' conferences—how, as they saw it, he always seemed to get out of the meetings in order to get into places to be able to get in front of the television cameras first. "They got mad because he was just better at doing the political thing than they were," is how one of Carter's aides once expressed it. Perhaps. At any rate, he was not the most popular man inside the meeting rooms of the governors' conferences.

Calvin Rampton, Utah governor for years, was once quoted as saying: "Of the forty some Democratic governors that I've known personally, I'd rank Carter about thirty-nineth."

Governor Patrick Lucey of Wisconsin said: "A number of the governors are upset about Carter's statements on revenue sharing. He thinks states should be excluded from the program. We are surprised to hear that from a former governor. . . ."

Wendell Ford, a former chairman of the Democratic Governors' Conference, was quoted as saying: "I don't know of any governors or former governors that he has contacted for support. That might indicate how much support he has among his former colleagues."

Among the governors not fond of Carter was Florida's Reubin Askew. Askew reportedly felt he had been led to believe at a meeting that Carter would back him for the chairmanship of the Southern Governors' Conference. But Carter wound up backing Dolph Briscoe of Texas, who had been endorsed as well by Wallace.

In the Florida primary, Askew was under considerable pressure to back Carter as an alternative to Wallace. Instead, Askew, still bitter, took no position. (After the Florida primary, he came out for Jackson).

Carter could have used Askew's help in Florida. But he found help from other sources. Among them was the United Auto Workers. Jackson was the man with the union ties in the Florida primary, and so the Georgian and his advisers were pleased at being able to wind up with some union help of their own—from Florida UAW people. And even the UAW's powerful president, Leonard Woodcock, showed up at a dinner party Carter attended in St. Petersburg. Woodcock emphasized to reporters that he was not making any endorsement at the time. Not yet. But he also spoke very warmly, very openly, about Carter.

▬   ▬   ▬

THE RESULTS: *Election night in Florida was the first of the big election-night gatherings of the Carter clan. Twenty-five or thirty relatives and friends gathered in the Carter suite at the Carleton House Hotel outside Orlando.*

They wound up celebrating a victory. Years ago, Carter and his men had figured that Florida would be the place where they could knock off Wallace and show Carter to be a viable southern alternative. And Florida was the place where they did just that. Carter finished with 34.3 percent, Wallace had 30.6, Jackson 23.9. Jimmy Carter was a born-again frontrunner.

Some of the Carter people celebrated through the night, but the candidate had a busy schedule ahead. He was getting ready for bed at 12:30 A.M. when there was a knock at his door. Someone passed the word that several of his Florida UAW people were outside. Carter put his pants back on and went out to chat with them. Barefoot.

▬   ▬   ▬

Interlude: The Morning After

The morning after his dismal fourth-place finish in Massachusetts, Jimmy Carter had been testy. The morning after his stunning first-place finish in Florida, Jimmy Carter was . . . testy.

"He was in a testy mood," recalled Greg Schneiders. "He discovered that he had been booked on 'Issues and Answers' and that an interview had been promised to Hunter Thompson [the sage of *Rolling Stone*], on the flight to Chicago. He complained to Betty [Rainwater, an assistant press secretary] that he was being overscheduled. He'd planned to sleep on the flight." Carter gave Thompson forty-five minutes and slept the rest of the time. Thompson turned out to be much enamored of Carter, and wrote an article highly favorable to the Carter campaign.

It is one of the things about Carter that he can fall asleep anywhere, anytime. A deep, good sleep. He can sleep right up until he reaches his stop, then wake up, straighten his hair, and go out and shake a few hands and make his speech.

March 16/Illinois

To say that Richard J. Daley is a mayor and be done with it is like saying that MacArthur was a soldier. Richard Daley is a master of the uses of power—power at the local level where it affects people directly, where people see what you are doing for them and see what they can do for you in return—the sort of power that makes a person something more than just a mayor; the power that makes a boss.

Richard J. Daley is a boss, but he is not without his problems, some of which have been visible at Democratic National Conventions. In 1968, when the convention was held in his city, the police turned disturbances into major riots with head-smashing billy clubs and brutal tactics. "A police riot" was the official verdict of an investigating commission. Television at the convention caught Daley making a singularly dramatic and obscene gesture at Senator Abraham Ribicoff, who had the temerity to call the storm-trooper police brutality that was occurring in the streets what it truly was.

Then in 1972, a year of McGovern and reform, Daley lost control of—and was tossed out of—his own Illinois delegation. An unceremonious thing to happen to a man of his clout. Daley reacted in the only style fitting a political boss. He came back. Came back strong. He won reelection in 1975 to a sixth four-year term as mayor, renewing his political power.

Jimmy Carter has a fine appreciation for the uses of

political power. And so it is that he long ago developed a fine rapport with Daley.

Shortly before the Democratic Convention of 1976, Carter was asked to reflect on just how important the seventy-four-year old mayor of Chicago is in politics today.

"He's important," Carter said. "You know, the county chairperson of a south Georgia rural area and the county chairperson of a metropolitan county in Pennsylvania or New York, they look on Mayor Daley as a sort of surrogate for them. He represents [a Democratic Party] establishment figure . . . who supported McGovern after McGovern had kicked him out of the [1972] convention. He was a professional and his word was his bond, and they look to him as an exemplification of what they are. And his support therefore is significant in the eyes of the media, in the eyes of the delegates whom he can influence, and in his posture as a loyal local Democratic official. . . .

"So in many ways, Daley is important. I like Daley personally, I have known him for five or six years. As a matter of fact, at the Kansas City convention [the mini-convention the Democrats held in 1974], when we took a crucial vote on the . . . rules, I was sitting with Daley, talking to him about politics and government. When I went to the Illinois delegation to meet with them before the actual deliberations at the Kansas City convention . . . , Mayor Daley welcomed me and he introduced me.

"I made about a five-minute speech, and there was a tremendous response from the Illinois delegation. He insisted I bring my wife up to the stage and introduce her to them. And when I finally walked out of the room, they were still applauding. And that would not have been possible without Daley's friendship."

This was two weeks before December 12, 1974, the day on which Carter officially announced his candidacy for the Presidency.

＊＊＊

James Wall, editor of the *Christian Century*, led the fight for George McGovern in the suburbs of Chicago in 1972. In 1976, the primary scene in Illinois was being dominated by Daley, who was running a favorite-son effort in the name of Senator Adlai Stevenson. James Wall, meanwhile, was looking for a candidate to back.

First he thought he would go with Fritz Mondale. But Mondale decided not to run. Next he thought he would go with Sargent Shriver. He was introduced to him, but did not hear from Shriver again.

He also took Mo Udall on a tour of his suburban area. But he did not hear from Udall.

On May 1, he had met Jimmy Carter. The Carter people kept in touch, and as Wall explained: "I'm from Georgia originally. I went home and talked to his staff." Then on October 20, Wall said, "Jimmy came to my home and asked me to become his state chairman. That's exactly the way he functions. I told him the mayor thing has been my big trouble. Jimmy said, 'I will take care of that. The mayor and I have a good relationship.'"

According to Wall, Carter told the mayor that, even though he was going to put up a slate of delegates in the suburbs of Chicago, its members would vote for Daley to head the delegation. There would be no repetition of 1972. Daley, said Wall, was not dissatisfied.

▄   ▄   ▄

Dear Friends,

You may already know that my brother, Jimmy Carter, is running for the office of President of the United States.

My reason for writing you is to acquaint you with a most important facet of Jimmy, one that couldn't possibly be pursued with any depth by the press or television, and that is his quality of deep personal commitment to Jesus Christ and his will to serve Him in whatever capacity he finds himself.

A growing number of national commentators have stated that they are deeply impressed with Jimmy's grasp of national and international affairs and his proven capacity of governing with fiscal responsibility and compassion for human needs. What usually is ignored in such analyses is that our nation's greatest need is for a President who will render spiritual leadership. This, in my opinion, is one of Jimmy's greatest qualifications.

RUNNING FOR PRESIDENT

As one who knows the importance of Christ in your personal life and who I'm sure wants our nation to be under His blessings and guidance—please pray for Jimmy. And if you share my feeling that he is the best candidate, I urge you to actively support him.

On Tuesday, March 16, the Illinois Primary will be held. Please call your friends and neighbors to go with you and cast your vote for Jimmy in the Preferential Primary and for his delegates in your particular Congressional District.

> Sincerely in Christ,
> Ruth Carter Stapleton

Ruth Carter Stapleton is Jimmy's youngest sister, and she is a gospeler who specializes in a ministry of "inner healing." She does not specialize in politics but she does believe that politics and religion can—and should—mix. So it is that she wrote her letter, which was sent to a mailing list of a couple of hundred names; the above copy was marked to be sent to a Lithuanian Center.

A very attractive woman, blond and blue-eyed and always fashionable in wardrobe and makeup, Ruth Carter Stapleton campaigned hard for her brother, bringing an unusual religious element into the realm of politics. While others tried to sell Carter on the basis of his grasp of governmental issues, she sold Carter on the basis of his belief in Christ. America should be "under *His* blessings and guidance," was her message, so "please pray for Jimmy."

She came to the campaign trail as a corporate executive of sorts: she and her husband, Fayetteville, North Carolina, veterinarian Bob Stapleton, formed "Behold, Inc." as a nonprofit organization which is the umbrella for her practice of the ministry.

She had come to her present practice of the ministry as a mother of four, after experiencing a period of profound personal unrest. She had gone from being a daughter pampered and favored by her father to being a coquettish southern belle and then to being a superreligious Baptist who eschewed frilly clothes and all makeup. "I hated myself and subconsciously wanted to die," she told the *Washington Post*'s Myra MacPherson. "People lit candles, prayed for me. A psychiatrist said, 'You're suffering too much—there's no way to help you. You need medication.' After I exhausted every resource, I had to come to grips with the fact that the problem was inside me."

Stapleton also told MacPherson that she has since had a couple of religious "experiences," and she told her in the spring of 1976 of the most recent one, which occurred two years earlier. "I woke up in my sleep and there was this light, this glow in my room. Something inside me said I was moving into a place of 'unconditional love.' My total healing took place when I fully realized God was a God of love, not one who punished."

As she travels the country, giving speeches and practicing "inner healing," she professes a ministry that is an unusual mixture of psychology and religion. She takes her patients back to their childhood and then conducts them on a trip of faith and imagination, traveling through their troubled childhood, but this time traveling with Jesus. She talked about her work during a small press conference she gave at the Democratic Convention. Syndicated columnist Garry Wills was among those who gave wide circulation to her story of a person she called "Zeb," which she offered when asked to describe her greatest healing experience.

"Suddenly the idea came to have Zeb visualize Jesus walking through each room of his childhood home, filling it with his love and light. When Zeb refused to go into the upstairs bathroom, I knew we had the key to one of the locked doors of his past. After much encouragement and with the assurance that Jesus would walk with him, together they opened the door to that bathroom. Through sobs and mild hysteria, Zeb told me his uncle had walked in on him many years ago as he stood there masturbating for the first time. Memories of his uncle's roars and cursing rebukes flooded his mind in that moment. I repeated the words continually, 'Jesus, Jesus, Jesus,' throughout his story. As Zeb began to regain his composure, he visualized Jesus there in that room blessing him, blessing the room, blessing his life, and, most important, blessing the part of his body that Zeb had so hated and had rejected."

Late in January 1976 Ken Levine went into Illinois as the first Udall operative to enter the state. He was thinking about trying to set up something for Udall in Liberal Representative Abner Mikva's Chicago area district and in the liberal University of Illinois communities of Champaign and Urbana. Mikva told him to forget it, that the people of his district don't know Udall. It went the same way in the university town. The ex-McGovern people were either for Carter or did not want to get involved. Levine then tried the 13th Congressional District.

"I made a presentation in the thirteenth—Libertyville," Levine told a friend later. "I said, 'Hey, Mo Udall is a liberal guy.' They said, 'Hey, we're going to go uncommitted. We don't know Mo.' "

Udall passed on Illinois. So did Scoop Jackson.

George Wallace did not. Wallace campaigned hard in the weeks following his loss in Florida, trying to get his campaign together again. Illinois was March 16 and North Carolina was March 23 and his opponent in both places was Jimmy Carter.

Wallace fought gamely in Illinois, trying to convince people that he was physically capable to be President. He told a press conference the day before the election, "Some people are paralyzed in the head, but I'm only paralyzed in the legs. I wouldn't be involved in the primaries if I couldn't do this. My health is fine. Doctors have assured me I'm all right. But if you want an acrobat for President, then I'm not your man."

THE RESULTS: *Wallace was not the people's man in Illinois. Carter scored a substantial victory in the presidential preference vote, defeating Wallace 48 percent to 28 percent. Shriver polled just 16 percent and was finished as a candidate. Harris received 8 percent and was never a factor after that.*

But Carter's most politically impressive showing was not his victory in the preference vote, but his second place finish in the delegate voting.

Carter had not even fielded delegate slates in seven of the state's twenty-four districts in and around Chicago. He and his advisers had been saying how they would be happy if they won a total of 20 delegates in Illinois.

Instead, Carter won 55 delegates—second to the 85

pledged to favorite-son Stevenson. Wallace won only three. Carter delegates defeated Stevenson's in many downstate races, including areas where Stevenson delegates were popular local officials. Daley, who more than anything else admires people who can win, was impressed. And Daley said so in his own way: "His was a campaign that some respect must be paid to."

≡ ≡ ≡

Interlude: Reorganization

All of these changes combined to permit the slashing of the administrative costs of government more than [in] half. . . .
—Jimmy Carter, on his reorganization of Georgia's bureaucracy, in his book *Why Not the Best?*

Rick Cobb is a Jimmy Carter man. He is deputy director of the Georgia Office of Planning and Budgeting. He is a true Carter believer who originally came to the state for a few months to help Carter implement his famous government reorganization and who became converted and stayed on. He is a man who says: "I'd work for Jimmy Carter anywhere—anytime."

About the only thing Rick Cobb won't do for Jimmy Carter is vouch for all of the campaign claims Carter made about the success of his reorganization effort. Cobb definitely believes that the reorganization was a great success. But he concedes that it probably was not as great as Carter likes to say it was.

Example: Carter's claim in his book, his campaign speeches, and brochures that he cut state administrative costs by 50 percent. "I wouldn't be surprised if Jimmy really thinks that's true," Cobb said. "Was fifty percent of the state government's administrative costs actually cut? No, it wasn't. But more cuts were made in administrative costs than in any other area. . . . It's just that we have no idea how much was cut and it would take a special audit to find out."

Later, a Carter campaign spokesman, Rex Granum, said that the former governor has no statistics to back up his

50 percent figure. "It's just an estimate," Granum said. And Carter, when told of the comments by planning official Rick Cobb, conceded that perhaps the savings claims had been exaggerated. Eventually Carter stopped making the 50 percent savings claim in his campaign speeches.

Carter did stick to one other controversial set of re-organization statistics however. He has always referred to how he eliminated 278 of 300 state agencies, leaving Georgia with just twenty-two. Actually, there were only sixty-five budgeted state agencies, commissions, boards, and so on when he took office. The remainder were not receiving any funds and in many cases they existed on paper only. Also, according to Rick Cobb, the total of existing state agencies and commissions and such was reduced by Carter to thirty, not twenty-two. "Even when he was governor," Cobb said, "Jimmy would say in speeches how we'd cut it down to twenty-two." And then we'd meet with him and say, "No, Governor, it's really twenty-nine or thirty or whatever. But he just stuck with twenty-two, and it's a small point, really."

Carter's media adviser, Jerry Rafshoon, commented much later on the numbers controversy that Carter's reorganization claims touched off. "I guess it was a mistake to get into a numbers game on reorganization," Rafshoon said. "The point is that reorganization was good."

March 23/North Carolina

"I spent more time on my knees the four years I was governor in the seclusion of a little private room off the governor's office than I did in all the rest of my life put together because I felt so heavily on my shoulders that the decisions I made might very well affect many, many people."

Jimmy Carter was standing on a riser on a patio of a sprawling, modern, luxurious home in Winston-Salem, North Carolina. More than seventy-five wealthy contributors had come to this fundraiser. The night was chilly, but the party had moved out to the patio because it was the best way to accommodate such a large crowd.

They had come expecting to hear a political talk. Instead they were treated to the rare spectacle of a presidential candidate discussing publicly the intimacies of his religion and the relationship he feels he has with God.

He told them about "a deeply profound religious experience that changed my life dramatically" in 1967.

"I recognized for the first time that I had lacked something very precious—a complete commitment to Christ, a presence of the Holy Spirit in my life in a more profound and personal way. And since then I've had an inner peace and inner conviction and assurance that transformed my life for the better. . . . I don't think I'm ordained by God to be President. . . . [The] only prayer that I've ever had concerning the election is that I do the right thing. And if I win or lose, my religious faith won't be shaken."

Carter elaborated on his comments the following day

at a press conference. "In 1967, I realized that my own relationship with God, with Christ, was very superficial. And because of some experience I had that I won't describe . . . I came to realize that my Christian life, which I had always professed to be preeminent, had really been a secondary interest in my life.

"And I formed a very close, intimate personal relationship with God, through Christ, that has given me a great deal of peace. . . .

"It was not a profound stroke of miracle. It wasn't a voice of God from heaven. It was not anything of that kind. It wasn't mysterious. It might have been the same kind of experience as millions of people have who do become Christians in a deeply personal way. . . . I don't think God is going to make me be President by any means. But whatever I have as a responsibility for the rest of my life, it will be with that intimate personal continuing relationship. . . ."

On that chilly North Carolina evening, and in the days that followed, Jimmy Carter talked about the very intimate, very personal nature of his religious beliefs to a degree that perhaps no presidential candidate has before. It had been a question from one of the campaign contributors standing on the patio that night that had gotten him talking about his beliefs. But Carter had been questioned about his Southern Baptist convictions before and had limited himself in the past to short, simple replies about how religion is separate from politics. Why had he responded in such intimate detail this time?

"The questioner wanted to know if I was going to disavow my religion or my religious beliefs in order to get votes around the country," Carter recalled. "This question had come up several times before in audiences and I would try to give a brief answer like yes or no or that's the way I feel. I had talked to my wife a lot and that question was coming up with increasing frequency, so I thought for once and for all with all the reporters present I would answer the question a little more completely and have it over with. And there was no surge of questioning of me by the news media until after Richard Reeves wrote an article about me in *New York* Magazine, ascribing my political success to a spiritual desire on the part of the American people that I was meeting. I have never known how to assess the impact of one reporter's writings upon another reporter's, but apparently that article had a great deal of effect on the interest of other reporters in that subject.

Question: Does Carter regret having discussed his private religious beliefs so publicly, and in such detail?

Carter: "In retrospect I would have done the same thing. I don't see any legitimate alternative to it. The people have a right to understand the religious beliefs of their future President. And this was a legitimate inquiry when Al Smith ran and when John Kennedy ran, and when we have our first Jewish nominee that's going to become an issue and I think that is expectable and certainly proper. At the beginning it created very serious political problems for me among some of the Jewish voters and some of the Catholic leaders because of the past prejudice that had been exhibited in the Deep South against Jews, against Catholics, against blacks, and others, and there had to be a learning process on their part, a teaching process to some reticent degree on my part just not to bury the issue once it was raised. And I think that as people began to realize that the Baptists believe in strict separation of church and state and that Truman was a Baptist and that I have served in public life for about fourteen years and have never tried to mix our religious beliefs and public service in an improper fashion, I think that the problem has attenuated substantially."

So it was that Carter came to talk about his Southern Baptist beliefs during his campaign through North Carolina. It was a move that may well have helped him win that Bible Belt region. And while Carter maintains he does not think his comments turned out to be a political plus in that primary, he also conceded that he probably would not have gone into the matter of his religious beliefs in detail had the question come that day in a northern primary.

Question: "Would you have answered the question as fully at a fundraiser in Boston?"

Carter: "No, I doubt it. The people in North Carolina knew what I was talking about and I didn't have to define terms or explain to them the basic tenets of a

Southern Baptist or of the Methodist faith. So I was talking to a group of people among whom knowledge of my faith was very widespread already. I didn't have to define terms. I didn't have to tell them that the Baptists believe in separation of church and state and we have no hierarchical arrangement that might tend to dominate me from the church structure. They know that just as a normal part of their lives."

Carter's "deeply profound religious experience" came, he says, late in 1966, following his gubernatorial defeat, and in the early part of 1967. As a result, he now considers himself a "born again" Christian—the term means that he has had a spiritual rebirth, that he has thus begun a new life, committed to Jesus, with a new love for his fellow man.

Ruth Carter Stapleton has been widely quoted as recalling the day when her brother, Jimmy, underwent this "deeply profound religious experience." After Carter's 1966 defeat, she has been quoted as saying, he sat outdoors and "put his face in his hands and cried like a baby." As Mrs. Stapleton told it to Myra MacPherson of the *Washington Post*, Carter went for a walk with her through the pine woods and there Carter said to his sister, "You and I are both Baptists, but what is [it] that you have that I haven't got?"

"I said, 'Jimmy, through my hurt and pain I finally got so bad off I had to forget everything I was. What it amounts to in religious terms is total commitment. I belong to Jesus. Everything I am.'

"He said, 'Ruth, that's what I want.' So we went through everything he would be willing to give up. Money was no problem, nor friends, nor family. Then, I asked, 'What about all political ambitions?' He said, 'Ruth! You know I want to be governor. I would use it for the people!' I said, 'No, Jimmy.' But he really meant it and became connected with part-time religious work. So he went to Pennsylvania and New York on a Baptist missionary tour for less than a year. Jimmy's a Baptist and to commit to life Baptists think you have to go off and be a missionary somewhere."

Carter is not happy with the way his sister, Ruth, recounts the story of his religious experience. Quietly, and apparently a little uncomfortably, he takes issue with her on the question of his weeping and the profundity of that one walk in the woods. Carter said: "There was never any crisis in my life that took place in one single day, one single walk in the pine woods. There was never any time when I sat in my sister's presence weeping. That's been exaggerated grossly. I did walk in the woods and talk to my sister Ruth about that. The problem in my life that had been created by that 1966 loss was the fact that my life seemed to be without purpose and that I was overly concerned about the defeats, that I had lost an interest in other people, individually, to a great extent, that I didn't get any sense of accomplishment when I achieved success and I felt like my religious beliefs were shallow and just a matter of self-pride. And Ruth and I had a long talk and it was a very important conversation for me, but there was no flash of revelations, no weeping. But there was a series of circumstances during that period of about a year or two that was in the last part of '66, first part of '67, and it gave me a renewed insight and a much clearer understanding of what my religious teachings, throughout my life almost, had meant. But that one particular episode was exaggerated a little bit because of my sister's subjective involvement in it."

Carter also took note of that period of his life in a televised interview with Bill Moyers, former press secretary to President Johnson and now a journalist and commentator. "I was going through a stage in my life there that was a very difficult one," Carter said. "I had run for governor and lost. Everything I did was not gratifying. When I succeeded in something, I got no pleasure out of it. When I failed at something, it was a horrible experience for me."

Moyers, himself a graduate of the Southwest Baptist Theological Seminary, channeled the hour-long interview into a revealing conversation in which Carter talked at length about his view of God and religion.

Q: "What drives you?"

A: "I don't know exactly how to express it. As I said, it's not an unpleasant sense of being driven. I feel like I have one life to live—I feel that God wants me to do the best I can with it. And that's quite often my major prayer—let me live my life so that it will be meaningful. And I enjoy tackling difficult problems, and solving them, and the meticulous organization of a complicated effort. It's a challenge. Possibly, it's like a game. I don't know. I don't want to lower it by saying it's just a game—but it's an enjoyable thing for me."

Q: "How do you know—this is a question I hear from a lot of people—how do you know God's will?"

A: "Well, I pray frequently—not continually, but many times a day. When I have a sense of peace, and self-assurance—I don't know where it comes from—what I'm doing is a right thing. I assume, maybe in an unwarranted way, that that's doing God's will."

Q: "What do you think we're on earth for?"

A: "I don't know. You know, I could quote the biblical references, through creation, that God created us in his own image hoping that we'd be perfect. But we turned out to be not perfect, but very sinful. And then when Christ was asked what were the great commandments from God, which should direct our lives, he said to love God with all your heart and soul and mind, and love your neighbor as yourself. So, I try to take that condensation of the Christian theology and let it be something through which I search for a meaningful existence. I don't worry about it too much anymore. I used to when I was a college sophomore, and we used to debate for hours and hours about why we are here, who made us, where should we go, what's our purpose.

"But I don't feel frustrated about it. I'm not afraid to see my life ended. I feel like every day is meaningful. I don't have any fear at all of death. I feel like I'm doing the best I can, and if I get elected President, I'll have a chance to magnify my own influence maybe in a beneficial way. If I don't get elected President, I'll go back to Plains. So I feel I have a sense of equanimity about it, but why we're here on earth I don't know. I'd like to hear your views on that subject."

Q: ". . . Do you have any doubts? About yourself, about God, about life?"

A: "I can't think of any. I, obviously, don't know all the answers to philosophical questions and theological questions—the kind of questions that are contrived. But the things that I haven't been able to answer in a theory or supposition, I just accept them, and go on—things that I can't influence or change.

"I do have, obviously, many doubts about the best way to answer a question. Or to alleviate a concern. Or how to meet a need, or how to create in my own life a more meaningful purpose, and to let my life be expanded, in my heart and mind. So doubts about the best avenue to take among many options is a kind of doubt that is a constant presence with me.

"But doubt about my faith? No. Doubt about my purpose of life? I don't have any doubts about that. . . ."

Q: "What's the most significant discovery Jimmy Carter has made?"

A: "Well, I think I described it superficially a while ago. I think it affected my life more than anything else. This is embarrassing a little bit for me to talk about because it's personal, but in my relationship with Christ and with God, I became able in the process to look at it in practical terms—to accept defeat, to get pleasure out of success, to be at peace with the world. For instance, one of the things I derived from it, again in a kind of embarrassing way, when I stood out on a factory shift line like I did this morning [in Erie, Pennsylvania—the General Electric plant]. Everybody that comes through there, when I shake hands with them, for that instance, for that instant, I really care about [them] in a genuine way. And I believe they know it a lot of times. Quite often I will shake hands with women who work in a plant and I just touch their hands, and quite frequently they'll put their arms around my neck and say—God bless you, son, or good luck. I'll help you and good luck.

"But it's a kind of relationship with people around me, but I don't want to insinuate that I'm better than other people. I've still got a long way to go."

In every state, in almost every speech, Carter talked about a special relationship that he believed he had developed with the people. He said frequently that he felt he would be a good President not because of any special talents or managerial skills that he had, but "because of the close, personal, intimate relationship I have established with each and every one of you." He would say this in living rooms, where he was addressing a coffee klatch of two dozen people; and he would say it in large halls, where he was addressing hundreds—and where his words "close . . . personal . . . intimate relationship" would echo through the building as the people in his audience nodded affirmatively.

Wednesday, the morning after the Illinois primary. George Wallace is having breakfast in his room at the Raleigh, North Carolina, Hilton, and he is a very disappointed man. He had been hoping for 25 to 30 delegates out of Illinois and he got only three. Now he knows that it is the end of his era. He was beaten by Jimmy Carter in Florida and he was beaten by Jimmy Carter in Illinois. Now he is in North Carolina and he is not going to win there either.

During breakfast, Wallace summons his press secretary, Billy Joe Camp. He tells Camp that he is considering pulling out of the race and he thinks he probably should. He cites the futility of the effort and the difficulty in just getting around. He asks Camp for his view.

"I said I couldn't disagree with him," Camp recalled. "But I said that I felt he ought to first talk to others in his staff and his family—his son, his brothers."

Wallace consulted with the others by phone. Some argued that he could probably get a good number of delegates out of North Carolina. "They felt maybe lightning would strike," Camp said. Wallace relented and stayed in the race.

North Carolina was the first time, according to his aides, that Wallace was really depressed about his political prospects for 1976. "It just didn't hit until North Carolina," said Billy Joe Camp. "More than anything else, it was the fault of our organization. We just didn't have a polling firm. And that was a huge mistake. A huge mistake. We only could go by the polls we read in the papers— and we sincerely felt they were wrong. We just really felt we were going to win in Florida, and we felt we were going to do better in Illinois."

Wallace was also buoyed by phone calls he received during the Illinois and North Carolina campaigns from Hubert Humphrey, Scoop Jackson, and Bob Strauss (chairman of the Democratic National Committee). None of them wanted to see Carter walk away with the nomination, and Wallace had the impression that they all wanted him to stay in the race; they told him things about his effort being courageous and that he had gotten a good vote, all in all, and not to give up.

So Wallace kept on fighting. He had been running for years by attacking Washington's bureaucrats and politicians, making himself at least part of the legend of his time. Now he attacked, for the first time, the Deep South politician who had finally done him in.

"He talks one way today and one way tomorrow," Wallace said. ". . . Jimmy Carter is a warmed-over McGovern. . . . He's seen fit to talk about me in Illinois and in Florida, so I say turnabout's fair play, and I'll talk about him in North Carolina."

Wallace had long been bitter over the fact that Carter would not nominate him for President at the 1972 convention (Carter spoke for Scoop Jackson instead). Now, in North Carolina, Wallace's bitterness against Carter boiled to the surface. In a remarkable interview with Elizabeth Drew of *The New Yorker* Magazine, Wallace repeatedly mocked Carter's stump promise that "I will never lie to you; I will never misleeeeeed you." (It is something to hear George Wallace do an imitation of a southern accent.)

"He was my friend when I was popular," Wallace said in that interview. "He said he was for me when he thought I'd die. . . . He talks about spending all that time on his kneeeeeees. Well, I'm going to church tomorrow, but I don't go around talking about my religion."

THE RESULTS: *Carter won 53.6 percent of the vote; Wallace, 34.7. George Wallace never again would be a factor in the primaries.*

RUNNING FOR PRESIDENT

Memorandum

To: Governor, Hamilton, Jody, Bob, Charles, Jerry, Rick
From: Pat Caddell
24 March 1976
Subject: General Memo

. . . The single greatest danger in presidential politics is "hubris." The arrogance of early success can doom almost any campaign. In the flush of early victories there is too often the belief in the inevitability of a candidacy. . . . In those heady days we [the McGovern campaign of 1972] believed that in coming so far in the end we could not be denied. In doing so, we sowed the seeds for the campaign's destruction. . . .

[When a] campaign changes from a state primary campaign to a national campaign . . . the ability to control and dominate the media coverage—the extent to which these tools are utilized to send signals and broad messages to the electorate—becomes critical. . . .

I don't think there is any question that we must win Wisconsin, avoid embarrassment in New York, and beat Jackson in Pennsylvania, and then in Indiana, to effect a quick kill in the primaries. . . . My position is, unless we can put together a first-ballot victory or damn close to it, this party will deny us the nomination. Popular with the elites, we are not. . . .

Of immediate concern are the next few primaries and a summary of each from what we know follows:

Wisconsin — While we are ahead in Wisconsin, the situation is precarious. Udall has moved up in the last few weeks, and among the most likely voters in a 40 per cent turnout, we lead 27 per cent to 20 per cent. If the turnout were 25 per cent or less, we trail Udall 28 per cent to 22 per cent with 18 per cent for Jackson. . . . The voters who presently express "no preference" or "none of the above" seem to be Udall-inclined liberals. . . .

New York — Downstate city data indicates that we are only trailing Jackson by a small margin in the city. Indeed, among likely voters we were running even, 20 per cent to 20 per cent. . . . I fear that in a low-vote primary, though, where organization is crucial, we would do worse due to our lack of voter ID and get-out-the-vote effort. . . .

Pennsylvania — This state is [likely] to be the "OK" corral of the campaign between Jackson and us. With three weeks of campaigning, except for days needed in the states that follow, we should be able to defeat Jackson. We trail by a few points in the data we have, which was completed before Illinois and North Carolina. In this state, we must effectively find a way to cut Jackson's blue-collar employment issue. . . . This is the first major northern state where the black vote should reach 15 per cent or more. This is our greatest edge, and Ben Brown must work particularly hard on a massive get-out-the-vote campaign. . . .

Indiana — This should be the next state Jackson will contest us in, but I suspect with farmers, blacks, and Midwest labor folks, he may have picked the wrong place. . . .

Speech, Issue Themes — This area of the campaign is the one in need of the most attention. We have passed the point when we can simply avoid at least the semblance of substance. This does not mean the need to outline minute, exact details. We all agree that such a course could be disastrous. However the appearance of substance does not require this. It requires a few broad, specific examples that support a point and it requires a better definition of these priorities and approach. . . . We need to have set formal addresses—no matter how distasteful —maybe every 10 days, for the purpose of articulating thematic program approaches and priorities, and to satisfy the press, elites, and eventually the public that we are "presidential" and competent. Also, we need to utilize this approach to send "signals" to interested groups and particularly to the suspicious but open liberals. . . .

in lining up the prominent Democrats as delegates.

April 6/New York and Wisconsin

Patrick Caddell, at age twenty-six, has been around. He was twenty-two when he entered the ranks of the political geniuses, running the public opinion polls that helped George McGovern come from obscurity and win the 1972 Democratic presidential nomination. And he was twenty-two when he entered the ranks of the political losers, as McGovern was buried by a Nixon landslide.

Now he was the only experienced national campaigner in Carter's inner circle. His March 24 forecast of the upcoming campaign pointed up important problems. Later he summed up the Carter strategy for the simultaneous New York and Wisconsin primaries like this: "Our strategy for April 6 was to somehow avoid disaster."

April 6. A two-primary day. New York—to the Carter people working in their plastic modern offices down on Peachtree Drive in Atlanta, New York looked like foreign territory; hostile foreign territory. Wisconsin—for months it looked like the party would not even permit this primary to be binding on delegate voting because the state was allowing Republican–Democratic crossover voting.

"New York was frightening," Carter aide Greg Schneiders conceded months later. "We were intimidated. We started out not knowing what the hell was going on there. We didn't have any presence there." What was worse, the names of the individual candidates originally were not going to be on the ballot in New York. Just the names of the delegates—and Jackson had a big jump on Carter in lining up the prominent Democrats as delegates.

Jimmy Carter was uncomfortable about New York, too.

As early as December 1975 he campaigned upstate, but shied from politicking in New York City. "I'd have to walk down the street naked to attract any attention here," Carter said.

And as late as mid-June, after he had the nomination won, Carter was uneasy when he appeared at the Waldorf–Astoria before a meeting of the New York delegation. He mumbled some lines in his speech, blew others, and received only mild applause. (Moments after Carter left the room, California Governor Jerry Brown entered and was greeted with a standing ovation, cheers, and shouts.)

As Carter's plane flew south from New York that June day, a reporter noted that the candidate had not looked as much "at home" before the New Yorkers as he had before other groups. Carter replied, "I didn't."

Question: "Did you get the feeling that you're still trying to prove things to them, that they're still examining you?"

Answer: "I did. . . . There are some groups with whom I feel perfectly at home. And some I don't. But, in general, I'm able to accommodate different kinds of groups fairly well. But I'm not always successful."

■ ■ ■

New York

Early in the campaign, in 1975, back before Jimmy Carter was traveling with a large entourage and staff, Carter was forced to endure a wait of more than three hours in LaGuardia Airport because his plane had not arrived. Carter has this thing about punctuality—he insists on it, and so the delay put him in a sour mood.

Carter went into a small waiting room to pass the time. A sofa and some chairs were there and Carter, fatigued, saw an opportunity to at least make up for nights of lost sleep. He dozed off almost immediately. The one aide traveling with him, Jody Powell, sat watching. Soon it dawned on Powell he had a problem. There were some phone calls he just had to make and there was no phone in the room. If he left Carter sleeping alone and went to make the calls, the governor might awake and find nobody there. What would he think? But the calls had to be made.

So Powell hit on a compromise. He opened the door —it made an annoying thunk—and went out to make his first call. The door closed with another thunk. After the first call, Powell raced back and opened the door— thunk—just to check on his boss, saw he was still sleeping, so closed the door—thunk—and ran back to the phone booth. After the second call he ran back to peek in again. Thunk. Carter was asleep and all was well. Thunk. So he went back to the phones. Then back to his boss. Thunk. Thunk. Finally, Carter raised his head and squinted in the direction of his aide.

"If you want to come back and check on me every ten minutes, leave the door open," Carter said.

"Well, I just . . ." Powell said, launching into an explanation of just what he'd been trying to do.

Carter listened to his aide's concern for his well-being and offered a low-key reply: "Well, you've told me and I'm awake." And he rolled over to try to pick up where he had left off, as Powell returned to the phones. Thunk.

▄   ▄   ▄

In December, Carter's campaign manager, Hamilton Jordan, met with Theodore Sorenson, the former speechwriter for President Kennedy, and William vanden Heuvel, an attorney who long had been identified with the Kennedy crowd. Sorenson is said to have pushed hard for vanden Heuvel to head the Carter campaign in New York.

But Carter already had Midge Costanza on his team. He had met her in Rochester in 1974, when he was serving as the Democratic campaign chairman and she was trying to unseat Representative Barber Conable, a Republican who still holds the seat in Congress. The Carter people had Costanza run the upstate effort, vanden Heuvel the downstate campaign. Some people on the Carter national staff did not think much of vanden Heuvel's efforts, but Carter believes that vanden Heuvel was instrumental in

125

eventually securing the endorsement of New York City Mayor Abraham Beame (after the New York campaign, but when he needed Jewish support).

🏴 🏴 🏴

The Carter strategy for New York was to pick up as many of the state's 274 delegates as possible and to discredit the New York election so that it would not be considered a major primary.

Carter charged frequently that the New York primary system, which called for the use of ballots carrying the names of all the delegates but not the candidates' names, was a disgrace and represented an attempt by the party bosses to thwart the people's will. The system was changed three weeks before the vote.

🏴 🏴 🏴

The Jackson strategy was quite different. It was to get out in front early and win. Win big. Carter's strategy was to run in every state. Jackson's was to win in the big industrial states, where he would have plenty of backing from big labor and party regulars. New York was the core of his big-state strategy.

For years, Scoop Jackson had been a leader in the Senate on the making of policies foreign and domestic. He was particularly familiar as a hardliner in matters of military defense and—important for many New Yorkers —he was known as a supporter of Israel and of Jewish emigration from the Soviet Union.

Scoop Jackson did not have to feel uneasy about New York, and he did not have to tell New Yorkers who he was.

As early as November 1974, a year and a half before the New York primary, he was raising money in New York through a fundraiser in the large Fifth Avenue apartment of insurance executive Leonard Davis. It had been attended by a number of prominent New Yorkers: Governor Hugh Carey, Morris Abrams, William Zeckendorf, philanthropist Jack Goldfarb, union leader Gus Tyler, city Environmental Commissioner Robert Lowe, and Representative Ogden Reid. That night, $60,000 was collected, and Jackson had similar success throughout the New York campaign. He raised big money and he spent big money.

🏴 🏴 🏴

New York is a city of fine restaurants. When Scoop Jackson sought to do some political courting before the campaign got started, he chose the restaurant at La-Guardia Airport. Jackson sat unrecognized and talked with Queens Democratic Chairman Donald Manes. All of the candidates had been wooing Manes, but at this meeting he opted for Jackson, a decision which probably had more to do with Manes's interest in clout than cuisine. "I liked many of the things he was saying—and I thought he could win," Manes recalled.

Manes proved a key to Jackson's effort. With the New York ballot being kept deliberately confusing by the prominent state and county party leaders, who did not want the candidates' names on the ballots, it was imperative that a slate of big-name, easily identifiable people be corralled to serve as delegates for a candidate who hoped to win. Manes proved quite adept at putting together a list of prominent people.

🏴 🏴 🏴

The Carter people thought Midge Costanza did a good job in upstate New York, considering the limited amount of time and, mainly, money Carter spent in the state. "But," said one national Carter campaign official, "Midge made a couple of tactical errors." He cited her challenges, in Carter's name, of Jackson delegates in three upstate districts in a campaign where Carter was trying to discredit the process and trying to appear to be a victimized underdog. Carter was not aware of the challenges upstate and he held a press conference decrying the fact that Jackson was challenging his delegates and saying that this was dirty politics; when reporters asked him why he was doing the same thing, he looked surprised by their questions and said he was not. "This, then, undermined our strategy of trying to discredit the election process in the state," the Carter official said.

Greg Schneiders had known about the challenges made by the Carter people upstate but had not gotten around to telling Carter of them yet. "I probably should have told him about them earlier but I didn't think he was going to say anything about them in that press conference," Schneiders said. He went to Carter immediately afterward and said: "We have a problem here. We are challenging in three districts." Carter said that was not right, that vanden Heuvel had told him they were not challenging. Schneiders replied that was technically correct: vanden Heuvel was not challenging—downstate; but Costanza was —upstate.

Three weeks before election day, the legislature voted to change the election rules so that candidates' names would appear on the ballot. Looking back, some Carter advisers say this led them to pull back from their strategy of just trying to hold down their embarrassment on April 6 and go for a win instead. "We ran a public opinion poll in New York the week of the election and we were even with Jackson," Carter recalled later. "But the people didn't vote and the organization didn't turn out people. . . . The turnout is very important. Very important. I have always done better when the turnout is large. Because the ones who are casually interested in politics like me. . . ."

The change in the election ballot, putting the candidates' names on after all, turned out to be significant to the Jackson people as well. "It changed the game completely," said Ben Wattenberg, a Jackson adviser. "From then on we had to scrap our 'Palm Card' strategy and step up our media strategy."

The Jackson people had hoped to make use of a complex, computerized system for mailing postcards to every registered Democrat in the state, back when it appeared that the candidates' names would not be on the New York ballots. The plan was for these cards to serve as "palm cards," to be carried into the voting booth to serve as delegate voting guides. The cards were going to say: "If you're planning to vote for Senator Jackson, these are the delegates in your district and this is where you vote. . . ." The Jackson campaign spent $50,000 on the computer effort. "But we scrubbed the whole project and waved good-bye to all that money when the law was changed. . . ." said Dick Kline, Jackson's finance coordinator. "We went into a hurry-up media campaign, especially heavy upstate. So we not only lost the $50,000 on the mailing, but we had all the added, unexpected expense of the last-minute media things."

All through his New York campaign, Jackson—buoyed by his Massachusetts victory—had been predicting that he was going to win "by a landslide" in New York. He said it everywhere he went. At times, early on, he mentioned a two-to-one margin; later he scaled it back to saying his "landslide" could be achieved by just capturing a majority of the 274 delegates. Every time he spoke the word "landslide," his aides cringed. They urged him— even argued with him—not to say it; time and again in primaries past, candidates have faired poorly because they set their public goals so high that even a good victory that fell just short of the mark was treated as a defeat.

Jackson's words were the yardstick by which his campaign was judged, and in the end he did not measure up.

THE RESULTS: *Jackson finished on top, but won just 38 percent of the delegates (103 of the 274). Udall finished a surprisingly strong second with 25.2. Carter was buried deep in fourth place with just 12.8 percent—beaten even by uncommitted slates, which took 23.7 percent.*

But there was another set of New York statistics that proved to be even more decisive: the spending statistics. The Jackson campaign went unaccountably wild, spending big bucks at three times the rate of any of the other candidates—and while it won him New York, it eventually cost him later in Pennsylvania, when he simply went broke. Jackson spent $891,698 in New York. Carter spent $293,377 and Udall just $139,770. (Add in Wisconsin spending and Jackson spent for the combined April 6 primaries $942,002 compared to Udall's $600,002 and Carter's $462,103.)

Wisconsin

"The decision to go into Wisconsin was announced to Carter by Hamilton." Announced. Greg Schneiders had chosen the word carefully; it described precisely the way Carter's campaign operation worked.

Throughout most of the campaign, the major decisions about where Carter would go and how long he would spend there—even about which states he would concentrate on and which he would slough off—were made by Hamilton Jordan and Jody Powell, or, occasionally, another top aide. Financial decisions were left to Robert Lipshutz. Media decisions were made by Jerry Rafshoon —in fact, it was not until April, when Carter happened to be attending a meeting in Rafshoon's office, that the candidate even saw the television ads that had been running throughout the country and helping him win for months.

Many campaigns of past years were doomed in part because the candidate tried to do too much himself. Some insisted on at least reviewing all major decisions and all media efforts. Carter did not. He delegated authority.

"We did that sort of thing really in 1966 when I first began political campaigns and I found that it worked well," Carter said in an interview after the primaries were over. "I used the same procedure, the same attitude, while I was governor, in the management of the state's affairs, and it worked well. As you can well see, the details of campaign scheduling and emphasis on issues in the advertisements were worked out long ago there with my staff in the formative months of the campaign planning. So that we were fairly well agreed, compatibly, on what should be done. I trust them completely to do a good job. When a deviation from the basic concept was at issue, I was always consulted on it. But I did not want to be responsible for scheduling, or the wording of television advertisements, or emphasis on issues. I trusted my polling group and news secretary and campaign manager and advertising agency to do that thoroughly. And I never doubted their ability to do it."

* * *

Originally, Wisconsin national committeeman Don Peterson was the state vice chairman of the Udall campaign. But he had a falling-out with Stewart Udall and became independent. Then a friend of his told a story about another friend from Georgia who had worked in Carl

Sanders' campaign against Carter in 1970. Carter, once elected, asked the man to take a state government position; the man pointed out that he had, in fact, supported and worked for Carter's opponent. According to the story, Carter replied: "I don't care. Just integrate the parks, but do it without disrupting anything."

The story hit Peterson just right. "It impressed me tremendously," he said. Later, when a Young Democrats convention was held in his home town of Eau Claire, Peterson agreed to host a reception for Carter. He was impressed again. And he was impressed once more when he later got a personal note of thanks that began "Dear Don" and was signed by "Jimmy." Peterson wound up a Carter man and even journeyed to Pennsylvania to help the Carter cause there.

After the Florida primary, Hamilton Jordan had written a memo to Carter saying that the campaign was about to start a new phase. While still intending to run everywhere, it would now be possible to pick and choose among the states where campaign effort would be emphasized— targets of opportunity, where Carter had a chance to eliminate an opponent. The memo said the Carter campaign ought to look to eliminate Udall in Wisconsin April 6 and Jackson in Pennsylvania on April 27. At that time, most of the top Carter advisers had the staying power of the two men reversed. They figured Udall could soon be eliminated, but that Jackson, who had so stubbornly fought on in 1972 despite a clearly hopeless cause, would stay to the convention at Madison Square Garden.

Morris Udall did not have much to do after Massachusetts, back on March 2, except to think about and plan and campaign for the primaries on April 6. He had bypassed Florida and Illinois and North Carolina and was hoping to finally win in Wisconsin.

Udall desperately needed Wisconsin. There was a deep belief in his camp that the Carter vote was fragile; they remembered how soft Carter's support had been in Massachusetts. Udall stumped hard through the state that is a mix of Midwest progressive thought, farm vote, and ethnic blue-collar big-city vote.

Three weeks before the election, Udall returned to Washington feeling optimistic after three straight days of campaigning in Wisconsin and met with some of his top advisers—his brother, Stewart, his media adviser, John Marttila, and his pollster, Peter Hart. They were meeting in Udall's congressional office to go over a new poll Hart had done. The news was bad. Carter, 34 percent. Jackson, 24. Udall, 17. Wallace, 15. Undecided, 10. No matter how they tried to analyze and rationalize, it did not seem to help. Even if Udall captured every one of the undecided, it would only give him 27—still well behind Carter.

Mo Udall sat on the sofa, staring silently. "It was almost cruel," Stu Udall recalled. "To hit him with something like that after he'd just been campaigning there so hard. I wish they'd told me first so I could have lied to him a little, just to soften the blow."

The Udall brothers left the office and drove out to Mo's home together. In the car, the candidate offered a crisp analysis. "Well, it's all over, isn't it?" he said, making more of a statement than a question. Stu nodded. "Yes, I guess so."

Stu Udall later recalled, "We both agreed that, well, he's going to lose—but at least let's go down with class. Don't whine. We were just so sure that we were going to lose, and lose badly, in Wisconsin. You just can't come back from a 2-to-1 deficit in three weeks."

Udall, dispirited, returned to see the campaign through in Wisconsin.

At times, Udall found himself in the same city as Carter; and in these times, the Secret Service found the situation rather confusing. The Secret Service gives each candidate a code name to be used on its walkie-talkie bands, and, in fact, in all radio communication. And the Secret Service, in its collective wisdom, had given Udall the code name "dashboard" and Carter the code name "dasher." There were times when Udall agents would move into action thinking they had received a radio alert that their man was coming, only to discover that it was a smaller, sandy-haired man from Georgia who was headed their way instead.

Ten days before the election, Peter Hart gave the Udall camp a more encouraging report. Udall was coming on strong. He had passed Jackson and was closing in on Carter. The figures: Carter, 34; Udall, 30; Jackson, 15. The Udall advisers were pleasantly stunned. It was a chance for John Marttila to do his thing again.

Marttila heads the Boston firm that has handled media for John Lindsay and Boston Mayor Kevin White. His big television campaign for Udall in the Massachusetts primary had pulled the tall, lanky Arizonan to a surprising second-place finish—a showing that had forced Birch Bayh to abandon his presidential bid.

Now, Marttila's ads apparently were working again. Another big media push could put Udall over the top in Wisconsin.

Udall had planned to raise and spend $350,000 for Wisconsin. His fundraiser, David Thorne, had said it could be done. But ten days before the primary, only $100,000 had been raised. Udall's brother, Stewart, doubted Thorne's assurances that the remainder would be on hand by primary day. Stewart Udall argued that the television ads, which would cost $25,000, should be taken off the air in Wisconsin.

Stewart Udall met in New York with Thorne, Marttila, and Tom Kiley, a Marttila associate, on Monday, a week before the primary. He told them to turn off the Wisconsin television and radio advertising. Marttila argued against pulling the ads, but Stewart Udall was firm. Marttila was distressed. He had not expected to lose the argument. He telephoned Morris Udall, then campaigning in Wisconsin, to appeal.

Udall decided he had to review the figures. He flew to New York for a meeting the next day, Tuesday. The meeting, set for the morning, did not start until the afternoon. Mo Udall overruled Stewart. It was only $25,000 more, he reasoned, so let the ads roll. Marttila went for the telephone. But his call to the television stations was too late—just about forty-five minutes too late. The last of the television air time already had been committed to others.

For two and a half days, the Udall ads were off the air in Wisconsin while Carter's commercials were filling the airways. The delay in arranging Udall's funding turned out to have been the most significant thing in the Wisconsin primary.

Meanwhile, the slow trickle of funds had also forced a decision to cancel a Udall mailing to 100,000 rural households—Udall's only mailing of the Wisconsin campaign. The cost was budgeted at $20,000. Representative David Obey, a key Udall adviser, was upset; at least the mailing had to get to his district in the northeast corner of the state. A revised mailing plan was set covering 23,000 households at a cost of just $6,500. But it was decided that the money was not there. This too was scrapped.

The Wisconsin primary that Udall had once thought could not be won had turned out to be very winnable. But the Udall campaign was stalled by bad planning and bad budgeting—by bad staffwork and bad guesswork. In retrospect, it is easy to see that Udall money was misspent. Marttila remained upset that Stu Udall had refused to spend that comparatively small amount of media money in the last days of Wisconsin. Stu Udall, meanwhile, was upset that the Udall campaign had spent precious money in New York—$139,770—even though he had made the decision early on that the Udall effort would concentrate in Wisconsin in an effort to secure that vital, first primary win, and that spending in New York was to be done only after it was assured that Wisconsin needs had been met.

And, perhaps most puzzling of all, the Udall people eventually managed to spend $180,345 on the next primary down the line—April 27 in Pennsylvania, where Udall was never a major factor and was in fact destined to finish well off the pace. "We scraped up and borrowed to have $70,000 for media in Pennsylvania," Stu Udall concedes. Why had they not put the Pennsylvania money into Wisconsin? "We just weren't thinking that way," he replied.

On election night, the early returns were heavily Udall. So were television network projections of ABC and NBC. The two networks predicted a Udall victory.

As the television projections rolled in, the Marc Plaza Hotel's ballroom in Milwaukee was filled with the sounds of Udall joy. Beer and liquor and victory elated the crowd as it set about celebrating the first Mo Udall victory party of 1976.

Joining the shouting, and saluting all with upraised glass, was a man whose face was flushed and very familiar. Almost, but not quite the face of the enemy; it was Jimmy Carter's look-alike brother, Billy. Billy shook hands, laughed, and joked with Ella Udall.

"I'm good friends with the Udalls," Billy Carter said. "They're misinformed, but they're nice. I came down to say hello." Udall aides said that in Green Bay, Billy Carter cheerfully had helped them put up some Udall posters.

Billy Carter, the candidate's beer-bellied cherub of a brother, was, at age thirty-eight, more at ease sitting in the gas station he runs in Plains sipping a can of Schlitz than he was foraging on the campaign trail. Jimmy has always said that his brother was more like their father than he. And Billy agrees. "People say I'm more like my father than Jimmy. That's because we look alike. And I'm more outgoing than Jimmy. I enjoy a party, too."

People often ask Billy Carter about his childhood of growing up with Jimmy. "That was nonexistent," he says. "I was four when Jimmy left for college." But Jimmy did manage to leave a lasting impression on his younger brother. "He was a very good student, and every year I used to hear about it from the teachers. Put it this way. He finished at the top of his class. In a class of twenty-seven, I was number twenty-four or twenty-five."

Billy Carter was sixteen when Earl Carter died. "I was closer to my father than the rest of them [family]. They were all gone as I was growing up, and I was almost like an only child," he said.

"Right after Jimmy came back [following the death of their father], I joined the marines. It was right in between everything—after Korea and before Vietnam. I traveled to the Philippines, to Japan, and to Thailand. I didn't intend to come back to Plains. I gave a lot of thought to it, and planned to make a career out of the marines.

"But I was married with two kids then. When you re-enlist, it was for four years—at least that's how it used to be in the marines—you had to spend one tour of duty overseas and I didn't want to leave them and do that. I went to college [Emory University in Atlanta] and flunked out. Then I worked for a construction company that did work all over the Southeast. I can't even remember the name of the company. Then I came back to Plains."

He ran the family warehouse business while Jimmy was governor and prides himself on its growth while he was in charge. They expanded the capacity of the warehouses and bought a new peanut sheller. In 1976, the business was valued between $2 million and $3 million, and their agreement in July with the National Bank of Georgia, mortgaging the buildings to establish a $1-million line of credit is a reflection of the size of the business. "I have a tremendous cash flow," said Billy Carter. "One day I might go buy a farmer's crop and I might need $500,000. I might get it back the next day, or I might still need more on hand."

Father's Day is big doings in the Billy Carter household. For Father's Day 1976, his five children, ranging in age from eight to twenty, gave him a green football jersey bearing the number "6" and his nickname "Cast Iron," a reference to his protruding stomach and its ability to withstand all sorts of abuse—notably his fondness for beer.

Where there's Billy, there's beer. His Amoco gas station became a landmark in Plains because it was the only place to buy beer in town; some said he pumped more beer than gas. It was a place for Billy and his friends to gather daily, sitting on worn-out chairs and wooden boxes, drinking.

The other gas station in Plains, a Fina station owned by Frank and Albert Williams, dealt strickly in automotive needs. "That pretty much decides their business," said Plains Mayor A. L. Blanton. "Billy gets the drinkers and the Williams boys get the Baptists."

Jimmy and Billy have the same trademark Carter smile; but that aside, they are not likely to be confused. "I'm not a political person. I'm blunt and sometimes folks don't like it, I don't go to church because I wasn't pushed into church. I catch hell for my beer drinking from some folks ... but I don't mind it."

As the 1976 campaign progressed and as the national

media began to discover that the Carter family and home-town were good copy, Jimmy Carter's relatives and friends developed favorite stories and quotable *bon mots* that they become fond of laying on each reporter who passed through Plains. One of Billy's favorite lines: "I got a mamma who joined the Peace Corps and went to India when she was sixty-eight. I got one sister [Ruth] who's a holy roller preacher. I got another sister [Gloria] who wears a helmet and rides a motorcycle. And I got a brother who thinks he's going to be President. So that makes me the only sane person in the family."

Two defeats in one night—an upset in Wisconsin and a humiliating drubbing in New York—could have been disastrous to Carter's campaign.

Late in the night, Carter went to the NBC affiliate station in Milwaukee to do a taping for the morning news show. Carter was thinking about doing two tapes: one as if he had won, the other as if he had lost, so they could use the one that proved accurate. NBC insisted on just one tape.

Back at the Carter headquarters at the Pfister Hotel, Pat Caddell began analyzing the returns that were still out. They included paper ballots and a lot of rural votes. Caddell screamed at the Secret Service agents to contact Carter, contact Jody Powell. Stop Carter from conceding. Meanwhile, Greg Schneiders was at the television studio, telling Carter that he ought to give NBC a statement that would be acceptable, win or lose. The Georgian agreed. Carter fuzzed the issue in his taped interview.

Once back at the hotel, Carter had an idea. He asked if there was a newspaper that had done the same thing the networks had done—predict a Udall victory. Carter was thinking of the great moment when Harry Truman held aloft a newspaper—the *Chicago Tribune*—with the premature headline saying that Dewey had won the Presidency in 1948.

Carter's aides came back with the *Milwaukee Sentinel*. The headline said "Carter Upset by Udall." But the late returns gave Wisconsin to Carter. It was 2:00 A.M., and Carter's supporters were still waiting. Carter greeted them, and held the newspaper high above his head, Truman-style. That picture—of Carter's winning in Wisconsin—became the focus of April 6. "It obliterated that disaster in New York," Caddell later said.

The Udall staff members—and Billy Carter—were still in the Marc Plaza's Bombay Bicycle Club eating pizza and drinking as the Udall lead slipped away with the night. Shortly before 2:30 A.M., they were greeted by a group of cheering Carter supporters bearing the news that it was Carter who had won. Billy Carter joined his brother's backers and let loose a triumphant rebel yell.

THE RESULTS: *Carter won 37 percent of the vote; Udall, 36. Carter won by less than 5,000 votes out of the more than 670,000 cast.*

Two liberals stayed on the ballot in Wisconsin and received what could have been crucial Udall votes. Harris got 8,265 (about 1 percent) and Shriver got 5,139 (also about 1 percent). Had either man come out in advance for fellow-liberal Udall and had his backers followed his wishes and voted for Udall, either the Harris votes or the Shriver votes would have been enough to put Udall over the top.

Months later, Udall sat in his House office and reflected on how things might have been changed had he only spent the money right away for the media and the mailing.

"If I'd only known then what I know today," Udall said, sitting on a government-issue sofa, his face somber as he thought once more about this fact that will haunt him always. "I'd already gone into debt. . . . My wife was concerned. I'd seen candidates going on the lecture circuit [to bail themselves out of heavy debt]. . . . Maybe putting up my home for mortgage. . . . [But] I promised my wife I wouldn't. Ella, she loves her home. . . . We had hit all our friends. We were over our heads. All of the scrounging, the borrowing hadn't done it. . . . [But] one more turn of the wheel would have done it."

There is no doubt in the minds of most of the Udall people that the campaign was lost by the delay that shut Udall off the television stations in that final crucial weekend plus the mailing of 100,000 letters that were never sent.

And there is no doubt either in the minds of the Carter

men. *"That had to be the difference,"* Hamilton Jordan conceded in an interview a couple of weeks later. *"A weekend of television has to be good for 5,000 or more votes easily. It had to make the difference. That's how they lost it. That's how we won."*

April 27|Pennsylvania

Memorandum

To: Campaign
From: Pat Caddell
8 April 1976
Re: Implications of Wisconsin

Analysis of Wisconsin

. . . Our survey was completed on Thursday evening, when the weighted results stood Carter 38%, Udall 27%, Jackson 8%, Wallace 7%, 5% no preference, and 9% undecided. Another survey by an outside source, completed on Saturday, showed the results to be 38% to 28%. As I explained at the time, we expected the 5% no preference vote to go to Udall as they were far more liberal than the electorate in general and more favorable to him or not to vote at all. However, the analysis I have done also shows that the undecided votes went overwhelmingly to Udall and some to Wallace. Indeed, Wallace almost doubled his vote on Tuesday both from our survey and the other survey. . . . Why the wholesale defection of the undecideds?

In our survey on Thursday, we noted only two disturbing notes. First, the leading Carter negative on open-ended responses was the category "not specific, wishy-washy, changes stands," which went from 3% in our first poll to 11% in the last survey. Also, the agreement to the projective statement "Jimmy Carter always seems to be changing his positions on the issues" rose from 23% in survey 1 to 33% in survey 2. . . . More important, the CBS poll [taken as people left the voting booths] indicates that 43% of the voters agree to a question similar to ours that Carter was not specific enough and vacillated on the issues. This would suggest that the 33% figure we saw rose and may well have cut us.

. . . This problem must be overcome. We must defuse the 'no specifics and changes positions arguments.' They seem to be rising. And inevitably unchecked lead to perceptions of Carter as 'untrustworthy' and 'dishonest.' We can see some of that already in Pennsylvania. Also, Carter must no longer stay on the defensive—every time that happens, whether in Massachusetts, Wisconsin, or New York, we are hurt badly. . . . We must assume a national campaign posture and stay on the offensive on change of issues. Otherwise a vacuum emerges and our opponents and the press will rush to fill it with adverse attacks and issues.

One-third of the people were thinking Carter was fuzzy on issues, and Carter had not been able to win any of the "undecided" voters on election day. The Carter advisers moved to combat the problem. Jerry Rafshoon, who in this campaign has earned himself a reputation as one of the most savvy in the business of political media, came up with a cut-rate plan to counter the image that Carter is a man who does not discuss issues. He took Carter's existing television spots and had an announcer read a new introduction: "Jimmy Carter on the issue of health care," he said for one; "Jimmy Carter on the issue of unemployment," he said for another; and so on.

Rafshoon also had the announcer read a new voiceover closing to the existing taped commercials: "If you see this *critical issue* the way Jimmy Carter does, then vote for him."

The specifics of Carter's now issue-oriented television commercial message had not been sharpened. But his image had. The spots were aired throughout the Pennsylvania primary campaign.

On April 2 Carter was interviewed by Sam Roberts, the chief political correspondent of the *New York Daily News.* An article based on the interview ran two days later. The sixteenth paragraph, on page 134, said: "And, asked about low-income scatter-site housing in the suburbs, he replied: 'I see nothing wrong with ethnic purity being maintained. I would not force a racial integration of a neighborhood by government action. But I would not permit discrimination against a family moving into the neighborhood.' "

Ethnic purity. Jimmy Carter had said it, and the *Daily News* had attached no special importance to it, and the New York and Wisconsin primaries came and went without the matter's being raised.

But a CBS official saw the phrase and suggested that correspondent Ed Rabel, who was traveling with the Carter organization, question him about it. Rabel did, at a press conference in Indianapolis on the day of the New York and Wisconsin primaries.

Question: "What did you mean by ethnic purity?"

Answer: "I have nothing against a community that's made up of people who are Polish, Czechoslovakians, French-Canadians, or blacks who are trying to maintain the ethnic purity of their neighborhood. This is a natural inclination on the part of people. . . . I've never, though, condoned any sort of discrimination against, say, a black family or other family from moving into that neighborhood. But I don't think government ought to deliberately break down an ethnically oriented community deliberately by injecting into it a member of another race. To me, this is contrary to the best interests of the community."

The questioning continued at South Bend, Indiana, and at Pittsburgh. Carter kept talking about the value of "ethnic purity" of neighborhoods. And he elaborated—warning of "black intrusion" into white neighborhoods and of "injecting into [a community] a member of another race" or "a diametrically opposite kind of family" or a "different kind of person."

Only two staff members, Greg Schneiders and Betty Rainwater, were with Carter. Rainwater was one of Jody Powell's assistant press secretaries. They were alarmed. Carter was not.

As soon as the questioning began, Schneiders wrote Carter a memo. It said that there was nothing unacceptable about Carter's basic points, but that, as in the abortion controversy in Iowa, the specific language should be clarified. The problem, he said, was the use of "ethnic purity" and the other phrases that are emotional and generate controversy. Don't use them, Schneiders said.

Schneiders gave the memo to Carter in South Bend. He and Rainwater got in the car with Carter. Carter said he did not think the words were offensive. He didn't intend them to be; he didn't think they would be taken that way. There is no telling whether the issue will prove to be good or bad for his campaign effort, Carter said.

Schneiders reasoned with Carter to no avail. Rainwater did the same. Later Schneiders and Rainwater separately called Jody Powell, who had stayed in Milwaukee after the Wisconsin vote. "Betty called first," Powell recalled. "She said, 'I think we've got a real problem developing here.' Greg called. It was a situation that was hard for me to make a persuasive argument [with Carter]. It was relying on their perceptions, which were clearly different from his—and I was arguing through them to him."

Hamilton Jordan was among those not overly concerned. "I thought it would pass," he said. "I felt it was a serious mistake, but that it wouldn't last. I was surprised when Betty Rainwater called from South Bend and told me how Jimmy's explanation [at the press conference] went over."

And then there was the view of Kirbo.

Charles Kirbo is a down-home country gentleman from the farmlands of Georgia. He is Deep South. Up until just a few months before he had been a familiar sight, driving his 1967 green weathered Chevy pickup truck into downtown Atlanta and parking it in the garage of an ultra-modern new building, taking the elevator up to one of the South's most prestigious law firms, where he worked in wood-paneled, expensively furnished elegance. He switched to a sedan—"they kidded me so much about that old truck that I don't use it anymore."

Kirbo is easily the slowest-talking man in the Carter campaign. He seems to weigh each word carefully before he says it, and gives it one more good look as it's coming out of his mouth. Kirbo used to drop by for consultation regularly when Carter was governor. "I never did have a parking space," he recalled. "So I'd just park my truck next to Jimmy's car. And sometimes there'd be a new young policeman on the beat and he wouldn't know and he'd make me move. It just got me in trouble."

It was Kirbo who first tutored the young aspiring politician when they took some of his votes away years ago when he was running for the state legislature. Kirbo represented Carter in a voting fraud case and won and he's been tutoring Carter ever since.

Kirbo has no staff title, no official responsibility. "I just kind of float in and out and help a bit if someone asks me to," he said. He is most commonly described by the members of the Carter staff as a father figure to the candidate. The Carter men and women call each other Jody and Hamilton and Betty and Jerry. They call Carter Jimmy. They call Kirbo "Mister Kirbo." He is gray-haired, tall, always courtly; he walks with a gait slowed by age; his nose is red and weathered. Yet he is just fifty-nine—just eight years older than his "son figure," the candidate.

When Kirbo heard about the ethnic purity situation, he decided to go out to the Carter headquarters—a place he then rarely visited—to be available for consultation. "I knew a flap was going on, so I came out," he said. "I just happened to walk in on a meeting. Well, they asked my views, and I said it was my feeling that if we keep on going with the issue—you know, issue an explanation and all that—it would just keep it going on. I've just seen it happen time and time again—you make a mistake, and then you keep fanning it, and it just keeps hurting you. So then they said that some of Jimmy's black supporters were embarrassed because they'd stuck their necks out for Jimmy, and all that.

"Well, I thought about that, and then I said that is different. If Andy Young wants him to apologize, then he ought to."

Andy Young is Andrew Young, a black Democratic congressman from Atlanta and a former top aide to Martin Luther King, Jr. According to his staff members, Young was distraught after learning of Carter's initial comment, and was upset even more by the candidate's subsequent explanation. Young had been Carter's first and only prominent black backer, and his credibility, as well as Carter's, was at stake.

"This doesn't mean to me he's a racist," Young said

publicly. "It means he made a terrible blunder that he's got to recover from. I just think it's an awful phrase. I don't think he understood how loaded it is with Hitlerian connotations."

The next night Carter was in the Bond Court Hotel in Cleveland. He washed out his socks and underwear in the bathroom sink; he called his wife; and he called Young. By the next day, he was convinced that he had to admit he had made a mistake. He had to apologize.

"I think most of the problem has been caused by my ill-chosen agreement to use the word ethnic purity," Carter said in a statement upon arriving in Philadelphia. "I think that was a very serious mistake on my part. I think it should have been the word 'ethnic character' or 'ethnic heritage.' . . . I do want to apologize to all those who have been concerned about the unfortunate use of the 'ethnic purity.' I don't think there are any ethnically pure neighborhoods, but in response to a question and without adequate thought on my part, I used a phrase that was unfortunate. . . . I was careless in the words I used. . . . I have apologized for it. It was an improper choice of words."

It took Carter days to switch from his original view about his remarks, but he finally apologized. His backers had been saying that it was just a case of his saying something while overtired. His critics had been saying it was a veiled appeal for the Wallace vote in the suburbs. No one knows Carter's motive for sticking so long with his original phrasing—except Carter. "The reason for the delayed reaction," said one of Carter's close advisers, "was in part because he is stubborn when under attack." Looking back, Jody Powell later said: "The situation made Greg [Schneiders] more forceful in the future and willing to go to the mat with Jimmy."

■   ■   ■

Hamilton Jordan had seen that the Pennsylvania primary could provide Carter's best chance to make a big impression in a northern industrial state. "After the Massachusetts primary," he added in an interview, "it became clear that Pennsylvania would be more than that. It would be our chance to take on Jackson man to man." So im-

mediately after the Massachusetts primary, Tim Kraft—
who had engineered Carter's Iowa victory—was sent to
Pennsylvania. He had almost two months to organize support for his candidate there.

One of Kraft's easier tasks was winning endorsement
for Carter from Pittsburgh Mayor Peter Flaherty. Kraft
asked him if he intended to be an observer or get involved.
Flaherty said that he would strongly support Carter. "You
should meet Jimmy Carter," Kraft said. Flaherty flew to
upstate New York to meet him. And then he made his
endorsement.

In Massachusetts, Kraft's efforts had been surpassed by
the Jackson staff's, especially by the get-out-the-vote work
of twenty-six-year-old Bob (Skinner) Donahue. But the
Jackson people then rejected Donahue's request that he
be put on Jackson's national campaign staff, and Donahue
was unhappy. Kraft heard about it and contacted Donahue.
The ex-Jackson man wound up running the Carter get-
out-the-vote campaign in Pennsylvania.

Kraft hired a professional telephone service and set up
a 100-phone bank in Pittsburgh and another 100-phone
bank in Philadelphia. The two banks were used in making 250,000 to 300,000 calls.

But on paper, at least, no one had an organization to
match Scoop Jackson's. Philadelphia's Mayor Frank Rizzo
had come out for Jackson. So had I. W. Abel, the head
of the steelworkers' union, most of the state's prominent
labor leaders, and most of the state's Democratic organization.

But it did not come together for Jackson. One reason
was that the Jackson people just did not see the situation
as clearly as Carter's. "I don't think Pennsylvania [was
considered] a crossroads state until it was upon us," said
Bob Keefe, Jackson's campaign manager. "Until mid-March
it was not clear that Wallace would not be a factor. . . .
We should have invested more heavily in building an organization in Pennsylvania."

Abel and his steelworkers and the other unions never
really came up with the hard-working day-to-day campaign
work necessary to make a man a winner. Keefe said he
was surprised at the failure of Abel and the other labor
leaders to deliver. "We believed Abe was going to help to
a greater degree than he helped," he said. "Hubert had

suggested to him that he help. Labor leaders suggested that he help. He suggested back that he was doing all he could. But we started working in a crazy season. He had his own [union] election coming up. Abe's handpicked successor bombed out and another handpicked successor had a couple of opponents. The steelworkers have a real election with ballot boxes. . . . So he was worried about his election. That's the nature of our business. . . ."

In Reading, two days before the election, another Jackson official recalled asking the business agent for an 11,000-member steelworkers local what it was doing for Jackson. "Nobody ever contacted me," was the reply.

"Fred Lebder, the Fayette County commissioner, was our key guy in Pennsylvania," Keefe said. "Fred Lebder is a typical local leader. He runs Fayette and he was supposed to worry about everything outside of Philadelphia. He filed for Congress . . . and he was running for a month before we knew about it. A lot of his reports, shall we say, lacked substance." (As it turned out, Lebder's attempt to divide his efforts between Jackson's campaign and his own proved unsuccessful. He lost the congressional primary.)

During the Pennsylvania primary, Keefe said, he kept talking to Hubert Humphrey's administrative aide, Dave Gartner. "It was their opinion that helping us was the best thing they could do," Keefe said. Later, however, Jackson men would be bitter over the Humphrey connection—stung most of all by the Pennsylvania labor men who admitted to Joseph R. Daughen of the *Philadelphia Bulletin* that their first choice was Humphrey, and that they were working for Jackson mostly because it was the best way to help Humphrey.

Udall, who had not spent the extra $30,000 on media and mailing in Wisconsin, was spending money again in Pennsylvania. He was campaigning hard despite a survey by Peter Hart two and a half weeks before the election which showed Carter with 34; Jackson, 25; and Udall, 15. "We kept telling ourselves, 'If we can just get the liberals,' " Udall recalled. "We thought the liberals might coalesce in Pennsylvania—that the liberals were going to rally there."

Paul Bereswill/*Newsday*

Governor Jimmy Carter of Georgia.

Paul Bereswill/*Newsday*

Jimmy Carter arrives in New York for the 1976 Democratic National Convention. Just to his right is New York Mayor Abe Beame.

Paul Bereswill/*Newsday*

In New York for the convention, Jimmy Carter addresses a crowd at a rally in front of the Americana Hotel.

Dick Yarwood/*Newsday*

Amidst reporters' cameras a laughing Jimmy Carter tries to watch the Democratic National Convention on TV.

Amy Carter, her father Jimmy, and her mother Rosalynn Carter.

Jimmy Carter is hugged by women of the Georgia delegation to the Democratic convention.

Dick Yarwood/*Newsday*

Jimmy Carter on his way to address the California delegation to the Democratic convention. With him are Governor Jerry Brown (**left**) and Senator Gene Tunney of California.

Dick Yarwood/*Newsday*

Jimmy Carter and New York Congressman Herman Badillo prepare to address the Chicano Caucus at the Democratic convention.

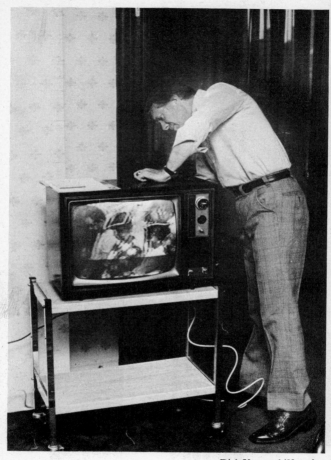

Dick Yarwood/*Newsday*
Trying to tune in the convention, Jimmy Carter fiddles with the TV set in his New York hotel suite.

Jimmy Carter talks with reporters at a press conference during the 1976 Democratic National Convention.

Senior PR man Jody Powell.

Dick Yarwood/*Newsday*

Dick Yarwood/*Newsday*

Carter pollster Pat Caddell.

Senior PR man Jody Powell with his aide, Betty Rainwater.

Carter staff member Greg Schneiders.

Jimmy Carter and his grandson, Jason, ten months old.

Dick Yarwood/*Newsday*

Miss Lillian Carter addresses a press conference at the Democratic National Convention.

Dr. Walter Stapleton, Billy Carter; Sybil Carter, and Jimmy's sister Ruth Stapleton in their hotel suite in New York City. Dr. and Mrs. Stapleton wear their convention ID cards.

Just before he makes his acceptance speech, Jimmy Carter gets a kiss from his wife. Daughter Amy looks on.

The entire Carter clan and assorted Mondales wave to the packed hall at Madison Square Garden as the Democratic convention draws to a close.

Rosalynn and Jimmy Carter at a press conference after Carter's nomination for president.

Amy Carter talks with her mother at the end of a news conference Mrs. Carter has held with Mrs. Mondale.

Joe Dombroski/*Newsday*

Jimmy Carter and Walter Mondale acknowledge cheers at Madison Square Garden. Their wives and Amy Carter are behind them.

Udall recalled how he was working a street in Philadelphia when a couple came out of a doctor's office with a two-year-old son who was wearing an eye patch. He had had an eye removed due to cancer. Udall stopped, talked to them, told them he too had lost an eye and asked them to keep in touch if they needed help. He said it not only made him feel good, but it got him great publicity.

If it was Philadelphia publicity he wanted, why, he was asked, did he spurn a rare invitation to address the city council at its regular meeting? Charley Bowser, a black lawyer, had arranged the opportunity for him. No other candidate had access to the council. It could have meant big television coverage in Philadelphia and even statewide. Instead Udall had gone to a fundraising breakfast in Washington. Udall looked genuinely amazed. "I didn't know about that [the city council invitation] until this minute," he said, almost two months after the Pennsylvania election.

Perhaps the most significant development in the Pennsylvania primary happened three months before the election, well outside the state boundaries, when the U.S. Supreme Court issued a ruling that prevented the Federal Elections Commission from disbursing matching funds to the presidential candidates until Congress reconstituted the commission on a constitutionally acceptable basis. The last checks were sent out on March 22. A month later, the candidates were in a cash squeeze.

Jimmy Carter managed—thanks to some prudent planning and good fortune. Scoop Jackson did not.

The Planning: Bob Lipshutz, Carter campaign treasurer, had insisted during the Wisconsin primary on saving some money for Pennsylvania. "That was the decisive break," Pat Caddell said later. "We had a big jump on the media. We were the only ones with the money for it. We were on for about ten days unchallenged."

The Good Fortune: When the Carter campaign committee needed money for Pennsylvania, it was able to quickly borrow $100,000 from the Fulton National Bank of Atlanta on the strength of Jimmy Carter's personal financial statement.

The Carter campaign also borrowed another $175,000 from Citizens Southern National Bank on the basis of its accounts receivable—money due it from the Secret Service and the press for airplane charter trips. And they borrowed another $500,000 from the Fulton National Bank against matching fund submissions awaited from the Federal Elections Commission.

Still, Carter needed more.

"In Pennsylvania we had to have about $350,000 in a hurry," Morris Dees, Carter's national finance chairman, recalled. "So I called a national finance committee meeting in Georgia and invited 650 people to come. We sent out Mailgrams and asked each person to raise $1,000 and bring it with them. We had about 400 people show up and they brought $150,000 with them. Had at least that much more in pledges which came in very quickly. So the week of the Pennsylvania primary (two weeks before, actually) we were able to put over $300,000 in the bank."

For Jackson, the situation was much different. "Pennsylvania was not prepared to go," Bob Keefe recalled. "We had not put the energy and resources there. We had applied them to New York, Massachusetts, and Florida. We spent way too much money in Florida."

The Jackson for President Committee spending records on file at the Federal Elections Commission tell the story of the faulty planning of the Jackson campaign.

In Massachusetts Jackson spent $657,393.

In Florida he spent $558,437 (in an election he was not really trying to win).

In New York he spent $891,698.

In Pennsylvania, his showdown with Carter state, he spent just $163,305.

"If we spent the same money in Pennsylvania as we did in Florida, we'd have won it. We didn't have any money to spend in Pennsylvania in the last three weeks."

Jackson would have been helped by smart planning and budgeting in a number of other states as well. Jackson officials spent $36,267 in California and $23,740 in Ohio—but Jackson had been blown out of the race long before those June 8 primaries came. He spent $13,866 in Iowa, in a half-hearted effort; $50,304 in a third place effort in Wisconsin when he was really concentrating on New York that same day; $44,728 in New Hampshire in a belated effort to win some delegates while staying out of the popularity vote (all he got out of this was a little media exposure in Massachusetts).

Jackson had a reputation for being a dull candidate and dull public speaker. But in the end he blew the election not on the stump but on the drawing board.

"By the time we got to Pennsylvania, it was a pity," said Hershey Gold, Jackson's national finance chairman. "But had we built the grass-roots organization, we could have made a good showing despite a dry bank account."

"Money isn't the ultimate weapon," he said. "How do you make $13 million do the work of $20 million? You do it by adding people—volunteers. Carter had the volunteers. He had the ability to do a literature drop of 50,000 pieces in a couple of hours," Gold said. "We used to struggle and flail around trying to get a little literature drop made— trying to find people to do it."

From their vantage point in Atlanta, the Carter people had always figured that Jackson had a bottomless source of wealth in that foreign place, New York. And Keefe, who had given Hamilton Jordan his start at the Democratic National Committee a couple of years earlier, was certainly a pro. So in Pennsylvania, the Carter people were amazed to find themselves facing what seemed to be a phantom opponent in Jackson. They had expected to find Keefe's presence everywhere, but they saw little evidence of his work. It was only then that they came to believe stories that had been circulating about how Jackson, that veteran of Washington back rooms, was hurting for money—how Jackson was left to depend on the unions to keep their word and deliver for him. But the unions did not deliver and Kraft's Carter organization did.

THE RESULTS: *Carter's "ethnic purity" controversy turned out to be no handicap. Carter won 37.2 percent of the vote; Jackson, 24.7 percent; Udall, 18.8. "In Pennsylvania it was a genuine pleasure," said Tim Kraft later. "It was like being in the cockpit of a powerful jet."*

Jackson took the train from Philadelphia to Washington on Wednesday morning with his press secretary Brian Cor-

coran. From Washington's Union Station, they walked several blocks to Jackson's office.

There, on the red chairs in Jackson's large inner office, they sat and contemplated what was left of the future. With them were Bob Keefe; Sterling Munro, the campaign administrator; Ben Wattenberg, an adviser; Dick Kline; and Walter Skallerup, the controller and legal adviser.

Wattenberg was the only man who wanted to continue the campaign. The group estimated that it would take another $1 million; the Federal Elections Commission had $400,000 for Jackson, but where would the additional $600,000 come from? The financial men offered no encouragement.

Labor leaders wandered in and out. They said they would do whatever Jackson wanted.

Ahead lay Indiana. Tough by any odds. Carter would win the southern part of the state. Jackson recalled how in 1960 he had been stumping the state for Kennedy and how people kept asking him: "Are you another one of those Catholics for Kennedy?"

No decision was reached Wednesday. Keefe said that he and Hubert Humphrey had talked, and that Humphrey asked him what was happening and that Keefe said honestly he did not know. Keefe called Humphrey at 8:10 A.M. the next day and said that Jackson was likely to drop out. Humphrey asked if Keefe had read the *Washington Post*'s editorial page. No? Humphrey read him the last paragraph of an editorial that said Humphrey could only bring discredit upon his career by entering the race now.

On Thursday afternoon, Jackson, Keefe, and some Jackson supporters watched live television coverage of Humphrey's press conference. Humphrey was teary-eyed as he said he had decided not to get into the campaign.

The Jackson people thought it all out again. Indiana, Keefe recalled, "would be bum. There was no money spent there. Texas was going to be bum. It would be another two weeks before we could see anything. Connecticut looked promising. Nebraska, Maryland, Michigan might be good." But, he added: "Scoop felt there was little likelihood that he would be the nominee." It wasn't worth going deep into debt. He decided to drop out. His active campaign was over.

152

Interlude: HHH

In 1948 a young, idealistic mayor of Minneapolis electrified the Democratic National Convention. "To those who say that this civil rights program is an infringement of states' rights . . . the time has arrived in America for the Democratic Party to get out of the shadows of states' rights and walk forthrightly into the bright sunshine of human rights," Hubert Horatio Humphrey declared in firm, ringing tones. Strom Thurmond and his fellow archright southerners walked forthrightly out of the Democratic Party and founded the Dixiecrats as a strong civil rights plank was passed. At age thirty-seven, Hubert H. Humphrey had catapulted to national prominence as a leader among liberals.

In 1960 a now-established senator mounted an energetic campaign for the Democratic presidential nomination. Hubert H. Humphrey criss-crossed the country lining up support, but was defeated first in Wisconsin and then in West Virginia by a well-oiled, well-financed John F. Kennedy machine. "I am no longer a candidate for the Democratic presidential nomination," a crushed Hubert Humphrey declared. "I shall run for reelection to the United States Senate."

In 1964 a fiery veteran of sixteen years in the Senate stumped hard after being chosen as the Democratic vice-presidential candidate. Hubert Humphrey rode into office on the tail of Johnson's landslide victory over Barry Goldwater.

In 1968 a vice president shackled to a hated war policy that ripped the country apart won the Democratic presidential nomination. But Hubert Humphrey could not bring himself to cut his ties to the Johnson war policy until it was too late. He was edged by Richard Nixon and he left Washington a crushed and crying man.

In 1972 a sixty-one-year-old freshman senator fought again to win the Democratic presidential nomination. But Hubert Humphrey was now Old Politics. He was thrashed soundly by a young, liberal crowd that rallied behind Senator George McGovern.

In 1976 the juices were flowing once more. The quadrennial glands that had secreted in sync with the presidential campaigns for so many years were pumping once more in that venerable and politic body that was once home to the young Turk of 1948. Powerful people in labor and within the Democratic Party had been urging the sixty-five-year-old Happy Warrior to make still one more run at the White House. "I get tempted. I get tempted because people call me. But I've gone around many times already asking for help. Asking people to please help me. And I'm tired of it. I don't want to have to go around and ask people to help me. I don't want to go to people anymore," Humphrey said back in March.

He preferred then to let others make the run, hoping for a deadlocked convention. But then Jackson collapsed in Pennsylvania, and Jimmy Carter appeared to have a clear field, and the pressures from labor people and party people mounted again. And so on Wednesday, April 28, Humphrey called nine advisers to his office to figure out what he should do.

In his office, Humphrey took off his suit jacket and outlined the possibilities. There were three options open: an all-out campaign which included entering the New Jersey primary; the authorization of an "exploratory committee" that would gather funds, assemble supporters, and lobby uncommitted delegates for votes; and, finally, nothing.

Humphrey asked each person to give his views. Most argued for an all-out fight, starting with the New Jersey primary with its filing deadline of 4:00 P.M. the next day.

A few argued against this. It would be hard to build an organization, to raise the money needed so desperately to mount an effective campaign that would win the voters in time for the June 8 New Jersey vote.

Then, if he announced he was going to wage an all-out fight, there would be intense pressure for him to enter the Nebraska primary, where the vote would be held May 11. His name was on the ballot there but he had absolutely no organization in the state. Senator Frank Church (D–Idaho) already was campaigning hard to win Nebraska. It would be tough, very tough.

Max Kampelman, the lawyer who had been Humphrey's legislative aide some years ago, showed the senator a draft of a speech he had prepared announcing his candidacy.

Humphrey scanned it and thanked him. He already had received memorandums from at least two congressmen, and a senator had outlined what he could say in giving his reasons for campaigning in New Jersey.

One of his secretaries entered the meeting and handed him a note. Humphrey smiled and read it out loud. It was from his wife, Muriel, and it said: "Whatever you decide to do is all right with me. And wherever you decide to have dinner is all right with me."

Muriel Humphrey had been reluctant to have her husband try again. Humphrey remembered his wife's attitude as he read the note. The secretary, he thought, "must have gotten the message wrong."

Despite the obstacles, Kampelman wanted him to fight it out in New Jersey. So did Walter Mondale, the other senator from Minnesota, who had voluntarily withdrawn his own presidential bid months before. So did Minnesota millionaire Robert Short, former owner of Washington's baseball Senators, who took the national pastime out of the nation's capital and moved it to Texas (a capital flight by a rich baseball man who wanted to get richer).

Erie County Democratic Chairman Joseph Crangle of New York also urged Humphrey to enter the race actively. He didn't really know the senator but he long had been a supporter of his. "Certainly," Crangle said afterwards, "he could win New Jersey."

But would New Jersey be enough, particularly if Carter sailed through the other primaries? Crangle counseled that Humphrey could be the issues candidate—a dramatic figure who could effectively counter Carter's anti-Washington, anti-big government themes.

After each of the nine spoke individually, there was a general discussion. Humphrey asked a lot of questions but did not reveal his inclinations.

Almost everyone present wanted Humphrey to enter the race. But then, the senator said: "Now put yourself in my chair. What would you do?"

The answers were somewhat different then. The nine were divided about evenly on the subject. Those against, according to one person present, basically said: "You've already served your country and the party. It'll be a terrible grind and strain on you to do it again."

Another person at the meeting said: "There was a recognition underlying the whole thing that this was an intensely personal decision. I could not tell at the end of the meeting which way he was leaning. He said, 'I will go home, talk to Muriel, and sleep on it.' "

On Thursday morning, Humphrey and his wife sat down in their library. They discussed the strain on their personal lives that such a campaign would bring. "I told her that as far as I could see, I should not enter the primaries," Humphrey said.

Still, he left the question open and left for the office, arriving at 10:40 A.M. His physician and confidant, Dr. Edgar Berman, had talked to him the evening before and was convinced he would run. Berman was so certain that he telephoned John Y. Brown of Louisville, the former owner of Kentucky Fried Chicken, to come up to Washington and run the Humphrey for President campaign.

Brown promptly boarded a plane and flew there. Meanwhile, Humphrey telephoned Henry Jackson and Morris Udall, two of the Democratic presidential contenders. He encouraged both to stay in the race. He did not call Carter because the former Georgia governor's campaign manager, Hamilton Jordan, had called him—making Humphrey think that Carter would be telephoning later. He did not.

Humphrey telephoned New York Mayor Abraham Beame, who told him to run in New Jersey. He called AFL–CIO President George Meany.

At 11:45 A.M. he called his wife and, during a ten-minute conversation, decided that he would not, after all, campaign. He called his daughter, Mrs. Nancy Solomonson, and told her of the decision. At 12:20 P.M., he dictated a statement announcing his intentions to his secretary, Marsha Greenwood, and went off to a labor committee luncheon.

"There was no overriding factor," said his administrative assistant, David Gartner.

"It was a personal decision," John Y. Brown said. "He didn't want to expose himself."

"Hubert is a gentleman," Dr. Edgar Berman said. "To be cut up by the press again would have been pure anguish. He thought it [the primaries] would be a very iffy affair among three candidates. It just didn't happen."

But Berman added that he thought that despite all of that, with two or three more days to think about it, Humphrey might have entered anyway. Deciding to stay out, Berman said, "I think was a mistake."

On Thursday afternoon, Hubert Humphrey stood next to Walter Mondale in the Senate Caucus Room and read the statement his secretary had typed. So momentous was his announcement that network television had cut into its soap operas to carry Humphrey live. The senator pulled a white handkerchief from his pocket and wiped tears from his eyes. "Really, I'm not crying," he volunteered. "Those [television lights] are really bright on my sensitive eyes. I've cried before but that's when I lost. This time, I prevented that."

Hubert Humphrey would not run for the Presidency, he would not pursue once more the goal which had forever eluded him. "One thing I don't need at this stage of my life is to be ridiculous," he said. "I haven't thought about a deadlocked convention since eleven A.M."

He actually had not come to a decision until 11:45. On Tuesday, two days earlier, one month before his sixty-fifth birthday, the voters of Pennsylvania—considered his most loyal followers outside his home state—had turned overwhelmingly to Jimmy Carter in the presidential primary.

But he did say there was always the chance of a miracle —a chance that the convention would deadlock and that the nomination might somehow still be his. "I shall not seek it," Humphrey said. "I shall not search for it. I shall not scramble for it." Then he paused. "But I'm around."

Another Interlude: Fiasco

From Pat Caddell's memo of March 24, 1976: ". . . This campaign needs now at least one excellent, brilliant writer, who can pull together ideas and statements for the governor and who has good political sense. Someone who knows how to capitalize on opportunities and also how to avoid disaster. This person needs to work with Jody, and may need to travel. I think under the right circumstances Shrum may be available."

Back in 1972, Robert Shrum was known as a very heavy,

very talented, very liberal political speechwriter. He was a 290-pound, twenty-nine-year-old man who had written for New York City Mayor John V. Lindsay and for the unsuccessful presidential campaign of Edmund Muskie. He had eventually joined the George McGovern staff. In April, 1976, Shrum had lost 140 pounds (through the discipline of lots of exercise and little food) but none of his talent and none of his liberalism. On the advice of Pat Caddell, he was brought into the Carter inner circle.

Shrum was recruited during the Pennsylvania primary campaign in an effort to defuse the charge that Carter was fuzzy on issues. He quit just nine days later and eventually made his dissatisfaction public, charging that not only was Carter fuzzy on issues, he was *deliberately* fuzzy on issues.

It was, in all, a rather short political metamorphosis. On Monday, April 19, Shrum sat in on his first staff meeting devoted to issues. And by Thursday, April 22, he recalls, he was a discouraged and disillusioned man; he sat on the steps of a Holiday Inn that night talking with Caddell until three A.M., unburdening himself of his doubts. On Monday, April 26, Shrum wrote a victory statement for Carter to use after the votes were counted the next day; but he didn't wait around to join in the celebration. Instead, he took the 5:41 Metroliner from Philadelphia to Washington, where he sought the advice of friends.

"After I wrote that victory statement, it all came back to me again—all the doubts and uncertainty," Shrum recalls. "It wasn't any blinding revelation that let me know what I was going to do—I don't believe in stuff like that. But the more I thought about it, the more I became certain about what I had to do. I believed at that point that Carter was going to be the nominee and then be elected the next President. But by then, the only thing I kept trying to calculate for myself was "Has this been long enough for me to make the decision to quit?" My initial thought was that I would quit but that I just would never say anything publicly about why I was quitting."

Caddell, who remained a friend of Shrum's even after the whole embittering experience, called at one point. In Shrum's words: "Pat told me if I was going to resign, to please shut up, at least." But in the end, Shrum says, he was most persuaded by a Washington friend who offered this counsel: "If you talk about it publicly and you turn out to have been wrong, how will you feel? You'll feel a bit foolish. But if you *don't* talk about and you turn out to have been *right* [about Carter], how will you feel?" As Shrum saw it, he had a duty to let people know how things were as he saw them.

And so, less than a week after the Pennsylvania primary, Shrum went public by giving reporters copies of the letter of resignation he had written to Carter, charging the candidate with "an attempt to conceal your true positions." He talked in interviews of manipulation and deception, and later elaborated on his feelings in an article he wrote for *The New Times Magazine.*

Shrum gave a lengthy list of examples of cases in which he felt Carter had deliberately fuzzed issues. He said that although Carter had publicly pledged to cut the defense budget by 5 to 7 percent, he had been told privately that Carter "might favor a substantial increase."

He said that Carter had decided not to support a plan to give automatic eligibility for black-lung disease benefits to miners who had worked thirty years because "the plan is too radical." He said Carter told him: "It would offend the operators. And why should I do this for Arnold Miller [the United Mine Workers president] if he won't come and endorse me? . . . I don't think the benefits should be automatic. They chose to be miners."

When trucking executives had wanted to know where Carter stood on changes in trucking regulations, Shrum quoted Carter as saying: "I want to give them enough reassurances to satisfy them, but give them as little as I have to." He also wrote that Carter wanted to tell the trucking industry people that "I oppose the diversion of the highway trust fund to mass transit"—but that an aide reminded Carter that "you're already on record as favoring it."

Shrum said that while preparing what the Carter campaign labeled a "comprehensive" economic policy statement that was released during the Pennsylvania primary, Carter cautioned that he wanted his advisers to make sure that the statement did not "commit me too much."

And he said that Carter had rejected a suggestion that he make another statement on the Mideast situation. He quoted Carter as saying: "We have to be cautious. We don't want to offend anybody. . . . I don't want any more statements on the Middle East or Lebanon. Jackson has all the Jews anyway. It doesn't matter how far I go. I don't get over four percent of the Jewish vote anyway, so forget it. We get the Christians."

In his letter that was written to Carter—and released to reporters—Shrum also said: "You say you wish to keep your options open. Within reason that is understandable. But an election is the only option the people have. After carefully reflecting on what I have seen and heard here, I do not know what you would do as President.

"I share the perception that simple measures will not answer our problems; but it seems to me that your issue strategy is not a response to that complexity, but an attempt to conceal your true positions. I am not sure what you truly believe in other than yourself.

"I have examined my reactions closely. I have attempted to justify a different conclusion. But I cannot rationalize one. Therefore I must resign."

The Carter people were clearly stung by Shrum's decision to go public with his damaging accusations and comments. Jody Powell maintained to reporters that Shrum was not being paid the $23,000 he said he was earning, and said that in fact Shrum had not even been on the payroll. "I think what he is doing now is childish and hurtful," Powell said. "I don't question his sincerity. . . . He, like anyone else, has said things about people and things that would be embarrassing if quoted back to him."

Carter appeared upset when reporters questioned him about the Shrum affair during a stopover in Terre Haute, Indiana. "Shrum has never been on my payroll," Carter said. "I don't feel inclined to comment on this young man's statement. . . . [Shrum] obviously wrote the letter for the news media. . . . I'm not a liar and I don't make any statements in private contrary to those I make in public."

May/Ups and Downs

Jimmy Carter had defeated them all. Birch Bayh and Fred Harris. Henry Jackson and Milton Shapp. Lloyd Bentsen, Terry Sanford, George Wallace, and Mo Udall. With the exception of Udall, who would press to the end, propelled by a number of second-place finishes, they all had stopped running by the end of April.

But the primaries went on. Two fresh challengers, Frank Church and Jerry Brown, arrived. And a movement known as "ABC" (Anybody But Carter), which actually was an effort to win the nomination for Hubert Humphrey, was formed.

As it turned out, Carter's new opponents were simply too late. Jimmy Carter had won the nomination when he defeated Jackson in Pennsylvania. The new challengers would slow him, but they would not stop him. He would lose in ten primaries in May and June. But he would win in ten, and his delegate total would keep climbing. The new opponents did their jobs pretty well, and Carter at times did not do his very well, but in the end, he had too much momentum for it to make a difference.

On May 1, Texas held the year's only Saturday-night primary. Senator Lloyd Bentsen, who had dropped his national presidential effort before New Hampshire, was still running as a favorite son. The Texas primary was the most difficult to qualify for, according to Carter campaign director Hamilton Jordan. He told of a conversation he had about Texas with Charles Kirbo, Carter's closest adviser/confidant. "I told Kirbo early on that I couldn't see spending the extra $6,000 or $7,000 it would take to get on in all thirty-one districts in the state," Jordan recalled. "We were on in twenty-five, and I figured that was good enough, Bentsen being a favorite son and all. But Kirbo put things in proper perspective for me. He said, 'Never put yourself in the position where you can't realize your own potential. Spend the money.' We did."

Carter wanted Texas badly and he worked the state well, while Bentsen appeared unsure of whether he really wanted to allow the primary to be a test vote on his statewide popularity. Carter was proving a formidable opponent.

At a rally in Dallas sponsored by the Southern Methodist University Law School, a rally attended by a largely middle-class college and white-collar worker crowd, one person got up to apparently give the needle to the Georgia governor. The questioner noted that Texas had a large Spanish-speaking population and asked if Carter had anyone on his staff who spoke Spanish. The Georgian handled the question the way Ted Williams used to handle a lazy, hanging curve. He clouted it out of the park. Carter answered the question in Spanish: "Yes, I do. I speak Spanish myself. And my staff will be happy to send you a detailed position paper on any issue you wish."

The audience erupted in applause.

Carter's national staff members became fond of quoting their Texas coordinator, Bob Armstrong, who gave them comfort and confidence by saying: "We're riding a fast horse. All we have to do is hang on and wave our hats."

Carter swept Texas, picking up 122 delegates compared to Bentsen's mere 8. Three days later, Carter had another big day. He carried his home state of Georgia with 83.9 percent of the vote, smashing Wallace. He carried Indiana with 68 percent compared to Wallace's 15. He carried the District of Columbia 39.7 to Udall's 26.1. And he came a respectable second to Wallace in Wallace's Alabama, 50.8 to 27.4.

May 1 plus May 4 meant a whopping 258 delegates for Carter in a single week. "We were in another euphoria as we headed for Nebraska," Caddell recalled. "Euphoria Number Three."

■   ■   ■

Challenge: Church in Nebraska

The only campaigning competition Carter had for Nebraska's May 11 primary was Frank Church, a newcomer. As the Carter people saw it, Church posed little threat.

Frank Church had picked his spot and his strategy carefully, planning months ahead. At fifty-one, after spending twenty years in the Senate, Church had looked at the large early field and figured that many of the candidates would knock each other off. Then, he hoped, he would come on with a rush in the West, cap his crusade in California, and take a large bloc of delegates to Madison Square Garden in July.

"To those who say it's too late, I reply that it's never too late—nor are the odds ever too great—to try," Church declared in his Idaho City announcement speech, his voice searching for emotion and emphasis in the Boys State oratory style that he has never lost. "In that spirit, the West was won and, in that spirit, I announce my candidacy for the Presidency of the United States."

That was his plan. But the collapse of Scoop Jackson was a damaging blow to the Church strategy, and then the emergence of Jerry Brown knocked it haywire.

Church had counted on Jackson being strong throughout the primary season. "He figured Jackson would beat Carter in New York [he did] and beat Carter in Pennsylvania [he did not]," said one of Church's closest advisers. "Then he would be out front and then there would be an initial surge for Humphrey, and then people would begin to wonder whether they really wanted to be saddled with all that old baggage Humphrey brings with him, and then here would come Frank Church, a fresh face with years of experience, who had just done an impressive job with the Senate Intelligence Committee [investigating the CIA]. Church thought he would inherit the antiwar people of McGovern and the old-line Democrats. But the one thing none of us foresaw—the one astonishing thing of the campaign—was the Jackson catastrophe."

"The plan was to finish big in California," said Bill Hall, former press secretary to Church. But Brown's decision to run wiped out Church's California hopes. After the popular young California governor announced his plans to run, Church remarked dolefully, according to Hall, "I made a mistake in not patenting that late, late strategy."

In November and December of 1975, Church had considered making an early bid for the Presidency by jumping into the Massachusetts primary. He had earlier given his word to Senate Majority Leader Mike Mansfield, upon being named chairman of the Senate Intelligence Committee, that he would not use the committee as a launching pad for a presidential campaign. But he could have reasoned that the *public* hearings of the committee had ended before the Massachusetts primary, thus freeing him to enter. A couple of his advisers, Geoffrey Shields and Jerome I. Levinson, were said to have urged him to get into the race early. But Church opted to wait.

On March 10, six days before he announced his candidacy, Church seriously contemplated not making the run for the Presidency at all. This was well before the Jackson collapse in Pennsylvania; it was, in fact, just after Carter had defeated Wallace in Florida. Church saw Carter as being already stronger than he had expected the Georgian to be. He talked with his advisers about forgetting the whole thing and with his family as well. Church's son, Forrest, who is getting a doctorate from the Harvard Divinity School, urged him to make the race.

Church made the race. He came into Nebraska well before the election and worked the state hard. He campaigned there just as he had campaigned in his nearby Idaho. Jimmy Carter, in contrast, spent one day in Nebraska. He was, after all, in the middle of what Caddell called "Euphoria Number Three": he was fresh off a week that had given him 258 delegates; and he had a new Caddell poll, taken just a week before the Nebraska election, that showed him well ahead, with Church mired deep in the pack. So it was that the Carter men decided to spend the candidate's politicking time elsewhere, where he was needed. They were supremely confident about Nebraska.

The Nebraska ballot contained the names of all persons who had been mentioned anywhere, anytime in connection with a run for the Presidency. Caddell's poll a week before the election showed Carter in the low 30s, with noncampaigners Hubert Humphrey and Edward M. Kennedy bunched behind with a total of 25 percent. Church had just 16 to 18.

Good enough grounds for euphoria. And so the Carter camp stopped polling. None of the Carter men bothered to ask if the people who were saying they were for the noncandidates, Humphrey and Kennedy, would really wind up voting for a man they knew was not running. Not even Caddell paused to ask. "That was my major mistake," he said later. "Not concentrating on the second choices. Not asking if the Kennedy and Humphrey votes would stay there or would they go elsewhere. Well, they all went elsewhere—and they all went to Church."

The Church people were never confident. Their candidate spent at least twelve days in the state. "We were wondering right up to election night whether we'd just wind up packing it all in after Nebraska," said one Church aide. "After all, California had already been shot out from under us. So if we couldn't win in Nebraska, forget it."

It was not until just before election day that Caddell got the inkling that something was wrong. And that was not exactly due to his scientific skill and method. Rather, it was because Gene Pokorny called his mom and dad. Pokorny, Caddell's Cambridge Research, Inc., partner, just happened to call home to Nebraska and in the course of things asked his parents who they were voting for. Church, the parents said. Pokorny was stunned. Why? he asked; didn't they know he was polling for Carter? Yes, they knew. But, they said, it was just that Church had been out there campaigning and Carter didn't even care enough to come.

THE RESULTS: *Church wound up beating Carter by one percentage point (38.8 to 37.8)—a margin of less than 2,000 votes. Carter was in Washington on election night, politicking at a congressional fundraising dinner for Democrats. Peter Bourne, who was with Carter that night, told another Carter aide that the candidate had been really upset with that one. Carter said that if they had only spent one more day in Nebraska, it could have made the difference. His staff men, kicking themselves, agreed.*

"A clear case of misreading—a clear case of stupidity," Jody Powell said candidly. "It wasn't like New York, where we might not have known the political system. In Nebraska, we damn well should have understood. If we can win in Georgia, we damn well ought to be able to win in Nebraska. . . . Nebraskans got the impression that we don't care about Nebraska and screw you. I guess I don't blame them. In Georgia, we'd feel the same way if someone campaigned in Georgia the way we campaigned in Nebraska.

"All this crap about us having a well-planned, flawless campaign that moved from obscurity to stardom is—is ridiculous. But Jimmy delegates authority in areas like strategy, and the good thing about him is he can live with the mistakes his people make."

Said Carter: "None of us realized what was happening in Nebraska until it was over."

The same day, May 11, was the only primary in which Carter did not actively campaign. West Virginia favorite son Senator Robert Byrd ran virtually unchallenged in his home state and wound up beating George Wallace 88.5 percent to 11.5. Carter did not campaign against Byrd because he figured, correctly, that he would have Byrd's delegates in the end. It is the sham of the American political process that when Byrd announced his candidacy early in the campaign year, he swore that he was not just a one-state candidate, that he would be running a truly national campaign. It is proof of the strength of the American political process that no one believed him.

      📭   📭   📭

Challenge: Brown in Maryland

It is the legend of Jerry Brown that he is the antipolitician.

He shuns the new $1.3-million California governor's mansion and lives in a nearby apartment, sells the governor's limousine and rides in a Plymouth, cuts his top aides' salaries, and lobbies successfully against his own pay raise. He returns free passes, free memberships, and other gifts sent by special interests; he halts the giving of free briefcases to state bureaucrats because he hates paperwork. He gives state janitors the same $68-a-week pay increase he gives state judges, cuts spending requests for liberal favorites such as education, does not give autographs, does not go on out-of-state trips—not even to national governors' conferences—and shuns traditional party fundraising functions and party patronage pleas.

Yet one year after his election, the respected California Poll found that only 7 percent of respondents thought Jerry Brown was doing a "poor" job as governor.

Only 7 percent. Most politicians are born with a higher negative rating. At age thirty-seven, Edmund G. Brown, Jr. (don't-call-him-Pat's-son), is setting records for voter popularity.

Jerry Brown is—by the only measure that really counts—the ultrapolitician.

Sacramento politicians find it hard to peg Jerry Brown. He is the Jerry Brown of the Jesuit past (and, some say, Zen present) who stunned a senior state legislator during budget deliberations by sending a young aide to ask him, in effect, if he was guilty of knee-jerk thinking. "The governor wants to know if your belief that the poor are hungry is just a middle-class assumption."

When he campaigned for the governorship, a lot of people assumed that he represented a return to liberal causes after eight years of Ronald Reagan. "He was Pat Brown's son, and everyone figured that Jerry Brown's election meant that the faucets would start flowing again," said one of the state's most prominent Democrats. "Well, everybody was wrong."

Brown is not big on public speeches: his first state-of-the-state address lasted just seven minutes; his second, eleven. Antipol.

But he is adept at winning over liberals and conservatives with a style that is effective, but unaffected, and with rhetoric that sounds like recycled Reagan. "At the state level, I think we ought to be doing more of what the federal government is doing now. And in the state, I think more ought to be done at the county level instead of pyramiding a lot of these new agencies that are unresponsive, unelected, and rather obscure." Ultrapol.

When Brown ran for governor in 1974, a number of education and labor people grumbled privately that they kicked sizeable amounts into Brown's campaign fund because they assumed he was a liberal who would favor their spending requests. But Brown says, "I never promised them I'd be a big spender. When I kicked off my campaign, . . . I said I will not raise general taxes. So all of these people know that once you say you're not going to raise taxes, it obviously imposes a certain limit. Now some people said, 'Well, this is the son of Pat Brown, so people thought they'd get more programs and more money.' " But Brown admits he did not tell his education and labor contributors that he was going to clamp down on their programs either. Antipol/ultrapol.

Does he consider himself a liberal? "John Stuart Mill was a liberal," he says. "By the standard indices, I guess people would think I am. . . . But I am not restrained by the metaphors and mythologies associated with the term. . . ."

Sacramento politicians make no pretense of having adjusted to Brown's modus operandi. A bachelor with a lifestyle on the modified bohemian plan, Brown says he works best at night. He handled the prolonged farm labor crisis by calling management, labor, and state officials into his conference room at about 8:00 P.M., keeping them there until 3:00 A.M.—with a break for a meal of Japanese food. Meetings on two succeeding nights lasted even later, and when an agreement was finally reached, he stunned those present by having them sign copies of the written accord—so that no faction later could deny having agreed to any section that might have proven unpopular with the people they represented. Antipol/ultrapol.

In February of 1976, back when Brown was proclaiming "I'm not locked in and I'm not locked out" about running for President, a visiting Eastern reporter asked the young governor if he thought he would make a good President.

The governor exhaled and sagged back into the sofa like a collapsed balloon. "Gee . . . let me think . . . I have to give that one some thought. . . . I mean, I just don't know."

There was no ringing formal declaration when Jerry Brown got into the presidential race. He just sort of let the statement slip out—parenthetically—in a chat with a few reporters after an art exhibit that, by the way, he intended to run for President, at least as a favorite son. Later he confided that he would begin a national campaign by going into Maryland.

Maryland was to be a testing place for Brown. It was too late for him to field a slate of delegates, but he could still have his name placed on the ballot for the presidential preference vote. It would be a way of finding out whether people outside California were interested in the politics of lowered expectations that Brown had been applying to the California electorate in his appealing, Zen-conservative way. He was the most popular figure in California political history, if the polls are an accurate measure; but no one—not even Brown—was sure how his politics would play east of the Rockies.

While Jimmy Carter was making it on a pitch that said he was a peanut farmer/engineer/navy officer/husband/father/Christian, Jerry Brown was making it on a pitch that he wasn't even a traditional governor. No mansion, no limo, no five-point programs, no promises that things would get better.

On April 28, Brown made his first trip outside California since he had been elected governor eighteen months earlier. From the time he hit Maryland, his campaign was something different from anything that had transpired in Campaign '76. He did not have crowds, he had mobs. They were not warm, they were bobby-soxer enthusiastic. They were not like the crowds around Carter or Udall or Jackson or anyone else in this campaign. They were more like the jumpers and squealers that used to surround Bobby Kennedy.

The rise of Jerry Brown was phenomenal. Just two weeks after he had announced his candidacy, before he had made a single campaign speech or taken a single trip outside of his state, Jerry Brown had a higher nationwide rating than three of his rivals—Jackson, Udall, and Church.

Brown arrived in Maryland May 28 and was welcomed

at the Baltimore International Airport by Governor Marvin Mandel, a number of top Democratic and labor leaders, and what the *Washington Post* noted was the largest group of newspeople to gather in the state since the resignation of Spiro T. Agnew. Brown went to a nighttime rally in the ballroom of the Baltimore Hilton that drew 2,000 people, many of whom had been urged to attend by party and labor officials.

"I'm not a Santa Claus with a bag of tricks," Brown told his audience. "I'm just an ordinary guy who works hard and comes home late."

The Maryland politicians fell into line. "A West Coast Jack Kennedy," Lieutenant Governor Blair Lee III bubbled. "I like him. And it looks like a lot of other people do too."

"He definitely made points here—there's no question about it," Baltimore City Council President Walter Orlinsky, who had been wearing a "Holding for Hubert" button for weeks, told the *Washington Post*. "We're getting a media star here. Everyone wants to see him. The question is: will he wear?"

Brown wore. His headlines read like political Horatio Alger. "Brown Gets Big Welcome in Maryland" . . . "Motorcade by Brown Is a Blitz." He was different; when a television interviewer stuck Brown with a long, boring question, Brown replied with a long, boring answer—and then added: "I don't know if that answers your question, but at least it fills up some air time."

Sally Quinn of the *Washington Post* caught a number of the Brown irreverencies in a lengthy piece in the paper that serves Washington's populous Maryland suburbs.

The article was widely read and its anecdotes widely quoted, and people saw a politician who offered them a refreshing change of pace.

Like the time Brown led a group of reporters on an inspection of a garbage dump and said: "What is the inner meaning of this? Why are we here? What are we doing?"

Like the time in a Westinghouse plant when he was shaking hands, saying absently, "I hope you'll vote for me." And one woman replied, "I will," and Brown did a classic double-take. "You will?" he blurted. "But you don't know anything about me."

Like the time he was asked which political philosopher

he looked to for inspiration and he replied somberly, "Thomas Hooker." Reporters wrote down the name and finally someone asked just who Thomas Hooker was. "I'm just being facetious," replied Brown. "He's the only obscure name I could remember from political science class."

Brown had the Maryland Democratic political machine, headed by Governor Marvin Mandel. The party regulars were backing Brown in part because Mandel does not like Jimmy Carter and in part because the labor-backed party officials do like Hubert Humphrey. He was, then, Jerry Brown, the machine antipol. It was Stop Carter politics well played. The only person who did not play the game well was Carter. The Georgian had never succeeded in checking the "soft-on-issues" label and it was starting to catch on, and this was reflected in the polls.

There were two primaries going on May 18—the other was in Michigan, where Carter felt he was doing very well against Udall, what with having such diverse endorsements as those of United Auto Workers President Leonard Woodcock and auto industry giant Henry Ford, and Detroit's black mayor, Coleman Young. They represented constituencies that at times would barely speak to one another. Carter and his strategists felt good about Michigan; they chose to tackle Brown head on in Maryland.

Caddell's Maryland polling showed Carter behind Brown by 4 points. Nationally, Carter negative ratings were starting to climb, from the low 20s up to 30 to 33—and up to the mid-30s in the West. Nebraska had shown that Carter was indeed still vulnerable. "Now we were getting pounded all over the place," Caddell said.

Carter moved to stop the slide by stepping up his efforts in Maryland and stepping up his rhetoric as well.

Carter stumped the state attacking Brown head on, attacking him for being against government reorganization. Carter said that reorganization is essential, that it must be done and that he intended to see that it was—that 1,900 federal agencies be chopped down to just 200. He gave no examples. But he pressed this argument, even in the suburban areas outside Washington, which are heavily populated by people who work in the bureaucracy Carter was promising to whittle down to size.

The last Carter polling, done the Thursday before election day, showed Carter 7 to 8 points behind. "We were getting killed by the Catholics, by the women, and mainly by Brown," Caddell said.

       🏴   🏴   🏴

"I made a mistake—that was a serious tactical mistake I made in Maryland," Carter said. "Going in and running against Brown and running against the establishment . . . if ever there was a state in the nation that has the political establishment that's still dominant, it's Maryland. It worked well in Pennsylvania and we didn't understand Maryland well enough to analyze it. So that was a mistake. . . . I should have run a positive, statesmanlike campaign in Maryland. I ran just the opposite. . . . As I said, it was a mistake. We finished with Pennsylvania and did the polls in Maryland. We were behind and we could either write off Maryland or run against the political machine. That was a mistake."

       🏴   🏴   🏴

Jimmy Carter had at least one fan among the government workers living in Maryland. William Richard Salter, who was active in the American Federation of Government Employees and who worked at the Department of Corrections, Washington, D.C., was a Carter man. He figured it would be nice to have a President he could talk to.

"Jimmy and I used to debate every Friday afternoon," said Salter, who called himself "Richard" when he grew up with Carter in Plains but who now is called "Bill" by his friends. "We were the captains of our teams [each year from eighth to eleventh grades]. There were usually three on a side. I don't remember the things we debated, except that Jimmy was always a stickler for the facts."

Salter recalled that Carter—"an excellent student . . . tops in his class . . . a natural leader"—once played hookey from school. "One day in the spring of 1941, about fifteen of us, we went to a movie—some kind of a clown movie—over in Americus about eight miles away. We had to submit to a good whipping from the principal before we could get back to school. [A wooden paddle.] Then we got a whipping from our parents as well. Our parents made us abide by the rules."

In fact, young Carter was frequently out on a limb. "Part of our life was spent climbing trees," Salter said. "One of the things we used to do was two of us would climb about thirty to forty feet up a young pine tree and bend it to the ground. Then one would jump off and the other would fly off to another tree. Four or five of us would get together and do that."

Challenge: Udall in Michigan

Three weeks before the Michigan primary, Peter Hart did a statewide poll for the Udall people. The results were not bad; they were disastrous. Hart showed Udall trailing Carter by a whopping 52 percent to 19. "We just went out there to lose," Stewart Udall said later. "We just assumed we were going to lose and lose badly. . . . But we also thought we just might be able to hang on to the end—because if we did, and if the convention was truly an open convention, we though Mo just might be able to end up as Vice President."

Once he got to Michigan, Mo Udall played hardball. "Udall's Quick Carter Quiz" was one of his biggest ploys, a checklist his campaign circulated asking questions about where Carter stood on welfare reform, right-to-work, and the reduction of specific federal agencies. Then there was the Udall cartoon—a thirty-second TV spot narrated by actor Cliff Robertson (John Kennedy in *PT-109*), showing two cartoon faces of Jimmy Carter, smiling and frowning at each other as conflicting Carter statements on issues were read.

The cartoon was negative advertising at its best—biting and effective. It also infuriated the Carter forces. And they responded with their version of hardball politics, low and inside. On May 14, addressing a group of black Baptist ministers on behalf of Carter, Detroit Mayor Coleman Young, who is black, said: "I am asking you to make a choice between a man from Georgia who fights to let you in his church, and a man from Arizona whose church won't even let you in the back door."

It was a blatantly unfair, bigoted attack aimed at discrediting the man because of his religion (in fact, Udall had long been unhappy with his church's views on the role of blacks and he had said he left the Mormon Church—Church of the Latter-day Saints—as a youth because of its policy of excluding blacks from the church hierarchy; but all of that is really beside the point now). Carter was asked repeatedly to repudiate Coleman Young's comments, but he would not. The Carter people felt that Udall's cartoon advertising was unfair. "Let Udall stew—he deserves it," one Carter aide said. Carter let Coleman Young's comments stand.

On Tuesday, election day, Hamilton Jordan flew from Washington to Detroit so he could be with his candidate when the returns came in. It was one of the few election nights that he bothered to make the trip. Usually he let others stay at the governor's side, but this time there would be some meetings and decisions to make. And besides, this was looking like a very uncertain night.

Jordan was wearing blue jeans and a windbreaker and he drummed his fingers nervously as he contemplated the night ahead. "I don't like it," he kept saying. "I just don't like it. I'm starting to feel good about Maryland. Jimmy spent a lot of time there and I think he may pull it out. But this Michigan thing is something else. It's slipping. Slipping away. It's that damn crossover."

Caddell had picked it up in Sunday night's polling. Democrats were deciding to cross over and vote Republican in this primary. To vote in the Ford–Reagan contest. And most of those Democratic crossovers were coming away from Carter.

Back in early May, Caddell had found Carter beating Udall decisively—45 to 20. He surveyed daily. Crossovers were running steady at 7 to 8 percent. But another 15 percent were saying they would consider crossing over, and they were prospective Carter voters by a 3 to 1 margin.

"Sunday night it all came apart," Caddell recalled. "We'd lost eight percent in crossovers. I really hit the panic button. Soon ten points of our twenty-point lead was gone in a matter of twelve hours."

Caddell projected the trend. If it continued at its present rate for the next twenty-four hours, Carter and Udall would be breaking even. Or worse. "The Udall people weren't polling," Caddell said. "They didn't even know what was going on until I finally told some of them over a drink."

On the plane, Jordan was figuring that as in the past the crossover would be conservative Wallace Democrats who wanted to vote for Reagan. A reporter flying with him bet that they would be more liberal Democrats, interested in helping out home stater Gerald Ford and seeing to it that Michigan did not boost Reagan toward the White House. Jordan was wrong on that, and he was wrong on Maryland.

He had been basing his hopes on a poll from an outside source.

🏴   🏴   🏴

On Monday, the day before the election, the *Baltimore Sun* published the results of a poll that brought encouragement—false encouragement, it turned out—to the Carter forces. The *Sun* poll said that the contest remained tight and that Carter was gaining strength more rapidly than Brown; a 3-point climb for Carter compared to just a 1-point rise for Brown. ". . . However, the separation between the two candidates appears to be of less significance than the slowing down of the impressive growth of voter support for Mr. Brown over the past month," the *Sun* reported.

🏴   🏴   🏴

THE RESULTS: *Carter forces felt they had narrowed the gap in Maryland. But on election night, it turned out that the gap was moving the other way—it had become a grand canyon, as Brown smashed Carter by 48.3 percent to 36.9.*

🏴   🏴   🏴

Detroit, election night. Carter campaign television adviser Barry Jagoda is making arrangements for the use of the Sheraton Cadillac Hotel's ballroom for a Carter election-night victory gathering. The hotel manager says he will need payment. Jagoda tells him to send the bill to the

Carter headquarters in Atlanta, Box 1976. No deal, the manager says. It must be cash. Jagoda tells him not to worry. The manager does not reply, but instead takes the Carter man over to a file cabinet and extracts a folder marked "uncollected." Inside is a bill, still unpaid, made out to the John F. Kennedy Campaign, dated 1960.

Jagoda rounds up the cash.

In Detroit, the Carter people were undergoing what Caddell later called "the worst night of the campaign." This was not supposed to be a close race; yet here was Carter, close to blowing it, close to suffering a disastrous double defeat at a time when he was supposed to be pulling away with the nomination won.

CBS—perhaps because they had been right in delaying the Wisconsin prediction when the other networks trumpeted Udall—was holding off in declaring Carter the winner. In the hotel bar, Jordan was saying how he was happy to have the 2-point victory they seemed to have shortly after midnight. Jordan by then was calm. Caddell was a nervous wreck; he did not get to bed until 5:00 A.M. (which proved awkward since he wound up having to rush back to New York to give a speech Wednesday morning). Carter says he fared better that night than his wife. "Well, I have to admit, I don't suffer when I think I'm going to lose," he said. "My wife does more than I do. In Wisconsin when we thought we had lost, I felt good. I had done the best I could. . . . I never thought I was going to lose in Michigan all through the night. . . . I went to bed fairly early when I was ahead, and when I woke I knew I'd won."

THE RESULTS: *Michigan went to Carter by less than 1 percent—43.5 to 43.2. And by a margin of just over 1,000 votes out of 659,000 cast. Democrats—mostly Carter Democrats—had crossed over into the GOP primary in large numbers to help home stater Gerald Ford defeat Ronald Reagan.*

On election night, Carter sat in his suite watching the returns. He sat slumped in a chair, staring at the television, his face mirroring concern, frustration, and disappointment. But when he went downstairs to greet his supporters in the hotel ballroom and to be interviewed by reporters he was smiling, apparently happy and confident and very much turned on.

He told reporters about how his delegate totals had climbed significantly that night and about how he had now received such a large number of votes throughout the long primary season. He smiled, he waved, he shook hands, and then he rode the elevator upstairs and went to bed, an unhappy winner.

For Udall, it was the fifth time in six primary contests that he had finished second—and the third time he had missed beating Carter by a few thousand votes or less. Udall said later that he had never realized how close he was to defeating Carter in Michigan. Had he known, he said, he would have done one thing different: "I should have pushed my colleagues [from Michigan] in Congress."

ABC: HHH

In the year of the American Centennial, 1876, the country was treated to the spectacle of at least nine prominent politicians vying to be the next President. On Friday, May 19, 1876, *The Daily Graphic,* an illustrated evening newspaper in New York, ran a front-page cartoon entitled: "Merry-Go-Round for the White House Bound." The cartoon featured each candidate on a hobbyhorse, trying to spear with his lance the brass ring labeled "Presidency" as the merry-go-round spun. Accompanying that cartoon was a poetic caption that summed up the campaigns of each contender:

> What time the newsman turns the crank,
>   The riders, in a whirl,
> From BAYARD, with his Bourbon bounce,
>   To CONKLING, with his curl,
> On hobbies mettlesomely high,
>   Career before the public eye.
> See TILDEN, saccharinely sly,
>   Come beaming to the tilt,
> With trophy called canal reform,
>   To deck his lance's hilt.

RUNNING FOR PRESIDENT

While thoughtful THURMAN, just behind,
   To ALLEN's anger rides resigned.
And BRISTOW brave, to battle borne,
   Another prize parades—
A badly broken Whiskey Ring;
   But, HAYES, by recent raids,
Has made a yet more gorgeous gain
From fierce Inflation, faced and slain.

Then mighty MORTON, martially,
   Whom Ku-Klux-Klans would kill,
Rides hot upon the track of BLAINE,
   Who, staunchly seated still,
At all unknightly knaves can scoff,
And parries Slander's serpent off.

Upon his lithe and legal lance
   Each wears a riven king;
Yet hangs there one on high each
   Would fain as victor bring:
The Presidency goes with this,
And what a joke if all should miss!
                    —O.C.K.

The punch line of that political cartoon-poem of 1876 was the strategy of Hubert Horatio Humphrey in 1976. He would sit on the sidelines while the crowded field of Democrats rode the circuit, sticking their necks out, trying to spear the presidential ring with their lances and—he hoped—sticking each other in the process. It was a strategy that would work only if the primary elections proved truly divided, with no one emerging as a frontrunner. When Carter beat Jackson in Pennsylvania, Humphrey was under great pressure from labor people and other long-time supporters to get into the race. But he decided he would not.

On April 29 at a press conference in which he announced this decision, Hubert Horatio Humphrey had declared: "The one thing I don't need at this stage in my life is to be ridiculous." But a few weeks later, Humphrey was reconsidering. It was just a month ago that he had ruled out an active candidacy. But now, his spokesmen were saying, Humphrey was going to take one more look at the political picture.

Urging Humphrey to make a final effort was the "ABC" movement. On May 18—as the Carter people were awaiting their election-day fate in Maryland and Michigan—a group gathered in a suite at the Hay Adams Hotel in Washington bent on sealing Carter's fate for him.

There, over breakfast Danish and coffee, they held the first meeting of what became known as the ABC movement. It stood for "Anybody But Carter," but this was a misnomer, since it really meant Humphrey instead of Carter.

The meeting was in the suite, just across Lafayette Square from the White House, belonging to Joseph Crangle, the Buffalo Democratic chairman who was trying to put together a movement that would carry the nomination to Humphrey. Jackson's man Bob Keefe was there; so were Udall's men Jack Quinn and Mark Shields; and McGovern's aide Alan Baron, who ironically had been the man who helped Carter's two aides get in to see the then McGovern pollster Pat Caddell back in 1972, when they were trying to convince McGovern to pick Carter for Vice President. (This time, Baron was not seeking to aid Carter but to bury him.)

"It was a meeting to take inventory," according to one of the participants. "To see where things stand, where there were holes for Carter." A second meeting took place one week later in Baron's apartment. All but Shields attended, plus several newcomers: Representative Paul Simon (who was working with Crangle on the Humphrey project); Arnie Miller, formerly an aide to Representative Allard Lowenstein and later a McGovern aide; and Steve Ross, a political adviser who was with Humphrey in 1972 and Jackson in 1976.

They gave advice to Crangle on how he could set up a boiler room operation for Humphrey and where to go looking for uncommitted delegates and Humphrey support. (A boiler room operation of about thirty people was eventually set up.)

They suggested people for Crangle to hire, and talked about how some Humphrey contributors ought to back Udall in Ohio. The machinists' union did.

The ABC people had a few moments of satisfaction in Rhode Island: an uncommitted slate beat Carter's delegates—largely through the campaign of Jerry Brown. A two-headed slate favoring Humphrey would result in New

179

Jersey voters electing more uncommitted delegates than Carter delegates.

But by then it would be too late.

▬ ▬ ▬

On St. Patrick's Day, novelist Patrick Anderson was celebrating, perhaps in part out of his affinity for the Irish, but probably more because the paperback rights to his latest book had just been auctioned off for a healthy $250,000. His book was *The President's Mistress* and it was written, according to Anderson, "to entertain the reader and enrich the author."

Patrick Anderson, a talented writer, was becoming a man of books. He had written *The President's Men,* a well-respected study of the White House staff of Lyndon Johnson; two highly acclaimed novels—*The Approach to Kings* and *Actions and Passions*—and he had ghost-written the Watergate tell-all of ex-Nixonite Jeb Magruder.

Anderson was also known to the Jimmy Carter crowd. At a Washington, D.C., party months ago, Anderson had met two Carter advisers, Peter Bourne and his wife, Mary King. Anderson had worked in Virginia for George McGovern while Bourne had worked with the Veterans Against the War in Vietnam and King had worked actively in civil rights causes, so they had things to talk about. Bourne and King began to tell Anderson how impressive they thought Jimmy Carter was (Bourne earlier had been brought to Georgia by then Governor Carter to set up state drug rehabilitation programs). They told him about how Carter liked to read Dylan Thomas and listen to Bob Dylan. At about that time, the *New York Times Magazine* had been talking to Anderson about doing a piece on a prominent political person—maybe Rockefeller, they said. Anderson countered, how about Carter? The *Times Magazine* agreed and soon Anderson was off to Plains, where he was courted in true Carter style. "I spent the night at Jimmy's home in Plains," Anderson recalled. "I was very favorably impressed."

Anderson's cover story article on Carter appeared in the magazine on December 14, 1975, titled, "Peanut Farmer for President." It reflected the author's admiration of the candidate. "It was certainly a very favorable article," Anderson said. "People much later would come up and tell me that it was that article that turned them on to Carter."

Now, on St. Patrick's Day, with the paperback rights to his latest book safely auctioned, Anderson decided that he could take a rest from his personal writing to devote himself to the politics of 1976. He called Peter Bourne and Mary King and told them to pass the word that he would be willing to do some political writing for Carter if the candidate wished.

It turned out that the Carter people had just made their move on another speechwriter, Robert Shrum, and so nothing was done. But on May 11, almost two months later, after the Shrum fiasco—and after the storm cloud it produced had settled—Jody Powell called Anderson and asked if he was still interested in writing for Carter. Anderson was. He and Powell conferred, and then Anderson drove into Washington, D.C., from his home more than an hour away in the rolling Virginia farmland community of Waterford, to get things settled and meet briefly with Carter. The candidate was in Washington for a Democratic congressional fundraising dinner at the Washington Hilton, and his conversation with Anderson was brief. It occurred in an elevator.

Anderson: "Governor, I hope I can help you."

Carter: "Well, we'll have some fun."

Anderson caught up with the Carter campaign on election night in Michigan and rode the candidate's plane out to Oregon to politick the West Coast. One of his first tasks was to help Carter with a speech he was giving in the heart of Jerry Brown country—an address to the California State Legislature in Sacramento. Carter entered the capitol by walking through the old wing, through the door where the sign is posted warning that the building is not structurally sound and that people enter at their own risk. His speech contained this central message: "If I had to sum up in one word what this campaign is all about, that word would be faith."

Another early task of Anderson's was to write a speech on conservation and the environment for Carter in Oregon, a truly independent and environment-minded state. Anderson soon discovered that traveling with the candidate was not the best place to write an issue-oriented speech. The campaign suffered from a lack of research at hand; there was Anderson, sitting just a few seats away from the candidate (who was busy reviewing memos and giving interviews), and he was unable to find out just what the candidate had been saying on the environment and just what new positions had been recommended. Someone in Atlanta had that information, but it was difficult if not impossible to pass the detailed issue material rapidly to a speechwriter traveling with Carter. Anderson wound up going home to work on the speech. Anderson was well into the writing when the Carter strategists changed their minds. Carter already had the environmentalist vote in Oregon, they figured; but he needed to go after the business people. "No need to antagonize the business community with more conservation stuff," said one Carter official. Anderson was told to forget about the speech. "I was getting a little depressed," Anderson recalled. "I felt I wasn't doing much to help the campaign."

At noon Wednesday, May 26—the day after the primaries in Oregon and five other states—Jody Powell telephoned Patrick Anderson's home in rustic Waterford, Virginia. "You've got to come back," Powell, who was in New York, said. "We've lost our theme. The thing is adrift. You've got to come back and write a new speech."

Powell and Patrick Caddell felt that the soft-on-issues stuff was crippling Jimmy Carter. Back in Atlanta, Hamilton Jordan was less concerned. But he was content to leave the issue decision-making up to others, and so it was that Powell put out his call for Anderson.

Within a couple of hours, Patrick Anderson was driving in his well-worn, well-rusted old Buick convertible along the highway that goes through Leesburg and to Washington's National Airport. Ideas came to him as he drove and he began scribbling notes on a pad at his side as he sped toward the airport.

"I see an America that . . ." Anderson wrote on his pad and continued it with a visionary ideal of the future. "I see an America . . ." he wrote again and he added another visionary goal.

The speech was good. Impressive.

William Safire would later write that the "I see an America" construction was nothing new—that it had been written by him for Richard Nixon and before him it had been used by Franklin D. Roosevelt in 1940, and before him by James Blaine, who was running for President 100 years before Carter, in 1876.

"I don't think I was consciously aware of it having been used before," Anderson said later, laughing. "I thought, as I was driving down that highway, that I had hit on a brilliant new idea."

Anderson caught an Eastern Airlines shuttle to New York and went directly to meet with Powell at the Madison Avenue office of Barry Jagoda, Carter's television adviser. There he turned his scribbled notes into a speech.

Meanwhile, Carter was engaging in a form of rare but essential politicking that night. He had driven from Newark to the Waldorf Towers Hotel, in Manhattan, to a meeting he had requested with former Israeli Prime Minister Golda Meir. Carter had met Mrs. Meir when he was in Israel before becoming a candidate for President (Hamilton Jordan's 1972 memo had suggested a visit to the Middle East). Now, at a time when the Carter strategists were very concerned about Carter's ability to win and hold the Jewish vote, the audience with Mrs. Meir was looked on in the Carter camp as a much-needed coup. The former prime minister was sensitive to the fact that she might be used for political purposes. She did not want any photographs taken of her meeting with Carter and would make no statement about it. "It's purely private," her secretary said. But the next day's newspapers still carried photos of Carter leaving the Waldorf Towers after his meeting with Mrs. Meir. And they quoted Carter describing her as "an old friend."

After the meeting, Powell, Anderson, and Jagoda rode in Carter's limousine back to Carter's hotel in Newark. Powell remembered that he had left his briefcase in Jagoda's office, which is in a five-story brownstone. Carter said it would be all right to go there to pick it up. The limousine drove up to the curb and Jagoda, who is in his calmer moments a whirling dervish of activity, burst out the door and raced into the building—just as a neighbor who lives there was walking down the stairs carrying a basket full of laundry with a box of Cheer balanced delicately on top.

"What's the matter, Barry? Running for President?" the neighbor asked.

"No, I'm not," Jagoda replied, and jerking a thumb toward the limousine at the curb he added: "But that guy is." The neighbor peered at the long black car and Jimmy Carter leaned toward the window and waved.

    🏴   🏴   🏴

In the limousine, on the way back to Carter's hotel, Anderson handed Carter a copy of the speech he had written and had shown to Jody. Typed across the top was a note:

> JODY: HERE ARE SOME IDEAS AND PHRASES THAT GOVERNOR CARTER MIGHT PLAY WITH. I THINK THE IMPORTANT THING IS THAT HE MOVE FROM ANY ATTACK ON THE STOP CARTER MOVEMENT TO A POSITIVE AND PASSIONATE STATEMENT OF HIS VISION OF THE AMERICAN FUTURE. THIS SHOULD BE INSPIRATIONAL, KENNEDYESQUE IF YOU WILL, BUT I THINK IT IS WHAT A LOT OF PEOPLE ARE HOPING FOR. PAT.

The speech was the one that became known as Carter's "vision of America" speech. Carter liked it and used it in the future on a number of occasions—including as part of his acceptance speech. This was the core of the message:

> I have a vision of an America that is, in Bob Dylan's phrase, busy being born.
> I see an America that is poised not only at the brink of a new century, but at the dawn of a new era of responsive, responsible government.
> I see an America that has turned her back on scandals and corruption and official cynicism and has finally demanded a government that deserves the trust and respect of her people.
> I see an America with a tax system that does not cheat the average wage earner and with a government that is responsive to its people and with a system of justice that is evenhanded to all.
> I see a government that does not spy on its citizens but respects their dignity and their privacy and their right to be let alone.
> I see an America in which law and order are not a slogan but a way of life, because its people have chosen to bind up their wounds and live in harmony.
> I see an America in which your child and my child

and every child, regardless of its background, receives an education that will enable him to develop to his or her fullest capacities.

I see an America that has a job for every man and woman who wants to work.

I see an America that will reconcile its need for new energy sources with its need for clean air, clean water, and an environment we can pass on with pride to our children and their children.

I see an American foreign policy that is consistent and generous and openly arrived at, and that can once again be a beacon for the hopes of the entire world.

I see an America on the move again, united, its wounds healed, its head high, an America with pride in its past and faith in its future, moving into its third century with confidence and competence and compassion, an America that lives up to the nobility of its Constitution and the decency of its people.

I see an America with a President who does not govern by vetoes and negativism, but with vigor and vision and positive, affirmative, aggressive leadership.

This is my vision of America. It is one that reflects the deepest feelings of millions of people who have supported me this year. It is from them that I take my strength and my hope and my courage as I carry forth my campaign toward its ultimate success.

This was the "inspirational" and "Kennedyesque" and "positive" and "passionate" statement Anderson had wanted Carter to make. But the writer had set up this message with an introduction that attacked Carter's opponents.

My critics . . . want to stop the people of this country from regaining control of their government. They want to preserve the status quo, to preserve politics as usual, to maintain at all costs their own entrenched, unresponsive, bankrupt, irresponsible political power.

At a labor meeting in Cincinnati, Carter read the speech virtually as Anderson wrote it. But as Carter and Anderson should have expected, reporters covering the event naturally focused their attention on Carter's harsh, name-calling attack on his opponents, rather than the uplift rhetoric Carter and Anderson had wanted.

"We blew it," Anderson said later. "So we did the next best thing, and went with the new vision again." Carter read the vision of America speech again at a gathering in Akron. But after the speech, a reporter asked Carter something about Udall's television ads, and Carter lashed out against the Udall ads, and the vision speech was bumped out of the news for a second day. "The new vision had bombed again," Anderson observed. Eventually Carter got his vision speech into the news. And when the Carter advisers decided to buy five minutes of nighttime television on all three networks for Sunday, June 6, the "I see an America . . ." theme was a strong part of the message. It was delivered by Carter in a setting unlike his previous television ads; it was not Carter talking while on his farm or politicking with voters; it was just Carter sitting in front of a bare backdrop, staring at the television camera, giving a speech. It was costly, and it was not one of Carter's most impressive campaign tools despite the quality of the words Carter was saying.

Much later, when Carter, Powell, and Anderson were lunching at the Carter house in Plains, the former governor turned to his press secretary and said: "The thing Shrum didn't like about me—one of the things Shrum didn't like about me—is that I always wanted to change and rewrite his speeches. Pat's the only writer I've ever used who didn't get his feelings hurt when I changed things."

May 25/Oregon Plus Five

The Western Forestry Center is a magnificent, modern wood-and-glass structure that sits in the midst of the great stands of Douglas firs outside Portland. Jimmy Carter's motorcade pulls up to the door at lunchtime and the candidate, beaming as always, emerges and handshakes his way inside. This is a Carter fundraising luncheon and the candidate himself is the drawing card. "It would be suicidal if I was to say one thing in one state and another thing in another," Carter says during his luncheon address. "If anyone would play a tape showing I'd made different statements in different states, I'd be proven a liar. I'd have to pull out of the race"—he pauses—"almost."

Carter is pleased to note that the large and airy room is virtually filled with about 200 people. But, in fact, it is a paper crowd. There just had not been enough tickets sold for the event and so many of the audience were recruited at the last minute to attend the Jimmy Carter campaign luncheon free of charge.

Oregon was just one of six primaries being held on May 25. But it was the only one that was being vigorously contested. The two prime candidates on the ballot were Jimmy Carter, who was from faraway Georgia but who had a national reputation as the Democratic frontrunner, and Frank Church, who was from neighboring Idaho—so close a neighbor, in fact, that there are parts of eastern Oregon which are fed by Boise television stations and have come to know Church as well as they know their own senators and congressional representatives.

Church had a national reputation that was well known in Oregon. He was a dove in a state that had produced some of the great antiwar leaders of the United States—the late Senator Wayne Morse was one of only two senators who opposed the Gulf of Tonkin Resolution, which became the justification for Lyndon Johnson's buildup of the U.S. war effort in Vietnam; its senior senator, Mark Hatfield, was a Republican moderate and staunch opponent of the Vietnam War effort.

Other primaries being held on May 25 offered little contest. In the West, there was Idaho, where Church would win overwhelmingly. And there was Nevada, which has so many economic, geographical, and personal ties to California that Brown would win easily.

⚑ ⚑ ⚑

Las Vegas. Pir Marini of the Thunderbird Lounge is looking splendid in his white-on-white suit, and, as the candidate walks into the auditorium rally, he strikes the piano keyboard with what he considers an appropriate theme: "What the World Needs Now Is Love Sweet Love." Later he says, "It was my own idea. Did you like it?"

The music was appropriate. For "love" is a dominant theme of the standard Carter campaign speech. The former Georgia governor tells voters at every stop that he expects to be a good President because of the "intimate personal relationship" that he has established "with each and every one of you" during his campaign swings throughout the country. And he has carefully chosen as the closing line of his speech the message that what the United States needs is "a government that is as good, honest, decent, truthful, capable . . . and filled with love . . . as the American people are."

⚑ ⚑ ⚑

In the Southeast, on May 25, there were Tennessee, Kentucky, and Arkansas, where Carter would win by huge proportions.

Only Oregon offered a true contest.

Mickey Kantor, campaign manager of Brown for President, was at home and in bed at midnight when the telephone rang. It was his boss, the candidate, calling. Jerry Brown was in the East, where it was 3:00 A.M., and he was up and awake and thinking politics—Oregon primary politics. Brown needed some answers. "What is the situation and the law for write-ins in Oregon?" Brown asked.

Kantor recalls that he gave Brown some general, factual answers. "No, that's not good enough," Brown replied with the clear hint of annoyance in his voice, according to Kantor. "We've got to be specific. We've got to know all the details. We've got to know if we need computer mailings and how to go about them. We've got to know just how we can tell every Oregonian precisely how he can vote for Jerry Brown."

Brown was upset and Kantor says he had a right to be. The Brown forces were about to mount a difficult write-in effort in Oregon, where Brown had gotten into the race too late to get on the ballot. "We had been at it up there only thirty-six hours and we didn't have the detailed information for Jerry," Kantor recalled. "But he was right. We couldn't afford a single delay or a single error. We only had nine days to do everything."

Kantor hung up the phone after finishing his talk with Brown and immediately called the campaign's computer specialist, Frank Tobe, at his hotel in Oregon. Tobe was not in his room, but he had left word of his whereabouts. It was after midnight and he was still in the offices of an Oregon computer company, checking out procedures. Different counties had rules for just what they would accept as valid write-in vote—"Brown" or "Jerry Brown" or "Brown for President," etc. The Brown campaign needed a computerized mailing to tell each voter just how to write in Brown in his precinct.

The Jerry Brown write-in effort in Oregon was for real. It was a skilled, computer-age effort that was attempting to capitalize on Brown's extensive West Coast press notices and appeal, realizing that the drive was bound to suffer from the last-minute nature of it all and the fact that many people just did not perceive Brown as a genuine presidential contender—although his Maryland victory did much to compensate for the latter.

■   ■   ■

Betty Roberts, a leading liberal Democrat in the state senate, was one of the Carter co-chairpersons in Oregon; Fred Heard, a leading conservative Democrat (a converted Republican) in the state senate, was the other. Together they gave Carter the political contacts and philosophic diversity that were definitely helpful in that beautiful, green, independent-minded state. But what they did not bring the Carter campaign was a smooth-running operation; it was the sort of thing the Carter brass had found in most of the states where they opted for using established state politicians to head their effort rather than importing someone of unknown political reputation but known organizing skills, such as Tim Kraft in Iowa and Pennsylvania, Chris Brown in New Hampshire, and Phil Wise in Florida.

Two weeks before the Oregon election, a Carter official came into the state and was shocked by what he later termed "a real lack of organization—people who should have been contacted, including name Democrats, just had not been called; there just were no good lists."

At one point Hamilton Jordan called a leading Carter official in California, Rodney Kennedy-Minott, and asked him to get some California volunteers up to Oregon to help campaign. Kennedy-Minott did, and he showed up himself to help with some of the last-minute fundraising. "I asked for the names of the potential donors—they handed me a shoebox," he said. "It was full of cards, but there were no notations as to who had been called already and who had not. So I just took the cards and began calling."

Several weeks earlier, the Carter strategists had looked confidently ahead to Oregon. Early in May, the *Portland Oregonian* had published a poll showing Carter cruising ahead of the pack with 32 percent. Trailing were noncandidates Humphrey (15 percent), Kennedy (10), Church (8), Udall (7), and Jackson (5).

But that was before Church and Brown had scored their upset victories in Nebraska and Maryland. It was before Carter's scare in Michigan. And it was before Brown had begun his write-in effort in Oregon.

Carter had planned to fly home from the West Coast to rest in Plains on the weekend before the Oregon primary. But on Thursday, Carter's strategists told the governor to change his plans, and then they announced to reporters traveling with Carter that the candidate would remain in the West throughout the weekend to campaign, primarily in Oregon. Jody Powell, and later Carter himself, unabashedly told the reporters that the reason Carter had changed his plans was that things were looking even more promising for Carter than they had anticipated, and they wanted to capitalize on this good fortune. They said they had learned of this new prosperity from a poll by Patrick Caddell. They flatly refused to release the figures of the Caddell poll, though they were willing to talk about it. "Our political strength is much greater than we had anticipated," Carter said, strolling the aisle of his chartered jet and explaining the schedule change to reporters. "We discovered a much more likely prospect of picking up delegates . . . than we had anticipated. . . . The poll shows I'm in a good position in Oregon."

It was much the same language that Jody Powell had used the night before in talks with reporters. And it simply was not true.

In fact, Caddell's secret poll had shown that Carter's lead had slipped dangerously—and that there was now a real possibility that Carter might suffer the political humiliation of finishing third to a write-in effort, the last-minute effort of Jerry Brown. The figures of the Caddell poll were published back East in *Newsday* that Saturday, and they were subsequently confirmed by Caddell after the Oregon primary had taken place.

The Caddell poll showed that Carter's lead over Frank Church had plunged to just two points, 24 to 22, among the candidates whose names were listed on the Oregon ballot. And when the polltakers had added the name of Brown to the list, the results had been even more startling: Brown finished first with about 24 percent, with Carter a couple of percentage points behind and Church trailing Carter by several more points. The Carter officials realized that there was no foolproof way of measuring anticipated votes for a write-in effort, because the mere action of putting Brown's name before the people being surveyed gave Brown more of an advantage than he would have in the voting booth, where his name would not be listed, and where the voter would have to go through a rather involved write-in procedure to cast a ballot for Brown. Still, the Carter strategists were clearly concerned about what the results showed. None of this justifies the unprofessional efforts of Carter and Powell and others to mislead reporters about the nature of their poll.

The episode of Oregon and the poll was one of the few times Carter and his advisers yielded to temptation and compromised integrity in the swirl of campaign pressure. Just why they acted as they did can be understood, but not justified, by recalling what they were going through at that time. After Pennsylvania, it had seemed that they had the nomination won; they had defeated every Democrat in the race. But then came the new faces of 1976—Church and Brown—the crumbling of what had once seemed so safe in Michigan, and now the erosion of their base in Oregon.

"We were all kinds of off balance in that couple of weeks beginning with Maryland and Michigan," Hamilton Jordan said later. "The Maryland thing—I thought we'd do better. And I was really uptight about Michigan. I mean, we'd just come so far and now all this—it seemed like a bad dream. I kept saying to myself, 'This can't be happening. We're not really going down the tube. Not after all this.' But then, every time I got to feeling uneasy during that time and after, I'd always go back to the figures. I'd look at the delegate count and the delegate projections. And then I'd feel better. I got back on my feet mentally. I knew the numbers were there. I knew we'd be all right."

What Jordan did on those days when he was feeling depressed about what was happening to his campaign was go over to his locked files and pull out a memo dated March 18, 1976, which was from him to Carter.

The memo contained a section on "Carter Delegate Projections." Jordan and Carter's brilliant young delegate coordinator, Rick Hutcheson, had put together a set of projections that Jordan said in the memo were "realistic and, if anything, conservative." Jordan's memo listed low and high estimates for each state. The figures gave Carter a total low projection of 969 delegates by the end of the last round of primaries on June 8 and a high of 1,509—four more than were needed to win the nomination.

The March 18 memo was based on an erroneous assumption: that Jackson would probably stay in the race until the end (in 1972 he had, after all, stayed in so stubbornly and for so long in his winless effort) and that Udall and Wallace would stay in for a while but would eventually fold. It turned out that Udall stayed but Jackson pulled out early, as did Wallace.

The Jordan memo had some projections which proved too low, some which proved too high, and many which were right on target. "It was those figures that gave me faith in May," Jordan recalled. "Every time I got worried, I went back to the numbers."

THE RESULTS: *The numbers in Oregon did not bring Carter a victory, but at least they saved him from disgrace. Church won with 34.6 percent of the vote. But Carter beat back the Brown write-in by 27.4 percent to 23.3. Idaho went to Church, as he beat Carter by 80.3 percent to 12.1. Nevada went to Brown, 52.8 percent to Carter's 23.3 and Church's 9.0.*

But Carter more than offset these defeats with decisive victories in three delegate-rich border states. He beat Wallace in Tennessee, 78.0 percent to 11.0; he beat Wallace in Kentucky, 59.3 to 16.9; and he beat Wallace and Udall in Arkansas, 62.8 to 16.8 to 7.5, respectively. Carter won 90 delegates in these three states, plus 20 in his defeats in the West, giving him a total of 110 for the day, compared to Church's 30 delegates won that day and Brown's 13. As Jordan said, it was the delegate numbers in that month of May and on May 25th in particular that cushioned the crushing fact that Carter had fared poorly in the only real contest of the day, in Oregon.

Jimmy Carter was weak out West. He learned that in Oregon, where he had campaigned hard, passing up a weekend at home to politick, but was lucky to escape the humiliation of showing third behind a Jerry Brown write-in. In fact, he would go the entire primary season without ever winning in the West. He took Texas away from Lloyd Bentsen in a strong showing in that southwestern state. But he went on to suffer defeats in Oregon, Idaho, Nevada, Montana, and California. It was a matter that would worry his campaign advisers throughout the primary season and into the fall presidential campaign as well.

Jimmy Carter was in New York City on May 25, the night of the elections in Oregon and five other states. It was careful planning that brought him there. Carter was in the East because, among other reasons, Oregon is in the West; he wanted to make sure that the television stations that night and the news stories in the morning would reflect as heavily as possible on Carter's victories in the border states, softening the blow of the defeats that were to come in Oregon, Idaho, and Nevada.

As it turned out, the emphasis on the television networks and in the newspapers the next morning reflected the fact that Carter had won three out of six rather than the fact that Carter had been beaten in the only real contest of the night. Had Carter stayed in Oregon to wring his hands and fret, the balance of the stories just might have shifted.

"We got by a lot lighter on the Oregon primary night than I was expecting," Hamilton Jordan conceded later. "I was afraid we would get hit over the head about that Oregon defeat. But the way it was played, it came out okay."

In his suite at the New York Sheraton, Carter was watching the returns on television and talking with his aides. One reporter, David Nordan, political editor of the *Atlanta Journal,* was permitted by Carter to sit in the suite and watch the governor watching the returns. An aide told Carter that Ted Kennedy had said earlier in the day that Carter was "intentionally . . . indefinite and imprecise" on issues.

"A hint of anger" flashed in Carter's eyes, according to Nordan, as the former governor replied: "I'm glad I don't have to depend on Kennedy or Hubert Humphrey or anyone like that to put me in office."—pause—"I don't have to kiss his ass."

Indeed, he did not. Carter had just summed up in a single phrase a strategy that had once taken his campaign manager seventy pages to explain in a 1972 memo, and which had taken pundits many column inches to analyze. Jimmy Carter was done with the May primaries. He was in the home stretch of a race that he had been running everywhere. He was winning some and losing some, but winning delegates all the while. He figured that if he finished the primaries on June 8 with 1,200 delegates, the delegates he needed to finally reach the 1,505 required for the nomination would eventually drift his way; he would be so far ahead of the rest of the candidates that they would have nowhere else to go. They would come to him. He did not have to kiss anyone's ass.

June 1|The Little Three

Late in May, Jimmy Carter conferred by telephone on a couple of occasions with one of his prime political advisers. The conversations led Carter to make two key changes in his campaign schedule.

"Everybody here in Rhode Island is going to vote for you," Rosalynn Carter told her husband in one of the telephone conversations. "But they're going to vote for you in November. I think you ought to come up here and create some enthusiasm . . . so people will come out and vote in the primary."

"We can carry South Dakota," Rosalynn reported to her husband in the other phone conversation. "We've got great support . . . people are working day and night . . . but they've never even seen you or met you." If he would just touch down in South Dakota once or twice, it could make a tremendous difference, Rosalynn told her husband.

On both occasions, Carter took his wife's advice and had his schedule changed to include quick visits to Rhode Island and South Dakota. The moves proved to be important, and as other members of the campaign staff would say later, they proved to be correct. Carter and his staff had been looking past June 1 to June 8, when the primary season would wind up with three big state elections: California, Ohio, and New Jersey. But the three small state elections on June 1—in Rhode Island, South Dakota, and Montana —had to be dealt with first. The amount of delegates they would pump into the overall nomination process would be few. But the damage that could be done by suffering severe setbacks just a week before the three big elections of June 8 could prove substantial. And this is why, most of all, Carter took his wife's advice and made stops in Providence and Sioux Falls and Rapid City.

"Jimmy would always tell me, 'If you go to something that's been planned for you, you'll never get a true feeling for what the situation in that area is really like,' " Rosalynn Carter said as she reconstructed the phone conversations she had with her husband back when she was in Rhode Island and South Dakota. "He'd say, 'If you get to the shopping centers and to factory shift lines, that's where you'll learn what people are really thinking.' And that's what I tried to do."

Rosalynn Carter campaigned across the country throughout much of 1975 and 1976 to help her husband win the Democratic presidential nomination. But rarely during the campaign was she at her husband's side. The Carters figured that they could cover more ground if they were in two places at the same time—Jimmy in one, Rosalynn in the other—and that is how they worked it for more than a year.

Over the years, Carter had come to greatly respect his wife's political judgments and instincts—"She has very good judgment of people in politics," he once told a member of his campaign staff. And in the 1976 campaign, Rosalynn Carter was a major asset to her husband's drive for the Presidency—and, in her own way, an aggressive campaigner as well.

It was not always that way.

Rosalynn Carter is a soft-spoken woman, very attractive, with dark hair and dark almond eyes, but also very shy. It is said that when he ran for governor in 1966, Carter had to push his wife to get her to campaign for him, coach her in such basic political arts as how to hand out a brochure on a street corner. One of Carter's deputy press secretaries, Betty Rainwater, recalls that years later Carter gave her similar instruction. "I was just sort of wall-flowering it," she recalled. "You know, standing on a corner and holding out brochures for someone to take if they wanted them. And Jimmy showed me how to do it in a pleasant but more forceful manner. He told me, 'You know, my wife, Rosalynn, used to have the same problem. But don't be afraid. She learned, and you can too.' "

Actually, Rosalynn had been used to getting things done, but in her own subtle way. Three years younger than Carter, she had been the best friend of Carter's sister, Ruth, and so she was in and out of the Carter house outside Plains frequently.

But she and Carter never went out on a date until Carter came home from Annapolis for a brief stay. In his book, Carter talks as if it were really his doing, how he and a friend had asked Rosalynn and Ruth for a movie date. Rosalynn recalls that it just did not happen that easily. "I had hung around his house for a month getting him to notice me," she said. "And he didn't ask me out until two nights before he was going back to Annapolis. Well, the next night he already had a date with another girl. But we had kind of a late date that second night. . . ."

Carter recalls telling his mother after their first date, "She's the girl I want to marry." Rosalynn recalls that when Carter asked her to marry him, she turned him down. "I was just eighteen and a sophomore in college," she said. "I was so young. I just wasn't thinking like that." The following February, she accepted.

When his father died, Carter wanted to give up his naval career and settle in Plains to run the family warehouse, which was just a very small business operation at the time. This provoked the first serious argument between Carter and his wife, Carter says.

"That's true," Rosalynn Carter says. She just did not want to give up the life that had taken her to Hawaii and New York and Connecticut and move back into the lap of the family in Plains. "I was young," she said. "I had been traveling, I had three babies. I think I liked the independence. It's hard to recall now just how it was then, but I think I thought that if I came home, I'd be more restricted . . . my mother, Jimmy's mother." She hastened to add: "I never did regret it, though."

During their first year back in Plains, Carter ran the entire business himself. "He kept the books, he loaded the goods, everything," says Mrs. Carter. But as the business grew, Rosalynn Carter assumed the bookkeeping duties for the Carter family operation. "Looking back on it," she said, "I can see where our give and take developed. I kept the books in the warehouse and he'd come in and ask my advice. He'd ask me, 'Should we do this or should we do that to make more money? Should we get more peanuts, sell corn?' That sort of thing."

But keeping books in a warehouse and politicking in a campaign were two very different things.

Edna Langford is a close friend and political traveling companion of Rosalynn Carter's. They met back when Carter was running for governor and the Langfords came to work on the campaign. The Carters' son, Jack, and the Langfords' daughter, Judy, met in the campaign and eventually married. Mrs. Langford recalls how difficult campaigning used to be for Rosalynn Carter.

"In the 1970 campaign, we set up a meeting over in the bank building in Calhoun and about fifty or sixty women were there in the audience," she said. "And then Rosalynn came in the back door and when she walked out front, her eyes got big and kind of fearful and she looked at me horrified and said, 'Do I have to make a speech?' She said she'd never made speeches before except to her missionary society and her garden club."

In April 1975 Rosalynn Carter and Edna Langford set out from Atlanta by car to work the Florida panhandle—to politick for a presidential primary that was almost one year away. "Jimmy just told us to go to Florida and make friends," Langford recalled. "Make friends in George Wallace's territory and show them that there was an alternative. So that's what we did."

In Tallahassee, they contacted Rosalynn's former fifth-grade teacher, Eleanor Ketchum, who had just been named Florida's Woman of the Year. "I said, let's have a get-together with thirty or forty of the active women in Tallahassee," Langford said. "Well, she sent out 400 invitations—and 308 of them came."

From there, the two women set out on a lonely trek through the small towns of the Florida panhandle, the most conservative, the most redneck, the most Alabama-like Wallace country in Florida. Quincy. Marianna. Bonifay. Chipley. They would hit the town and walk in unannounced to the local newspaper office and the local radio station and try to get Mrs. Carter interviewed and get her picture taken. "Sometimes nobody would know anything about Jimmy," Langford recalled. "So if we were told by someone in the newspaper to come back later, of course we didn't have time to wait around for that because we had to go on to the next place. So I would say, 'Wouldn't you like to get somebody to come out and take her picture—maybe take a picture with Mrs. Carter and you?' " And often they would, and then it would lots of times wind up on the front page. "We'd always have Rosalynn holding a Jimmy Carter bumper sticker, so people would get to know his name even if they didn't read the story. And at the radio stations, if the boy didn't know what to ask, sometimes we'd write down the questions for him.

"Once, we went into one newspaper office and there was only one person inside. It was about nine-thirty in the morning and so she called her editor—woke him up—and asked him what should she ask Rosalynn. Well, the editor said to ask her how she would restructure Vietnam. Restructure Vietnam! And so she did, and Rosalynn answered: 'I don't know anything about restructuring Vietnam.' "

In Panama City, the two women were eating in a restaurant near the beach when Rosalynn looked over and saw a car with a press sign on it. Then she saw another. "Where are the press people?" she asked. Edna Langford spotted a Rotary Club sign, and the two women got up from their table and left—even though they had just ordered their meal. (They paid the bill.)

"I just went in and went up to the president of the club," said Langford. "And I said to him, 'I'm Edna Langford from Georgia and my daddy was a Rotarian and my husband is a Rotarian and I've got someone here who I think you'd like to meet.' And he was delighted and we both spoke before the group. . . . And there was a woman there from a newspaper with a camera and she put it in the paper."

There were times during the campaign that Rosalynn Carter even advised her husband on the handling of thorny issue questions. For example, in March 1976 she let him know that he had botched the question on home mortgages and tax reform in Massachusetts and that he was continuing to botch the issue every time it was raised.

"I called him from Florida about that home mortgage exemption," she said. "Everywhere I went I was getting questions on what Jimmy had said about [perhaps eliminating] that home mortgage exemption. Jimmy would always answer the questions by going into all the details of how it was going to be part of his comprehensive tax reform program , . . and it just wasn't getting through. I told him he did not have to do all that. Just be brief. Say, 'I'm not going to raise your taxes' and explain that no tax reform proposal of his would cost them more money."

　　　　▄▄　　　▄▄　　　▄▄

There was a time, in Rhode Island, when the Carter people figured they would take the contest without too much difficulty. But then the new faces of 1976, Brown and Church, moved in. Both had scored impressive wins over Carter and together they had seriously shaken Carter's once-comfortable view of Rhode Island.

On the Wednesday before the Rhode Island election, Brown's official schedule showed him spending the next three days in California on "state business." But then on Thursday Brown decided to take another gamble, just as he had in Oregon—only with less time before the election to do his work. He announced that he would fly to Rhode Island and spend three days campaigning for the uncommitted slate, spending some $25,000 on a last-minute radio, television, and newspaper advertising campaign.

Along with his extensive media campaign, Brown put together a hurried, but effective, organization that managed to round up a group of uncommitted delegates he could endorse. Brown and his people worked the small state vigorously, stumping for the uncommitted slate, and had considerable success in getting their message across.

Church, meanwhile, was helped by three of his Capitol Hill colleagues—one of them being Mo Udall. Church and Udall had worked out an understanding: Udall would concentrate on beating Carter in South Dakota and would not campaign in Rhode Island, even though he remained on the ballot there and had a slate of delegates pledged to him; Church, meanwhile, would not run in South Dakota. Dennis J. Robert II, Udall's Rhode Island state chairman, was quoted shortly before the campaign as confirming the existence of this meeting of political minds.

The other two Capitol Hill colleagues helping Church were Senator Claiborne Pell and Representative Edward P. Beard. The two men campaigned with Church through the state, helping him with voting groups such as teachers and the elderly. On Sunday, Church announced the endorsement of the officials from three unions: the vice president of the Rhode Island Federation of Teachers, and officials of the United Steelworkers of America and of the barbers' union.

Carter was still considered the favorite right up to election day in Rhode Island, but his lead was viewed as slim, and his concern was sufficiently larger. He took his wife's advice and scheduled a Memorial Day appearance in Providence, to march in a holiday parade and hold a press conference. He left Rhode Island and made two more stops that day—one of them in Rapid City, South Dakota— before turning in for the night in Sacramento.

▬   ▬   ▬

A few weeks before the South Dakota primary, Pat Caddell's people took a statewide survey and tabulated the results. Just as they had in Oregon, the Carter strategists decided once again—at all costs—to keep the poll results secret. Only this time the Carter people were not afraid of being embarrassed, as they had been in Oregon. Just the opposite. They just did not want Udall to know how well Carter was doing. Jimmy Carter had scored 45 percent, 12 to 13 points better than Mo Udall.

"It was the best kept secret of the primary," Caddell said later. "For us, South Dakota was really part of the Ohio [June 8] primary. Udall thought he would do well in South Dakota and have something going by the time he hit Ohio. But our poll showed us that those were our kind of farmers. And Udall didn't know it. The Udall people just kept thinking it was in the bag and we didn't tell the reporters or anyone otherwise."

The Carter people were careful; they kept looking

203

nervous about South Dakota, even as they brought Carter into the state twice, Rapid City and Sioux Falls.

THE RESULTS: *In Rhode Island the turnout was small, as Rosalynn Carter had warned, but it was large enough for Jerry Brown. His uncommitted slate upset Carter by a 798-vote margin, 19,035 (31.4 percent) to 18,237 (29.9). Church came in third with 16,423 (27.6). "We gave a home to a lot of people who were homeless," said Brown Campaign Manager Mickey Kantor. "A lot of our people were Jackson people in Rhode Island."*

In Montana, Church easily defeated Carter, who did not try to make it much of a contest, 59.9 percent to 24.8

In South Dakota, Carter kept Udall's winless streak alive. He beat Udall 24,573 to 20,055—41.1 percent to 33.5. "It took the wind out of Udall's sails," Caddell said. In fact, it did more than that. It gave Frank Church an argument for going into Ohio along with Udall and Carter, rather than letting Udall have a clean shot at trying to knock off Carter in that large midwestern industrial state.

June 8|The Big Three

June 8. It had always been clear that this would be the most important date on the Democratic primary calendar. June 8. A three-alarm climax to the primary fight for the presidential nomination—540 delegates on the block in three populous states, California, Ohio, New Jersey. June 8. The date was so well known throughout the primary season, that politicians did not refer to it by month or numeral. Some called it "Big Casino." Others called it "The World Series."

Jimmy Carter and his aides had visited California early and had prepared for months—even years—to make that a major fight. California was, after all, the traditional end-of-the-primaries contest, with the convention's largest delegation as its prize. But when Jerry Brown got into the picture, California pretty much got out. The state would go to Brown, it became clear, and the only question was how many of California's 280 delegates could be won by the also-rans. With the delegates now being divided proportionally—no more winner-take-all—it was still possible to finish second and come away with a whopping 100-plus delegates. Possible, but not probable. For Jerry Brown was still rolling along with a record 85 percent popularity figure within his own state. And buoyed by his showings in the East, Brown could demonstrate to his home staters that people in Maryland and Rhode Island had taken him seriously as a presidential candidate and that they ought to as well. Brown figured to own most of California on June 8.

205

New Jersey, with its 108 delegates, offered a potentially appealing prize. There was an uncommitted state that had the backing of a number of the state's party bosses, and there were internal divisions and uncertainties and a confusing ballot structure and a separate beauty contest and delegate-selection balloting that clouded the outlook in the state.

And there was Ohio, with its 152 delegates, and its large industrial blue-collar and midwestern middle-class Democratic Party. "It became clear by the beginning of May that Ohio was going to be the big windup of the primaries," Hamilton Jordan said. "And that was fine with us."

Patrick Caddell explained why. "Ohio was always our strongest state," he said. "It had a lot of southerners who had settled there and a lot of rural voters. It was not as liberal as the other two states and it had no crossover voting provision." Caddell's organization polled constantly in Ohio, and the results showed that Carter was never in trouble in Ohio. He cruised along in the high 40s in the Caddell polls, a lofty position which left him able to look down with amusement at the Punch and Judy performance that was being waged by his opponents.

Mo Udall and Frank Church came roaring into the state in the beginning of June, each suggesting that the other pull out.

Church: "He [Udall] cannot be a viable candidate after having gone so many times to the voters [without winning] —and he must realize that himself. Those who are looking for an alternative candidate in Ohio will have to look for a winner . . . he's had ample opportunity to win." Did Church want Udall to withdraw? "That is a judgment he himself must make. . . ."

Udall: "He hasn't taken my advice [to stay out of Ohio] during this campaign and I'm not likely to take his, . . . I don't think Frank Church should be pronouncing me dead or out of the race. He has 50 to 60 delegates. I have over 300. I expect to win Ohio and go into the convention as a viable candidate. . . . If Carter slips and falters, I'm in a better position than anyone else to get the nomination. I know it's a long shot. I can recognize a long shot as well as anyone else. I look at one every morning when I shave."

▄▄   ▄▄   ▄▄

California

"I invented it and put it into a system. Five media markets in one day—a record for media politics. I was, and am, quite proud of it."

Kent Brownridge is an artist who works in the medium of message. He is by profession the marketing director of *Rolling Stone*. He is by choice "a politics junkie—a lot of us at *Rolling Stone* are politics junkies." So it is that in the spring of 1976, Kent Brownridge cooked up on Jimmy Carter. His specialty is the media event, and on June 1, 1976, he put on an art show of sorts up and down the state of California.

California is a sprawling state of more than twenty million diverse people who are linked together by a love of the sun, a fondness for the sea, and little else except a tenuous necklace of affiliated and independent television and radio stations. It is a state that is top-heavy with broadcasters and reporters and photographers and camerapeople, full-timers and free-lancers, and even media groupies. Candidates can politick and win in California without even shaking a single hand; but they cannot politick and win without holding a single media event.

A media event is a by-product of the performing arts that is often without cultural, social, or even aesthetic value. It is the sort of thing that does not necessarily look impressive in person—it may, in fact, look perfectly ridiculous and may even *be* perfectly ridiculous. But if it guarantees that the candidates will get on television in one of the local news shows that night, then it is good.

Once Jerry Brown said that he would run in California, that traditionally important end-of-the-campaign primary looked a lot less winnable, and therefore a lot less important, to the Carter people. The trick, then, was for Carter to get whatever was going to be his in California with as little expenditure of money—and mostly of the candidate's highly valuable time—in the state as possible. There were, after all, campaigns to be waged in Ohio and New Jersey. So a five-day visit to California was cut down to just two days, and Kent Brownridge had orders to do the best he could.

Brownridge was not a part of the Carter national staff; he was a volunteer who was experienced in politics, a a former Californian, and a Carter fan. He boiled a week's worth of publicity into a day's worth of politicking. Yet he says: "I don't think the governor even knows me. I don't think he knows my name."

Brownridge convened a quick school for advance people and trained Carter volunteers in the art of building crowds, screening the people the candidate would spontaneously meet while the cameras were rolling, and, in short, marketing the candidate. Index cards would be prepared, one for each person Carter would meet; flash cards telling him the name of the person, what they were interested in, and at times what to say.

"The thing was we had to hit all of the major media markets in what was really one day's worth of campaign," Brownridge said. "And what we wanted to do was focus on specific issues—show people that he was not wishy-washy on the issues. So we set up an extremely fast schedule. Go into one media market. Do one specific thing tailored to the one issue we wanted to emphasize. And get out."

This was Jimmy Carter's June 1:

7:15 A.M.—handshaking at Sacramento Municipal Utilities Truck Yard.

Carter talked about employment. Dozens of workers crowded around and the cameras caught the scene. "We bought out the coffee wagon. Gave free coffee to everyone, and they just crowded around and the governor talked to them. He was a real pro. We gave them a half hour and that was it. Cut it and on to the next place."

7:45 A.M.—en route to Sacramento Municipal Airport. 8:20 A.M.—fly to Oakland. 8:55 A.M.—arrive Oakland. 9:30 A.M.—tour Alpha Bates Hospital.

Carter talked about health care. "First he went upstairs, with the cameras following him, to meet some patients who couldn't pay for their bills. We introduced each patient. There was a card for each. [Sample: Patient John

Doe. Pneumonia. Illness is not covered by health insurance. Ask: Do you have insurance to cover this illness?] Then he went downstairs to make a statement before all of the press. It was a regular room in the hospital which we'd packed with people in white coats and stethoscopes— so it looked very healthish. . . . It wasn't hard to get them to come. After all, this was big haps for the hospital. If you had a boring job emptying bed pans, then this to you is big time. . . . The press just went bullshit. They'd never seen anything like it before.

"For the patients, we had to find people who could not pay and then we picked people with tubes running out of their noses and all sorts of medical contraptions strapped on their bodies. . . . I know we're taking advantage of people with hardships with what we're doing in a way, but a guy like the governor can do it in good taste."

Upstairs, Carter was led to the bedsides of five patients.

The last patient Carter was scheduled to visit was an elderly lady with tubes in her nose and an intravenous unit in her arm who apparently was so ill that her breathing came in difficult, raspy gasps. She was seemingly unaware of what was going on around her. Carter's television adviser, Barry Jagoda, who is modest in stature and a giant in energy and intensity, took one look at the woman while Carter was still down the hall and ran nervously for the nearest doctor. "Doc, tell me—is she going to die when he gets there?" Jagoda wanted to know, horrible visions clearly running through his head. The doctors assured him she would be all right. But Jagoda wanted to make one final check to satisfy himself. He raced back to the woman. Jagoda, who has dark hair and a full, dark beard, walked to the side of her bed and leaned over. The woman looked up at the swarthy Jagoda, reached her hand toward him, and asked in a thin whisp of a voice: "Governor Carter?"

Jagoda got Carter downstairs as quickly as possible. He was out the door less than an hour after he had arrived.

10:15 A.M.—*en route to airport. 11:00* A.M.—*fly to Long Beach. 12:30* P.M.—*reception with senior citizens at Bixby Park.*

Carter talked about senior citizen issues. "We had three thousand senior citizens at that park. Three thousand! It's always hard to build a crowd, and when you have a special requirement—that they be old—it's even harder. Well, we made three thousand phone calls. Put out forty thousand leaflets. And we had this little secret—we had buses bring them in, but the buses were kept very carefully hidden [from the press]. . . . And we also gave away a free lunch to anyone who came. That was also a secret. They'll always come out for a free lunch."

1:15 P.M.—en route to airport. 1:55 P.M.—fly to San Diego. 2:35 P.M.—arrive San Diego. 3:05 P.M.—brief remarks at Mae L. Feaster School.

Carter talked about education. "Attending were students, parents, and teachers—we got teachers to come who weren't teachers at that school. So it was a little hokey. . . . It was the least successful of our events." This was in part due to the fact that there had been in-fighting between local and traveling Carter staff people. And it was in part due to the booing. It seems that someone had reminded Carter that they were just a few miles north of the Mexican border, and so Carter, who is so fond of showing that he knows Spanish, tried out a few welcoming lines on the crowd. There was silence, and a few boos. Carter thought they hadn't heard him well enough, so he gave his little all-Spanish welcome again. More boos. The advance people had neglected to tell him that this was a conservative, virtually all-white neighborhood area of people who just did not think highly of Chicanos.

3:45 P.M.—en route to airport. 4:20 P.M.—fly to Los Angeles. 4:55 P.M.—arrive Los Angeles airport. 5:40 P.M. —arrive at Martin Luther King, Jr. Hospital dedication.

As the Carter entourage made its way down the state of California, from media event to media event, Patrick Anderson sat in the bus, writing. He had awakened at 3:00 A.M. in his Sacramento hotel with the idea and now, on the bus, he was putting together and polishing a speech for Carter to give at the last stop—a serious and meaningful stop at the end of a contrived-for-the-media day— a speech at a dedication of a wing at the Martin Luther King, Jr. Hospital in Los Angeles.

The speech was not a health-care speech, but a race-relations speech. It was a little bit of Carter's autobiography and a little bit of New South. It was a white southerner paying tribute to a black southerner. A rural

Georgian praising the coming of civil rights. "It was the best thing I've ever written for him," Anderson says. It may, in fact, have been the best speech Carter gave in the entire campaign, in content, in delivery (see Appendix). Anderson showed the speech to Carter and Powell at noon and they liked it.

Carter made only one substantive change. Anderson, a northern-thinking liberal, had written a dig at George Wallace: "When I started to run for President, there were those who said I would fail, because there was another governor who spoke for the South, a man who once stood in a schoolhouse door and cried out, 'segregation forever!' "

Carter, a practical southern politician, took a blue-ink pen and shortened the paragraph so it would simply read: "When I started to run for President, there were those who said I would fail because I am from the South."

Powell had the speech typed and distributed to the traveling press corps. In general, traveling press corps provide the nation with a vital and essential service: humbling those who are at the center of, or trying to get to the center of, power. With the writer, Anderson, clearly in earshot, the reporters read over the speech next and began singing, "We Shall Overcome."

In fact, it was an impressive speech.

       ▬   ▬   ▬

In his autobiography, in his speeches, and in his interviews, Jimmy Carter made note of the fact that *War and Peace* was one of his favorite boyhood books. He probably never stopped to think of it, but there was much about his California campaign operation that was reminiscent of Tolstoy's classic. Internally, the organization was often at war and seldom at peace; and its leadership ranks alone had more characters than a Russian novel.

All of this is not merely because of the people involved; it is due in large measure to the state in which they operated. California is a beautifully schizoid political place; it is at least two states in one: northern California, which is a world that looks to San Francisco for leadership, and southern California, which revolves around Los Angeles. Statewide campaigns usually find themselves in

211

a northern California versus southern California split, and the Carter campaign was no exception. They had problems putting together a smoothly functioning unit in 1975 and on June 8, 1976, they were still trying to get things organized.

Carter had met Rodney Kennedy-Minott early in his presidential travels, back in 1974 when he was out in Palo Alto doing his work as chairman of the Democratic congressional campaign committee and getting around the country in the process. Carter had grown to like Kennedy-Minott, and so had Hamilton Jordan and the rest of the Carter men. He continued to be close to the candidate and his crew throughout the campaign.

When the Carter campaign set up operations in California in 1975, Kennedy-Minott headed the effort in the north with the title of California Chairperson, and Terry Utterbach was then working as Southern California Coordinator. Technically, according to the Carter staff in Atlanta, Utterbach was under Kennedy-Minott; as Atlanta saw it, Utterbach wanted a larger share of the control, and then he wanted a salary, and soon he was no longer with the Carter organization.

Ben Goddard, a political adviser out of Colorado, was brought in. As the national Carter staff saw it, Goddard had a Number Two role to Kennedy-Minott, but he had the titles Western States Regional Campaign Coordinator and California State Campaign Coordinator, and their roles at times seemed to overlap. Meanwhile, various California political figures began making themselves available to the Carter organization; each sought a prominent role in the decision-making and each sought to advise the candidate on what he ought to do and when and how he ought to do it. State Senator Omer Rains and Los Angeles County Supervisor Ed Edelman were among the California political establishment figures who became active in the Carter campaign. Rains was titled Western States Co-Chairperson; Edelman was Co-Chairperson of the California Carter campaign.

"California was one state Ham [Hamilton Jordan] was intimidated by," said one of Carter's top national campaign officials. "Hamilton kept letting these people join and he kept giving them titles and each thought he was running things. They all fought most of the time and little grass-roots organization developed. They spent their energies on each other."

All of this left Carter and his national staff members in a difficult position. His administrative assistant, Greg Schneiders, was heard on at least one occasion to observe that he had a hard time knowing which advice to follow when one of the California hierarchy was telling him what Carter *had* to do. "I never knew who to listen to in California," Schneiders was quoted as telling a friend.

Consider the night of May 20. Carter had been the guest of honor at a lavish fundraising dinner at the Beverly Hilton Hotel and at 10:30 P.M. he had gone up to his room and was getting undressed for the night when State Senator Omer Rains appeared. He said that a group of Chicanos was waiting downstairs and Carter had to go talk to them, that Carter had not yet met with the Chicanos and it was imperative that he do so. So Carter put his shoes on and went downstairs to see the group.

The Chicanos had a list of questions they wanted answered; Carter gave them a general talk and told them to give him the list and he would have his staff issues people send them the answers. They presented Carter with the list and went on to complain that Carter California official Ben Goddard was not serving Carter well in California— that only State Senator Rains (who had set up the meeting for them) was doing a good job. Meanwhile, Goddard had by chance walked into the room and heard their comments; he walked in because he had been searching for Greg Schneiders to set up a meeting because he wanted to pass the word on to Carter that State Senator Rains and Ed Edelman were not doing their jobs well. Edelman, meanwhile, had cornered Schneiders three times that night to warn him that the other Carter officials had California screwed up. Edelman pressed that Goddard had been allowed to talk to Carter and was certain Goddard was complaining about Edelman; so Edelman said he wanted a chance to talk to Carter to present his side of it. Schneiders relented and scheduled Edelman to ride out to the airport with Carter the next morning.

Late that night, both Goddard and Kennedy-Minott talked to Carter's administrative assistant and expressed concern over what Edelman would have to say to Carter. But when Schneiders told them the conference would be at 8:00 A.M., on the way to the airport, Goddard and Kennedy-Minott were visibly relieved; Edelman will never make it that early, one of them said to the now thoroughly puzzled Schneiders. At 8:00 A.M. the next day, Edelman was nowhere to be found when Carter stepped into his car and left for the airport.

People in the California operation were constantly threatening to quit and go public with their dissatisfaction, according to people on the Carter national staff. The clash of personalities in the California Carter campaign continued right up to the end. Just a day before the primary election, in fact, Carter's national finance director, Morris Dees, dismissed Los Angeles attorney and fundraiser Herb Hafif, who had been involved in a dispute with several Carter staff members for some time, as co-chairperson of Carter's California fundraising committee.

In the end, the Carter campaign in California had more friction than fire. "Perhaps the basic problem was that none of us could make up our minds," Rodney Kennedy-Minott said candidly. "I couldn't and I don't think some in the headquarters in Atlanta could either. After Brown came in, I contacted Hamilton and I said, 'Now I don't think we should make a big effort out here.' And then later, I started getting excited about the way it was looking and I thought we should make the effort. And then, at the end, I knew we were right to concentrate on Ohio instead."

"We became mesmerized by the popular vote total," Kennedy-Minott said. "We booked Jimmy into San Francisco and Los Angeles on his last swing out here. I think that was a mistake. Had we booked him into Orange County and the Central Valley, the Sacramento Valley—rural areas—we probably would have picked up some more delegates per district. But we were mesmerized—we succumbed to the lure of all those votes in the LA area."

≈   ≈   ≈

Beverly Hills. Hundreds of people have paid $100 a plate to attend the Carter fundraiser. The festivities are opened with an invocation from a rabbi. The rabbi takes note during his remarks of the fact that campaign seasons necessarily produce "the painful banalities, the hectoring . . ." by political candidates.

Just before the fundraising dinner, candidate Carter met in a hotel suite with a group of Los Angeles Jewish leaders. There he made some remarks that are unusual when compared with most candidates' standard cocktail party commentary.

"I'm going to tell you something you don't like," Carter said. "I'm a devoted Southern Baptist. There has been a great deal of concern expressed to me by Jewish leaders about my beliefs. . . . I'm a devoted Baptist. . . . I ask you to learn about my faith before you permit it to cause you any concern. . . . There is no conflict between us [concerning the] separation of church and state. . . . I worship the same God you worship."

Carter and his strategists were concerned about the Jewish vote for much of the campaign, and they were especially concerned about it as they worked toward a big finish in Ohio, New Jersey, and California. They had gone to great lengths to set the meeting in Manhattan with Golda Meir and to secure the endorsement of New York City Mayor Abraham Beame.

"One of the leaders of the Jewish Community," Carter later said, ". . . explained to me that they'd been concerned about my stand on Israel, first of all. Then they were concerned about my Baptist beliefs. [Because so many southern rednecks had proved to be hateful anti-Semites.] But they were also concerned about the degree to which I was committed to the Great Society and New Deal programs. Because if there was social unrest . . . intersocietal conflict, quite often the Jewish people were the ones who suffered. Incipient prejudice there—that was something that was explained to me by a professor. I don't know whether it's true or not."

New Jersey

James P. Dugan was spending a four-day weekend of getting-away-from-it-all by sitting in his Sahara Hotel room in Las Vegas wearing a telephone in his ear. He was the chairman of the Democratic Party in New Jersey, and here he was in Las Vegas watching his grand plan for the June 8 primary come apart in his hands. Hubert Humphrey had just let him down by going on television April 29 announcing that he was not going to campaign for the Presidency. Dugan, an erudite and effective party boss, had carefully constructed a slate of big-name delegates that would be officially uncommitted, but would in fact be backing Humphrey. Then Humphrey had withdrawn and now Congressman Peter Rodino, the state's most prominent Italian-American office holder, and Newark Mayor Kenneth Gibson, the state's most prominent black office holder, were pulling their names off the slate. And Dugan was not happy about the whole thing, and he was having his problems.

"Rodino and Gibson abandoned ship the weekend I was in Vegas," Dugan recalled. "So there I was in the goddamned room all weekend talking on the telephone with Rodino—who always had been a willow in the wind —and with Gibson. And I was having real problems getting people to come aboard a sinking ship."

On the fourth and final day of his vacation, Dugan made it out to the poolside. If he could not cure his troubles, at least he would try to tan them. He was sitting there reading the *Las Vegas Sun*—"reading all those stories about the Howard Hughes wills"—when he saw a box that said that Jerry Brown would be arriving in town to make an appearance at a function with Nevada's lone congressman, James D. Santini. This set Dugan to thinking. "We needed a campaigner—someone to put some excitement into our race," Dugan said. He contacted Santini's office and found out that Brown would be arriving at about the same time that he would be departing, and so a meeting between the California governor and the New Jersey chairman was set up for the Las Vegas airport terminal the next day.

The meeting was brief. Dugan told Brown about how he had put together an uncommitted slate and how its delegates had been pro Humphrey. "I'd like to give you the opportunity of coming into New Jersey," Dugan recalled telling Brown. "But since you've come in late, you can only do it if you come in support of my uncommitted slate." Brown was interested and the two men agreed to meet sometime the next week in New Jersey.

It turned out that they met on May 15 at a party Diane von Furstenburg, the dress designer, threw for the Manhattan cognoscenti. The two men left the party and went to Brown's room in the New York Hilton. There Brown said he wanted to come into New Jersey, but that he wanted to come in and campaign for a de facto Brown slate. Dugan balked at this.

"No," Dugan recalled saying. "You're not going to get anything out of New Jersey unless we get our uncommitted slate in. If we elect them, then you'll get a fair shot at getting delegates out of the slate."

As Dugan saw it, he had put together an uncommitted slate and then had it pledged to Humphrey. He felt that he could not abandon Humphrey because (1) he had given Humphrey his personal commitment; and (2) "tactically, we would have looked foolish, starting out uncommitted and then going for Humphrey and then switching to Brown."

As Dugan remembers it, Brown agreed then to come in on Dugan's terms, but then—following Brown's impressive drubbing of Carter in Maryland—the Californian reinstituted his original demand that the Dugan slate come out as a Brown slate before he would agree to come in and campaign for it.

As the Brown camp remembers it, Brown never agreed to come in on Dugan's original terms.

"We just couldn't go with terms like that," Mickey Kantor, Brown's campaign manager recalled. "It made us look poor—lowly."

"So we talked with them again, and Dugan and the New Jersey people came up with the two-headed monster."

The New Jersey uncommitted slate, put together by Dugan and headed by Senator Harrison Williams, would be for Hubert Humphrey and/or Jerry Brown.

Among those pushing the uncommitted slate, however, was a knowledgeable carpetbagger, Joseph F. Crangle, Democratic Leader in New York's Erie County (Buffalo), and one of those who had been at the ABC (Anybody But Carter) meetings pushing Humphrey.

Carter had the support of one well-known party boss, Harry Lerner of Essex County (Newark).

Throughout the candidacy of Jerry Brown, people had speculated that he was really just Hubert's stalking horse —he would try to create a deadlocked convention; the convention would turn to Humphrey; then Humphrey would name Brown as his Vice President. Brown liked Humphrey and admired many things about him. But he and his people had strongly rejected the implication that he was Humphrey's stalking horse. And now, in New Jersey, he had become Humphrey's stablemate.

The Humphrey/Brown stable was bolstered by the return of a campaign warhorse who had seemingly been put out to political pasture. Edmund G. Brown, Sr.—Pat Brown—had volunteered to campaign for his son back in Maryland, but his offer had been spurned. The senior Brown, former governor of California and the man who had sent Richard Nixon down to defeat in the 1962 California gubernatorial contest, had reportedly heard the thanks-but-no-thanks not from his son, but from his son's campaign manager, Mickey Kantor. But in New Jersey, a state big on the boss system and old politics, Pat Brown was more than welcome. He was wanted. And he came back to stump for his son (and Humphrey).

Late in the campaign, Dugan and Jerry Brown were sitting in a car in Trenton.

"How did my father do campaigning here?" the young governor asked.

"Great—a lot of people think he should be the candidate," Dugan joked.

Later, Dugan elaborated on the role of Pat Brown. "The truth is, he went over like gangbusters. He was terrific. He went to Atlantic City and he did a fundraiser and he worked the boardwalk, and he went and spoke before the county pols, he spoke opposite one of Jimmy Carter's relatives, his wife Rosalynn or his sister. And he went over great."

Looking back, Dugan figures that Humphrey was both a plus and a minus in the New Jersey primary. "He helped us, but he also hurt us," Dugan said. "He hurt us because of that April 29th thing of his. He made four or five appearances in the state, and there would be times when Hubert would be standing next to me and he would make a statement to reporters that he was not a candidate. And then the reporters would turn to me and ask me, and I would say that he was going to be the next nominee and the next President.

"But Jerry Brown was all plus. He added that degree of excitement. He was the alternative to all the pols. A very electric candidate. Young, good looking. He takes a different view of politics and he does not make the classic political speech. He was very effective."

☰ ☰ ☰

Candidates campaign in New Jersey by making sure they get on television in Philadelphia and New York City. These are the stations that serve the south and the north, respectively, in that strange large industrial state-without-television. It is this televisionless fact of life that has made New Jersey politicians all the more dependent on strong party machines. The lack of television may have hurt political independents and challengers, but it has been a boon to bosses.

(A quick digression: There was a time years ago when Channel 13 was serving New Jersey on a commercial basis. In 1957, Democrat Robert Meyner was running in the gubernatorial election against Republican Malcolm Forbes, and he purchased the hour from 10:00 P.M. to 11:00 P.M. for a big windup to his campaign. Forbes, concerned that he would need a rebuttal, purchased the block of time immediately following Meyner. But after fifty-five minutes of his commercial, Meyner signed off with a thank you, the Star Spangled Banner was played, and for the last five minutes of his time, Meyner showed just the test pattern. Most viewers figured that the station had gone off the air. They turned off their television sets and went to bed, leaving a furious Forbes to beam his rebuttal to darkened homes.)

Carter was scheduled to leave New York City by train and go to Philadelphia—to make a time-consuming stop for a press conference—before doubling back to Trenton to get on with his genuine New Jersey politicking. But in New Jersey, Phil Wise, a young Plains, Georgia, man who has become in this campaign a savvy state coordinator and political operator, was more than a bit perturbed about the scheduling of that Wednesday. The Carter schedulers had booked the candidate into Trenton at 2:00

P.M.—after the Philadelphia media stop—to talk with government workers at the state capital. No good, said Wise; it has to be lunchtime so Carter can pull an audience from among state workers who are out strolling the capitol lawn. Wise wanted the Philadelphia stop scratched. The Carter men were assured by politicians wise in the ways of the Philadelphia media that the television stations would gladly come up to Trenton to cover Carter. So the Philadelphia press conference was cancelled and the candidate went directly to Trenton—and only one Philadelphia TV station showed up.

"The boss was pretty mad about that one," a Carter aide later acknowledged. Did Carter bawl out anyone on the staff or raise his voice in anger? "No," the aide said. "When he gets mad he gets very, very, very quiet. And he just glares right through you."

Southern New Jersey, the suburbs of Philadelphia, and the farm areas were Carter country. "But the further north we went, the harder it was for us," Wise said. "These were the areas to the north that were heavily settled with ethnic groups, Catholics, et cetera."

Carter continued to have problems with the Catholic and Jewish voters. Some Catholics were unhappy with his failure to come out for strong antiabortion measures. And both the Catholics and the Jews were still distrustful of this politician who would discuss so openly his personal religious convictions. But it was not until the primary campaign was over that the public had one of its most fascinating glimpses of the religious side of Jimmy Carter.

June 19. Jimmy Carter is preaching.

He is standing on an auditorium stage, before some 2,000 predominantly white Christian laymen, under a huge banner that reads "WHO'S IN CHARGE?" (there is a small cross painted in the center of the question mark). The man who is to be the Democratic nominee for President is preaching.

"The biggest blessing we have is our belief in Christ," Carter is saying. "It gives us an unchanging core around which our lives can function."

It is Saturday, midday, and Jimmy Carter has come

to this national gathering of the Disciples of Christ in the Purdue University auditorium in Lafayette, Indiana, to give a speech that is more evangelical than political. The Disciples of Christ is not his church, but it is the church of Charles Kirbo, his closest adviser. He had agreed about a year ago (before he was the Democratic frontrunner) to address this gathering that is the Department of Church Men, Division of Homeland Ministry, "Sessions '76 Program."

The program for the day had begun with music—a modern piano piece and a song led by a very rotund man in a white jacket, black shirt, bold black-and-white striped pants, and white patent leather shoes that glossed almost as much as his slicked dark hair. But the highlight of the day is Jimmy Carter, who is, in the words of one of his aides, *"witnessing*—witnessing his faith in Christ." An airplaneload of television crews and photographers and reporters and technicians—who travel with Carter because he will soon be the Democratic Party's presidential nominee—is also on hand to witness Carter *witnessing,* and report it all to the outside world.

He talks of Christ and God and government. "I think if you analyze the parables of Christ . . . Christ was concerned more than anything else, about pride. . . . I always thought my political leaders told the truth and that our nation stood for what was right in the eyes of God. Maybe it was too much for the national pride. . . . In the last few years, we've seen—with the Vietnam War, the bombing of Cambodia, the Watergate tragedy, the CIA revelations—that the goodness of our nation is not as sure anymore as it once was."

And he talks to the Christian laymen, perhaps more than anything else, about his own faith in Christ and how it developed and how he had been asked to do missionary Christian work in Pennsylvania but at first didn't want to go. "So I prayed about it and I decided to go." It is a carefully planned, carefully constructed sermon that is designed to show the virtues of both religion and himself. He talks at one point about how hard it is for men to overcome pride and actually show emotions such as crying, and at another point of how he found himself "with tears running down my cheeks" after doing some Christian missionary work. He talks about doing missionary work with Eloy Cruz, whom he describes as a "dark-skinned Cuban" and "the best Christian I ever saw."

He talks about how in Massachusetts, "I was asked to go and witness among Spanish-speaking people" and about how he was able to do this because he speaks Spanish; and then he proves this by speaking a sentence with careful emphasis, phrase by phrase—first Spanish and then English. "Nuestro Salvador tiene los manos que son muy suaves, y El no puede hacer mucho con un hombre que es dura." ("Our Savior has hands which are very gentle, and He cannot do much with a man who is hard.") He speaks this and translates it with pride; it is apparent—and understandably so—that Jimmy Carter of Plains, Georgia, who often says he is the first of his father's family to finish high school, considers it a badge of honor and accomplishment to be able to demonstrate his grasp of a foreign language.

His speech is quiet and low key, and his gestures are the same—he punctuates his soft comments with his favorite soft gesture, done mostly with the wrist, with his hand moving in a semicircle first toward his chest and then toward his audience. Yet he holds and impresses his audience of Christian laymen, and he moves them to scattered shouts of "Amen!" at one point when he says with emphasis: "What power lies in this auditorium! Four or five thousand men knowing a truth that never changes!"

Then his preaching is done and the man who will soon be the Democratic candidate for President adjourns to a nearby church bookstore so he can autograph for various churchmen copies of his book, *Why Not the Best?* It is almost 1:00 P.M. when Carter takes off from Lafayette and flies back to Georgia.

▪   ▪   ▪

Ohio

Jimmy Carter was not going back to California.

His spokesman, Jody Powell, announced this into the airplane's public-address-system microphone as the Carter charter was flying to Toledo. A last-minute swing west had been scrapped in favor of more campaigning in New Jersey and Ohio.

Later Carter was asked why. He told a press conference that it would be the best use of his time and so on. Finally he said: "I've already told you more than I know on the subject." That was probably true. For Carter was not involved in the crucial strategy decision to bypass California. Powell made the decision based on phone calls with Carter people in Atlanta and the states involved. He analyzed the situation and he made the decision and then he told Carter, who accepted it.

"That's the way things are done in this campaign," explained a Carter campaign official. "The single most valuable commodity we have is the candidate and his time. He needs to be at his best in his public appearances. So he trusts his staff to handle a lot of the decisions, strategy and otherwise."

Milton Gwirtzman, a Washington attorney and veteran of Democratic political campaigns, was along on the Carter charter primarily to give advice on issues. Sometimes Gwirtzman sensed the need to diversify. Such an occasion came as Carter was strolling the grounds of the Ohio capitol in Columbus, pausing for interviews and handshakes. Gwirtzman noticed a statue there paying tribute to General William Sherman, the Ohioan famous for having marched his Union Army troops through Georgia during the Civil War. Sensing a media field day and Carter disaster, Gwirtzman rushed ahead and deftly diverted the governor to a path that prevented photographers from snapping the obvious picture of Carter—who refused to sing "Marching Through Georgia" as an Annapolis plebe—marching past the huge bronze Sherman.

Carter was advised long ago about the importance of cultivating cordial relationships with individual reporters and influential editors and publishers. But he often seemed uncomfortable around the press. He is not given to the easy back-and-forth banter and joking that some politicians, such as Morris Udall and Edward Kennedy, find so easy.

One morning, Carter had scheduled an early press conference at a Holiday Inn, and most of the reporters were in the conference room waiting for him to arrive. Several others were in a separate anteroom, downing a last cup of coffee. Another reporter, who obviously had difficulty waking up, arrived at the same time as Carter; the reporter headed for the coffee room instead of the press conference and Carter followed, sensing an opportunity for a cup of coffee and fellowship before going in to face the cameras. The straggling reporter was dressed in a loud, almost garish, blue-and-white-check summer suit.

"Dressed for the beach?" a colleague asked. The late-arriving reporter replied, "No, I just got confused. I thought this was California." A third newsman interrupted: "This year Ohio is California." (The reference is to the fact that this year the heavily contested big last race of the campaign is in Ohio, not California.) Through it all Carter stood with the group, smiling, apparently happy to be part of the discussion but nevertheless silent and too shy to inject himself into it.

Finally, a reporter asked Carter if he was aware that one columnist had suggested that there ought to be still one more primary vote—this one to be conducted not in a state but at the upcoming National Governors' Conference. "That ought to be perfect for you," said the reporter with the loud suit. "You're bound to do well with them because they're so fond of you."

The reporter was needling Carter about the well-known fact that he is not popular with a number of the men who used to be his gubernatorial colleagues, especially the other "New South" governors. Carter understood the needling and it provoked his only comment, delivered with a good-natured laugh: "Yeah, I'll do real well with fifty guys who each want to be President." On this the coffee klatch dispersed, and the participants adjourned to positions on their respective sides of the podium.

On another occasion, reporters traveling with Carter spotted a T-shirt in a souvenir shop, bought it, and presented it to the governor. The shirt was symbolic of Carter's Oregon primary night statement concerning Ted

Kennedy and Hubert Humphrey. The T-shirt said: "KISS MY ASS" and carried the picture of a Democratic donkey.

Carter was working a group of well-wishers when someone, trying to make conversation, asked, "How's Amy?" It was the sort of question that is usually responded to with a standard "Fine, just fine." But instead, Carter offered a candid glimpse of the problems of a family on campaigning.

"Amy cried the last time we left home," Carter said. "When she had school to go to, it was not so bad. But now she's at home all day without us [she was staying at the home of Carter's mother while her parents campaigned] and she misses us. It's hard for her."

Rosalynn Carter remembered the incident as well. "She just kind of cried," Mrs. Carter said. "It was very unusual. She was two when Jimmy ran for governor and she's never done that. But that last Sunday that we left, she just kind of clung."

The incident was unsettling on both parents, and they decided that from then on, Carter's mother would come and stay in their home with Amy whenever both Jimmy and Rosalynn had to go out campaigning.

"Rhode Island—that was a mistake," said Frank Church's former press secretary, Bill Hall. "He should have spent more time in Rhode Island." As it was, Frank Church spent just enough time in Rhode Island to louse up what was already a too-late campaign. Church had hoped to campaign long enough in Rhode Island to continue his impressive streak of wins over Jimmy Carter to four out of four. But as it turned out, Church campaigned just long enough in Rhode Island to come down with an ear infection and strep throat, which proved the beginning of his undoing in Ohio.

After tasting defeat for the first time in Rhode Island, Church flew to California, where he attempted to campaign despite his illness. He wound up the worse for it, spending two days in bed in California instead of shaking hands at factory gates and shopping centers.

Finally, Church got his campaign in gear on Friday and headed toward a commitment in Toledo, Ohio. The heavily Democratic, heavily organized, heavily patriotic, decidedly Polish-American Fourth Ward of Toledo had turned out in large numbers to sit on the wooden bleacher seats of a high school football field and listen to the oratory of men who wanted to be their President. Mo Udall had sent word that he could not make it, but Jimmy Carter and Frank Church were expected, and that was enough to bring more than 2,000 people to the Fourth Ward Rally on this warm, summery evening.

Jimmy Carter arrived promptly—so promptly, in fact, that the crowd was just filing in when he got there. So Carter worked the entrance, which enabled him to shake hands with most everyone who was filing into the bleacher area. A high school band was playing, and high school twirlers were twirling, and there was a festive air to the rally when Carter finally began to speak, some twenty minutes after he had arrived and before the crowd had finished filing in.

Carter gave his old, standard stump speech, the one he had been giving throughout most of the campaign, the one which essentially answered the question, "Jimmy Who?"

Carter had finished, given a farewell wave, and left amid warm applause, and as the masters of ceremony looked nervously around, it was apparent that Frank Church was nowhere in sight. So local politicians got up to do some impromptu speech-making, killing time by talking at length in an overly patriotic and decidedly dreary fashion. Reporters mostly took the occasion to leave; a few stayed and interviewed people in the bleachers. Most of the people interviewed seemed to take the line expressed by Bob and Geneva Watson. He is a Jeep plant worker and he said they were "pretty much sure that we're going to vote for Carter" and his wife nodded her assent.

It was one hour later that Frank Church and his tiny traveling entourage swooped into the football field area. There had been a problem making connections in Chicago. In a remarkable show of political spirit, about half of the

2,000 people had stayed to hear the man who had served for years on the Senate Foreign Relations Committee and who had just headed the headline-making Senate Investigation of the Central Intelligence Agency. Frank Church had been hurrying—racing—to make it to Toledo's Fourth Ward, and the knowledge that he was so late had not left him in the best of moods. Yet as soon as he hit the field and got within sight of the crowd, Frank Church exploded into an enthusiastic—no, it was actually ecstatic—grin, laughing and waving as if this was the most fun he had ever had, campaigning an hour late with the remnants of strep throat and an ear infection. Church hit the field at about the 30-yard line and moved briskly around left end, picking up speed and smiling and waving all the while as he crossed the field from sideline to sideline, then turned upfield and picked up 20 yards before being stopped by the speaker's stand. At his side (as always), matching him pace for pace (as always), and grinning a grin that rivaled her husband's (as always), was Church's wife, Bethine, who functions variously as the senator's adviser, answer-prompter, security guard, and mother. (She has been known to answer questions for him in interviews and take the onion off his sandwiches. She is also an enthusiastic political running mate who works a crowd along a fence as energetically as her husband. She calls him "Frostie.")

Frank Church was a little out of breath, and probably a little thirsty (a dab of white formed at the left corner of his mouth as he began to speak and it remained there throughout his talk); but he was an orator of impressive talents. He had a good and simple speech, and he pounded it home eloquently. He had a hard-hitting view of what to do about unemployment and biting attacks on Gerald Ford and Ronald Reagan for having turned their Republican race into a jingoistic debate on the Panama Canal.

When he had finished, Church left the stand for a return dash across the field, once again smiling and waving as he went. Bethine had remained back to greet a few well-wishers, apparently assuming her husband had done the same; when she turned and saw him departing, she moved out like a pulling guard—albeit a dark-haired and pleasant-looking pulling guard—elbowing her way through the trailing band of people and a couple of security men until she caught up with her husband and fell into stride, and smiled and waved immediately to his right.

Frank Church had made a big impression with the some 1,000 who had stayed behind to hear what he had to say.

"Now I don't know," Bob Watson said as Church was finishing his speech. "That fellow Church was really something." Said his wife, Geneva: "He's a better speaker [than Carter] but what got us is that he spoke to the issues we wanted to hear." Her husband nodded and added: "We're back to undecided."

Had he started earlier and stumped the state hard, Frank Church might have made an impact in Ohio; he was that good on the stump. But there was too little time remaining between Friday night and election day in Ohio, and, as it turned out, Church would not even have much of the time that was left.

On Saturday, as Church was working a shopping center in a Cleveland suburb, he received word that there had been a disaster back home in Idaho. The newly constructed $55 million Teton River Dam had crumbled, releasing a torrent of water that swept through 400,000 acres, bringing death and destruction to at least a half dozen communities.

Church cut short his campaigning and prepared to return home. He flew from Youngstown to Cleveland, drove ten miles from the airport to a hotel downtown, and prepared to gather his belongings to depart. He cancelled plans to appear with the other Democratic candidates on ABC's "Issues and Answers" Sunday. Meanwhile, aides rushed to charter a thirty-three-seat, propeller-driven plane for a midnight flight west.

But even that plan wound up wrecked. Late that night, an airport baggage truck somehow ran amok—it was unmanned, the Church staff was told—and smashed into a propeller of the plane Church had just chartered. The plane was grounded, and Church was delayed.

Church, clearly haggard, moved to make the most of his time while aides tried to find another plane. He decided to videotape the interview for "Issues and Answers" so it could be used Sunday, while the others appeared live; at least he would get on the air. He went to a local television station shortly after 1:00 A.M. and taped the interview. (When it was televised on Sunday morning, while the other candidates looked relatively fresh and vigorous, Church looked like a man who was answering questions at 1:00 A.M. after a night on the town, a few rounds, with Muhammad Ali, and perhaps an invasion of Normandy.)

At 2:00 A.M., Church received word that his aides had secured two small Lear jets, each carrying six passengers, for Church and his wife and secret service agents and a few news media representatives.

At 5:00 A.M., the Lear jets left Cleveland, flying 1,850 miles to Pocatello, Idaho, in four hours. From there, Church and other state dignitaries flew over the dam and flood area, viewed the damage, and conferred briefly on how the matter should be handled by government authorities. That done, Church and his party turned right around and headed back to Cleveland.

It was 7:00 P.M. Sunday when the candidate and his small entourage entered the lobby of the Hollenden House in downtown Cleveland. There were puffy pouches under each of Frank Church's eyes, his face was ashen, and as he moved wearily toward the elevator he said to no one in particular, "Show me where my bed is."

He received no directions, but instead he received a request—demand, really—from an inebriated woman in the lobby who wanted an autograph and who got his attention by calling out: "Senator or congressman or whatever you are!"

Church, by now a pushover, signed her piece of paper, telling her softly: "You had it right the first time."

▄ ▄ ▄

There were those who thought that Church went into Ohio not so much because he thought he could win, but because he figured it could help Carter in, and that Carter might then be more receptive to picking Church to run as his Vice President. The Church people were all quick to dismiss this line of speculation. But Bill Hall, Church's former press secretary, believes that the Idaho senator had become somewhat tired and frustrated after serving twenty years in the Senate. (Church's wife used to kid him about having opposed the war in Vietnam for ten years without being able to stop it.) Was the Vice Presidency on Church's mind all along? "I think so," Hall said. "He seriously went after the Presidency but he thought he might get the Vice Presidency out of it."

≋   ≋   ≋

THE RESULTS: . . . *In Ohio, Carter swept to an overwhelming victory. He won 52.2 percent of the vote, compared to Udall's 21.0 and Church's 13.9. Carter came away with 119 delegates—more than he had expected.*

On the night of the election, Frank Church dined at a seafood restaurant in Cleveland. Church, who had repeatedly called himself the tortoise of the campaign and Carter the hare, ordered turtle soup. Then he realized what he had done. "My God," he said, "I feel like a cannibal."

In New Jersey, the Humphrey/Brown "two-headed monster" won; its officially designated uncommitted ticket picked up 82 delegates to Carter's 25 and Udall's 1.

The New Jersey ballot was so complex that it is quite possible that it did not promote, in all instances, a true reflection of the will of the people. Consider Essex County. There were some black precincts in which George Wallace received more votes than Jimmy Carter, despite the fact that Carter had drawn very well among blacks throughout the campaign. Perhaps the blacks of Essex County really were for George Wallace. But more likely, it was that the ballot was so constructed that Wallace headed the list of candidates—he had the place that was often the regular Democratic party line—and "they just went straight across voting that line," said one Carter man.

In California, Brown scored big, as expected. He won 59.0 percent of the vote, which brought him 204 delegates. Carter's 20.5 percent earned him 67, which was less than he had expected. Church got 7.4 percent and Udall 5.0, giving them 7 and 2 delegates, respectively.

"We were a little slow on the uptake—at least I was," Mickey Kantor said about the Brown campaign. "Four or five days before the election I *still* thought that if we won in New Jersey and won big in California the same day, we'd be in okay shape and would have a chance at the nomination. Here I was, I kept talking to the Udall people—Mark Shields and Paul Tully—and they kept telling us Ohio was going to be close, and so we went into June eighth feeling good. Shows you what we knew!"

Morris Udall. He brought class to the Democratic primaries in 1976. He was hard-hitting in his attacks on Carter—in Ohio his television ads featured a jack-in-the-box poking ridicule at Carter's positions on issues. But he was always, in defeat (after defeat after defeat), a man of wit and gentle disposition. Because he had lost so often by so little, he chose for his theme song, near the end, "Second-Hand Rose," inviting people to call him Second-Place Mo. And when reporters presented him with a rubber chicken, he took one look at it and said: "Is this campaign a turkey?" Yet losing was serious and painful to him; and when he finally returned to Washington winless after the last of the primaries and was greeted by a genuine surprise gathering of enthusiastic supporters, Mo Udall broke down and cried.

The next day, June 9, George Wallace, Richard Daley, and Henry Jackson padded the Carter delegate count with their endorsements and made it clear—Jimmy Carter would be the Democratic nominee for President of the United States.

"Skill and luck," Pat Caddell would say later, "—they're both key parts of the political process. And in 1976 we had the best of both."

From 1972, when Jerry Rafshoon outlined the image and he and Hamilton Jordan both outlined the strategy, the Carter men made the right calculations. They were right in figuring that the country was ready to accept a southerner, if he was a sophisticated and nonracist alternative to George Wallace. They were right in figuring that

Carter had to make a big initial splash outside the South—in Iowa and New Hampshire—and then show in Florida that he could take the South away from Wallace. They were right in seeing early that Pennsylvania would be their big casino, their chance to annihilate Scoop Jackson, when even Jackson did not see it coming until it was too late. ("What we were counting on," said Jackson man Ben Wattenberg, "was that we'd get the wind in our media sails after a big New York win. Then the reporters would all look at Scoop Jackson's worm farm and Jackson's peanut farm and Jackson's faith-healing sister.") And they were right in figuring that they could capture the nomination with a big win in Ohio, even if Carter was defeated in New Jersey and soundly whipped in California. All that was skill.

But the nomination could not have been won on skill alone. That was Caddell's other point. For even while Jimmy Carter and his men were doing so many things right, the nomination might well have gone elsewhere. . . .

If Jackson had run in New Hampshire, thus splitting the center-right vote with Carter, giving Udall the early victory and never letting Carter get off to his fast start.

If Udall and Bayh had campaigned in Florida, splitting the liberal and black vote with Carter and allowing Wallace to win, showing that Carter was not as strong in the South as he had been saying.

If Udall had been willing, right away, to spend $25,000 on television ads—instead of being off the air entirely during the last crucial weekend in Wisconsin, where he had been making such big gains and wound up just short of defeating Carter.

If Jackson had seen Pennsylvania early on as his big confrontation with Carter, and had planned and organized and spent there accordingly.

If Hubert Humphrey had made a real run early, instead of just sitting on Capitol Hill assessing and reassessing and re-reassessing.

If the liberals had gotten behind one man from the start, rather than siphoning votes from each other.

Ifs. It might have been different. But it wasn't.

For the last several weeks of the campaign, Jimmy Carter looked tired—bone tired. The lines in his face became pronounced, his skin faintly splotchy, his fragile-fair complexion marred by occasional pinkish patches. And the skin of his neck hung in loose excess.

Now Jimmy Carter was on his way to his last speech of the primary campaign, a talk at a shopping center in Cherry Hill, New Jersey. A Secret Service agent was driving the car and Carter was seated—slumped, really—in the right rear seat, where the Secret Service insists that the people it protects sit. Jody Powell and Greg Schneiders were in the car.

"I was there for your first speech," said Powell. "So I'm going to be here for the last."

Carter talked about the last sixteen months of campaigning. He had been in 110 cities and towns. He has been told that he made 2,050 speeches. Schneiders estimated that Carter had averaged 800 miles a day. Carter talked about how hard it all had been.

"If I had two more months to go, I probably could," he said. "But because it's near the end, I'm getting run down." He was looking forward to the end of the primary campaigning. Looking forward to a few days of rest and a few more days without speeches.

It had been a long sixteen months on the road. Carter, speaking very low to conserve his voice, shook his head and said: "If somebody told me right now that all I had to do was repeat what I'd just done for the last sixteen months and I'd have the White House—I'd tell him no."

A Lengthy Epilogue

It is 2:30 A.M. and out of the blackness of the night sky a small twin-engine plane floats in over the tall Georgia pines and bounces to a stop on a grass airstrip outside Plains that is used in the daytime by cropdusters. The door swings open and out steps a tall, familiar figure. Senator Edmund Muskie, one of the most famous members of the Democratic Party establishment, has come to call. More than that, actually; Senator Muskie has come hurrying—anxiously—to a job interview.

There was a time, just a few months before, when Jimmy Carter had a tough time getting his calls returned by the pillars of the Democratic Party. But that was 1,505 delegates ago, and now leading Democrats across the country are struggling to get calls through to this man who holds no public office, who is just a former governor now residing in Plains, Georgia. They want to offer their services and they want to offer advice and, mainly, they want to make sure they are on the in.

One of the main pieces of business on Jimmy Carter's mind in the days that followed June 9 was the selection of a vice-presidential running mate. He had instituted an elaborate procedure that included lengthy questionnaires on financial and medical histories, preliminary interviews by Carter's closest adviser, Charles Kirbo, detailed background investigations, and finally, for the finalists, a personal job interview with Carter.

Muskie was the first to be summoned for an interview. Carter had tried twice to reach the senator at a fishing

235

camp in Maine on Saturday, July 3, and it was late when Muskie finally got the second message and returned the call and learned he and his wife, Jane, were being invited to come to Plains.

On Sunday, the fourth of July, the Muskies got themselves to the nearest airport and began a series of commercial airline flights that brought them to Atlanta's sprawling airport at about midnight. Carter's youngest son, Chip, had been sent to meet the Muskies, and he escorted them to the small twin-engined craft that carried the party to their predawn arrival in Plains.

Ed Muskie, who had been the party's vice-presidential candidate on the 1968 Humphrey ticket and who had unsuccessfully sought the presidential nomination in his own right in 1972, looks solemn and haggard as he steps out of the plane and walks across the soggy airstrip to a waiting car. He is driven a few miles to Carter's home, where he and Jane are to be houseguests. There Carter and the travel-worn Muskie sit and talk for another hour before finally calling it a night at 3:30 A.M.

9:00 A.M. Carter cheerfully taps on the door of the guest bedroom, signalling it is time for the job interview to begin. For three hours the two men confer. Muskie is not too pleased with the fact that close to half the time is spent with Carter asking him for assessments about other men on his list: Senators Frank Church of Idaho, John Glenn of Ohio, Walter Mondale of Minnesota, Henry Jackson of Washington, Adlai Stevenson of Illinois, and Congressman Peter Rodino of New Jersey.

Reporters have gathered outside the Carter home. They have been told that the two men will emerge from the talks and hold a press conference on the front lawn. Instead, Muskie and Carter emerge and head for the center of the town, where Carter takes Muskie on a handshaking tour of Main Street and his depot headquarters. As they cross the tracks, Muskie's moccasin-style shoe catches on a rail and gets left behind. Everybody stops. The towering six-foot-four Muskie leans on the compact five-foot-nine Carter, retrieves his shoe, and the walk continues. Finally they drive to the airstrip where, beside the small plane, Carter and Muskie tell reporters that they have had meaningful discussions and discovered that they had no serious differences and that Carter intends to give new and broader meaning to the job of Vice President. And Muskie, the first of the establishment to be summoned to the Court of Jimmy the First, departs.

Carter's vice-presidential selection process was complex. In all, more than seventy people were involved before Carter made up his mind. In late May, Carter's staff had compiled a list of two dozen names. Unknown to Carter, Pat Caddell and Hamilton Jordan then selected fourteen of the names and ran a poll. The results showed that none of the fourteen would significantly help or hurt a Carter ticket. Among those ultimately considered by Carter, Church and Muskie and Glenn finished near the top in name recognition. Mondale finished near the bottom, with only 30 percent recognizing his name.

June 12. Carter was handed the results of the poll. He then began to confer personally, usually by phone, with a number of influential people—"distinguished Americans," his staff called them. He eventually talked to about forty leaders of politics, business, labor, and at least two journalists (who were apparently willing to depart from the role of observers even though it meant they had become partisan advisers.)

June 17. While vacationing on Sea Island, Georgia, Carter and Charles Kirbo began to trim the list. Carter concluded that since he was from outside Washington, his running mate ought to be from within the Washington establishment. Thus governors and mayors were eliminated. When Carter and Kirbo were done, Muskie was not on the list.

June 22. Kirbo met with James Rowe, Jr., long-time adviser of Democratic presidents and the man President Johnson chose to screen Humphrey's background before he was picked as Johnson's 1964 running mate. Together they drew up questionnaires on financial and medical matters—questionnaires designed to avoid the debacles of Spiro Agnew and Thomas Eagleton.

June 28. Kirbo went to Washington. He conferred with those on the list, interviewing each and handing each a set of questionnaires. Only one person interviewed, Senator Abraham Ribicoff of Connecticut, asked that his name not be considered. While in Washington, Kirbo talked with Muskie—but as one of the "distinguished Americans" who ought to be consulted, not as a potential Vice President. He asked Muskie about other candidates and learned in the process that Muskie himself wanted to be considered and that Muskie was, in fact, upset that he had not been on Carter's list. Kirbo later conferred with Carter by phone and eventually delivered questionnaires to Muskie as well.

July 2. Kirbo conferred in Plains with Carter about his interviews with the possible running mates. The list of potentials was cut to seven. Carter had come out of the primaries leaning toward Frank Church as his choice. Church had run strong campaigns in the West, where Carter had been weak; he had run what Carter viewed as fair and honorable campaigns; he was considered a liberal but he represented a rather conservative state; and he had extensive foreign affairs experience. But a number of the "distinguished Americans" did not rate Church as highly as they rated other possible candidates.

Kirbo, meanwhile, the slow-talking Deep South lawyer whose opinion was so highly valued by Carter, had thought Scoop Jackson would make a good Vice President. Others in the party—and in the Carter camp—argued that Jackson was too hardline and conservative on foreign affairs and defense matters; they talked about the political realities and about how the liberals would feel like outcasts and would not work for a Carter–Jackson ticket. All of this was thought to have an effect on Kirbo's thinking. Meanwhile, Kirbo came away from his Washington interview of Ohio's John Glenn very much impressed by the former military officer/astronaut who had ridden his Mercury space capsule to hero status and eventually to a U.S. Senate seat. Carter began to lean favorably toward Glenn.

July 3. Carter chose to speak first with Muskie, who was by now on his list of seven, and invited him to Plains.

July 8. Morning. Walter Mondale's turn. The senator and his wife, Joan, arrived at the small airport at Americus, Georgia. The car sent by Carter to meet Mondale had not yet arrived. "Do you suppose he is trying to tell me something?" Mondale asked reporters at planeside. Eventually the escort arrived and the Mondales drove to Carter's home in Plains. Carter had always figured that Mondale was too liberal for him. Yet they hit it off very well during their three hours of discussion. Carter felt the views expressed by Mondale were very similar to his own—on the issue of busing, where Carter had thought Mondale would be too far to the left, Mondale said he favored an approach similar to that taken in Atlanta. They seemed to mesh on a variety of domestic and foreign issues. Carter was also impressed that Mondale had apparently thought out what he was going to say so that he could present his positions in a crisp and straightforward way. Moreover, the two men found that they liked each other personally—a fact which perhaps surprised each of them. They emerged from the Carter house and conducted a press conference in a rarified atmosphere of easy banter and joviality, and then strolled among the residents and the tourists in downtown Plains.

July 8. Afternoon. John Glenn arrived for his interview. Their talk was concluded in less than two hours. They walked out to Carter's front lawn for a press conference that will be remembered for swarms of gnats and bees that hovered nearby and for Carter's petulance. Carter responded angrily when a television reporter asked if the questions could be delayed "a few seconds" until his cameraman was ready. "Do you want to come up here and run this press conference?" Carter snapped. "Do you want to take over?"

Glenn was a popular figure from a pivotal midwestern state. In part due to Kirbo's report, Carter had gone into the Glenn meeting expecting to be impressed. He left the meeting feeling somewhat down. "Jimmy commented that Glenn had certainly been well prepared," said one person close to Carter, "but that Glenn had gone into such detail that it was a little hard to sit there and listen to it all."

The two men parted without taking the stroll through town.

▨ ▨ ▨

The Democratic Party convened in New York City.

Come you busted city slickers,
Better take it on the chin,

RUNNING FOR PRESIDENT

Father Knick has lost his knickers,
Give it back to the Indians.

Rogers and Hart offered that message to New Yorkers
in 1939, in their musical *Too Many Girls*.

FORD TO CITY:
DROP DEAD

President Ford offered that message to New Yorkers—
embellished in the inimical style of the *New York Daily
News* headline writers—in 1976, in his hardline handling
of the financially crippled city's efforts to stave off bank-
ruptcy. The Ford position provided ample fodder for glee-
ful Democrats in July, as they convened for what promised
to be a convention unlike any of the stormy and divided
times the party has had at more recent quadrennial gatherings.

There was no bitter fight over the presidental nomination. There was no bitter fight over the party platform.
There was no bitter fight over the convention rules or over
the delegate credentials. In short, there was no way the
television viewers at home could be sure, at a glance, that
they were watching a real Democratic National Convention. It was, in fact, not a convention at all; it was a corona-
tion. The George McGoverns were there and so were the
Richard Daleys; the Jesse Jacksons and the George Wal-
laces.

Jimmy Carter and his entourage swept into New York
on Saturday, July 10, and the candidate took up headquarters on the twenty-first floor of the Americana Hotel.
In the week that followed, the nation's eyes and ears and
minds would be focused, through the miracles of network
television, on the red-white-and-blue convention hall inside
Madison Square Garden, where a week of oratory and
pageantry was being performed. But the true place of
power that week was the twenty-first floor of the Americana—in the pale, powder-blue corridor and the individual
rooms, and mainly behind the big, polished, wooden
double doors of the Americana suite where Jimmy Carter
had established residence.

"Governor Carter's Suite. . . . Governor Carter's Suite.
. . . Governor Carter's Suite. . . . Governor Carter's

Suite. . . ." A bank of receptionists had been set up in a room off the corridor, politely answering telephone calls coming in through the convention and hotel switchboards and taking messages that Carter would never see. "Every important political person and a lot of those you never heard of are trying to get through to Jimmy now," said one staff member. "You wouldn't believe it."

Carter did not return any of these phone calls. Instead, Greg Schneiders or Pat Caddell would stop by the switchboard on a regular, alternating basis and collect the messages. They would see to it that the calls were returned the same day by a high-ranking member of the Carter staff (not just a volunteer), and pertinent information was then passed on, if absolutely necessary, to Carter.

(Separate telephone lines were installed in Carter's suite. These phone numbers were given out to only a handful of people—perhaps ten—including Democratic National Committee Chairman Robert Strauss.)

Carter's official inaccessibility kicked a sizeable burden over to senior members of the Carter staff, especially Hamilton Jordan, his campaign director. Failing to get through to Carter personally, most of the Democratic dignitaries would try to score with Jordan. And this in turn placed a large burden on Jordan's administrative assistant, Caroline Wellons, who months before had mastered the art of maintaining unflappable cool and magnolia politeness in the most hectic of pressure circumstances. (Wellons was always Jordan's administrative assistant; but because she was a woman, she found herself often being called Jordan's "secretary"—and the problem with that was that many of the heavy politicos who called wanted to speak to someone who had more clout than just a secretary; they wanted to speak to someone like an administrative assistant, and it was hard for them to realize that few people in the Carter organization had more influence with Hamilton Jordan than did Wellons. "I wish you *were* a secretary," Jordan once mock-fumed at Wellons, who like most administrative assistants had neither typing or shorthand skills. "Then I wouldn't have to do all my own typing.")

The twenty-first floor. Elevators did not stop there. Access was gained by going to the twentieth floor, which was also staff headquarters, and then being screened and gaining clearance to walk around a guard-post table and walk up a bare concrete stairwell to the twenty-first. Members of the Carter entourage and been issued a variety of color-coded passes. But only a few of those were good for entry to the twenty-first floor.

The twenty-first floor. For all its aura of elite, it was not a very palatial place. There were Secret Service agents guarding doors and passageways; there was also a guy strolling the corridor barechested. There was a procession of dignitaries who were being granted appointments with the near-nominee; there was also a man with a grocery bag filled with six-packs, returning from a nighttime mercy mission for his friends.

Security was vigilant. When Hamilton Jordan arrived in New York, the Manhattan-based security operatives did not recognize him and would not permit him to enter his own offices or room until one of his assistants came down to vouch for the boss. So too with Jody Powell. He arrived credentialless and was permitted entry only when his wife, Nan, who had arrived ahead of time and had her proper pass, came down and assured security personnel that she would see to it that her husband behaved properly.

Security was fast. Pat Caddell, who can organize complex polling operations but has trouble with the monotonies of life, somehow managed to lose his color-coded credentials somewhere between the door of his room on the twenty-first floor and the bottom of the stairwell on the twentieth. Within an hour, security experts had changed the locks on Caddell's door, lest the credentials had fallen into the wrong hands.

And consider the case of the man with the bag full of beer. A middle-aged-looking woman with blond hair was staffing the checkpoint at the table on the twentieth floor and she had heard all of the lines before—a score of gate-crashers (some of them highly placed) had to be turned away at the checkpoint every hour. So she was understandably wary—but inexplicably rude—when the man came with the six-packs, just as Jody Powell had asked him to, so the Carter hierarchy could sit around and sip beer and watch the convention that night. The man with the beer told her that he was expected by Powell on the twenty-first floor and asked her to phone up and check with him. The woman instead lied: "Mister Powell's not here. He's at the convention hall." The man with the bag said he knew better. The woman made a telephone call and reported back: "You can leave the beer but you can't go upstairs yourself." The man with the bag said he was a friend of Powell's and Powell had invited him to come up too. Finally the woman agreed to make the proper phone call to Powell; she was told that indeed the beer man was to be escorted upstairs to see Powell and only then did she relent, unsmiling.

To the Democratic heavies and hangers-on down below, the twenty-first floor seemed to be the essential place to be, the citadel of what C. Wright Mills would have recognized as "The Power Elite." But those on the twenty-first floor saw little mystique. "Access to the twenty-first floor was sort of like sex," Greg Schneiders observed. "It didn't seem very important except to the people who didn't have it."

Among those who were granted audiences with Carter on the twenty-first floor were delegations of women, Spanish-speaking Americans, and prominent blacks. When the Latins came in, Carter did a little talking in Spanish. When the blacks came in, he spoke to them in plain English. The black delegation pushed two basic points: (1) they wanted Carter to keep Basil Patterson as vice chairman of the Democratic National Committee—Carter indicated that he would; and (2) they were unhappy that Carter had not at least considered Los Angeles Mayor Thomas Bradley, a black, among the finalists for Vice President. Carter said that he had concluded that he wanted a man from Washington, D.C., and that because of this he had excluded all governors and mayors. Jesse Jackson, one of the blacks, said, according to others in the room, something to the effect that he had not expected that Carter would wind up picking Bradley, "but it would have made all of us proud to see a black man get off the airplane in Plains, Georgia." The line of reasoning left Carter somewhat stunned and he said so. Carter told them that he had not wanted to act out a charade, that it would not have been honest to make it appear that the black mayor had a chance when in fact he did not because he had no Washington experience.

■   ■   ■

The only suspense at the Democratic Convention was the anticipation as to who Carter would choose as his running mate. In his Americana suite, Carter interviewed the four other Washington-based "finalists," although they were largely, by that time, pro forma interviews. There was Frank Church, who had once led Carter's list, but who had gradually slipped in part because of the reservations of some of the "distinguished Americans" and in part because Carter and his staff were turned off by people who had been lobbying hard for Church behind the scenes —among them Carter's finance chairman, Morris Dees. There was Senator Adlai Stevenson, who was considered too colorless, but who was being considered largely because he was Mayor Richard Daley's man (he was known by some politicians as "Dick Daley's pet rock"). There was Scoop Jackson, who had fought Carter and lost and had come out in support of Carter when he needed it; but Jackson was considered too conservative to be included on the Carter ticket. And there was Congressman Peter Rodino, who promptly took himself out of consideration by telling Carter he feared that a recurrence of glaucoma would make it difficult for him to campaign. Rodino asked Carter to keep the matter confidential; but at a press conference the next day, a reporter asked Carter a question and the former governor acknowledged that one of the seven finalists had indeed asked that his name be withdrawn from the list. Carter left the conference with reporters pursuing him to the elevator asking him to supply the name. Carter stepped into the elevator. "Maybe Jody will have something for you later," he said as the door closed leaving the reporters outside. Up in his suite on the twenty-first floor, Carter located Rodino by phone. He explained what he had let slip and said that he would like to supply the name, since he had gone that far already—if Rodino did not object. It had gone too far to stop. Rodino consented.

■   ■   ■

From the day he arrived in Manhattan, Carter had been getting hints that some of the party's leaders—principally Robert Strauss—would like to see him choose Muskie. Muskie would help him with the Catholics and people of European ethnic origins, where polls were showing Carter was weak; also, Muskie's extensive knowledge of the federal bureaucracy and budget problems would prove useful.

But in the last days before Carter was to make his selection, the vice-presidential finalists were all being careful so as not to make it appear that they were doing anything overt to try to campaign for the job. All they wanted to do was to drop out of sight and keep their names and faces out of the newspapers for a couple of days—lest Carter think someone was trying to mount a public relations pressure campaign. Television networks and some newspapers, meanwhile, tried to keep watch over the activities of the frontrunners.

Among those who tried to live a low-key existence was Muskie. *Newsday* Washington correspondent Myron S. Waldman was keeping track of Muskie, and he filed this report to his editors:

> On his way to his Gotham Hotel headquarters . . . Muskie told a reporter he intended to go to a museum with his wife, Jane, but didn't know which one. He added that he did not much care for modern art. About half an hour later, his press secretary told reporters that Muskie had decided not to reveal where he was going.
>
> Reporters walked out of the hotel and hired two taxis to wait with meters running. The sight of reporters and a television truck caused pedestrians to stop. As the crowd gathered, the doorman came out. He was nervous. "Please clear the sidewalk," he said.
>
> A television crew began to film the crowd it had helped to create. This brought more pedestrians to a halt. A policeman arrived to control the crowd. The excitement among reporters grew. Would Muskie go to the museum or not?
>
> Soon Muskie and his wife emerged. The crowd cheered. No, he would not tell a reporter where he was going. The reporter and his colleagues raced for the

cabs. Muskie got into a station wagon. The ABC television truck pulled out. And the chase began.

Up 56th Street and left on Madison Avenue the parade proceeded, cabbies cursing, running red lights and defying buses whose drivers tried to cut into Muskie's reluctant entourage. A technician leaned out of the ABC truck and filmed the fleeing station wagon. Finally, at Madison and 75th, the station wagon stopped in front of the Whitney Museum. "You're spoiling our fun," Mrs. Muskie complained.

Inside, the Muskies, tailed by television cameras and reporters, immediately began the tour of the exhibit, "Two Hundred Years of American Sculpture," conducted by Paterson Sims, curator of the museum's permanent collection. Sims, a young red-bearded man in a gray sweater and ascot, led the Muskies through the modern section first.

He showed them crushed auto parts. He showed them bricks. He showed them a Martinson's coffee can filled with paint brushes. "That's like your Hole In One Award," Mrs. Muskie said to her husband.

Someone mentioned that the exhibit had gotten a bad review. "I've never read a review as mean as that," Sims said. "Have you read any of mine?" Muskie asked.

Later, the Muskies toured primitives and older sculptures crafted in a style of realism, among them a statue of a beast in which was hidden a device which, when activated, expressed a single point of view.

"Interesting," Muskie said when asked afterwards how he felt about modern art now. "I enjoyed that animal who stuck his tongue out at us. His instincts were similar to mine."

      ▬   ▬   ▬

The drama of the Democratic National Convention had come down to this: Muskie or Mondale. Carter had narrowed the field down to the two senators. Carter had been leaning away from Glenn since they had talked in Plains—there was concern on the Carter staff about Glenn's use of income tax shelters; and there was some concern that a ticket that would feature two former military officers would provoke criticism. "That ticket didn't sound quite right," joked a Carter confidant. "Carter–Glenn sounds like a middle-income housing development."

There were powerful forces urging Muskie and powerful reasons to back up their views, primarily the Catholic ethnic balance he would bring, shoring up Carter where he was weakest among Democratic voters. But Peter Rodino had told Carter forcefully on Monday that he did not need to put a Catholic on the ticket to appeal to the Catholic and ethnic vote—as long as he had prominent Catholics campaigning for the ticket. Rodino said he would campaign for Carter regardless. Carter was also concerned about Muskie's legendary hair-trigger temper, and by reports that he was at times unnecessarily harsh on his staff.

"It was down to whether Jimmy should be safe and go with Muskie or politically bold and go with Mondale," one Carter aide said. "The chemistry with Mondale had been very good and, like Jimmy, he would be a whole new face on the national scene. That cut it for him, I guess."

July 15. As he had promised, Carter telephoned those he did not pick on Thursday morning to let them know the decision had gone against them. This was, in one instance, a difficult thing to do.

Jimmy Carter's personal assistant, Greg Schneiders, reached for the phone at 8:40 A.M. and dialed the New York Sheraton Hotel.

He asked for the room number John Glenn's staff had provided. Carter had to break the news to Glenn that he had chosen another to be his vice-presidential running mate.

The number rang. No answer.

Schneiders explained to the hotel operator, that "Governor Carter needs to talk to Senator Glenn right away. Is there another number where we can reach the senator?"

"We're not allowed to give out that information," the operator replied.

She agreed to ring the other number herself, however, But the number was busy. Schneiders waited. She tried again. Still busy.

Schneiders explained that this was a very important call

that Jimmy Carter was making to John Glenn and could she please break in on the busy line? Glenn would want very much to speak with Carter, Schneiders told her. No, she said, hotel policy.

Schneiders asked her to please send someone upstairs to tell Glenn to hang up the phone. The New York Sheraton operator refused.

Five minutes later, Glenn's phone was free, Schneiders got the call through and put Carter on the line, and Carter told Glenn the news he did not really want to hear.

Carter also called Fritz Mondale.

"Did I wake you up?" Carter asked. "Would you like to run with me?"

     🏴   🏴   🏴

Carter had won his nomination. He had picked his running mate. That night he would stand before the convention (and before America and the world) and deliver the most important speech he had ever made, before the largest audience he had ever faced. But before that, Carter had some friends to thank. So shortly after announcing his selection of Mondale, he walked across the street to the City Squire Hotel to the Georgia delegation's caucus. There, in a room crowded with more than 200 people, Carter offered emotional words of thanks. At one point his eyes filled with tears and his voice broke as he spoke to the people of his state.

"When I announced and began to campaign for the the highest elective office, perhaps in the world, nineteen months ago, not many people thought I had a chance, but a lot of you thought I had a chance [cheers].

"There were a lot of times when I was lonely. There were a lot of times when there was a great deal of doubt. We had some serious setbacks, and I made some mistakes, but I never had a feeling of loneliness or withdrawal or isolation or abandonment from the people of Georgia.

"For about eight months, I was by myself. But later, when the going really got tough, you just can't imagine how it made me feel to get off a small airplane in an isolated airport and see some of you, standing there—" his voice broke completely; he was on the verge of tears, but did not cry—"with signs waving back and forth in the snow and to see the expressions of friendship and support for me. I could not have carried New Hampshire, which was a close election, without you, and I could not have carried Florida, which was a close election, without you. I could not have carried Wisconsin, which was a close election, without you.

"The strength of our political effort has been the closeness between me personally and voters around the country. Women in the shoe factories and textile mills. And men driving trucks and making electronics equipment and working on farms and cutting hair and waitresses in restaurants. To a substantial degree they felt they could have confidence in me and that I was close to them. And there wasn't any powerful political figure that stood between them and, possibly, the next President. And I'll never shake that intensely personal relationship, because I want to be sure that when I am in the White House the American people feel: that's my President."

▨　　▨　　▨

Congressman Andrew Young, the bright, forceful Atlantan who was once a deputy of Martin Luther King, Jr., and who had been an early Carter supporter, also spoke before the Georgia delegation.

"Back in January, 1975, when Jimmy Carter announced he was running for President, I was there at the Hyatt Regency in Atlanta and I introduced Jimmy. Last week, when I was starting to get my notes together for the seconding speech [which Young gave for Carter at the convention], I thought it might be interesting to hear what I had said about Jimmy way back in the beginning. So I called my friend Aubrey Morris at [radio station] WSB in Atlanta, and I said, 'Aubrey, could I listen to your tape of that press conference?' Well, he laughed and he said to me, 'Andy, we didn't keep that tape because we didn't think Carter was going anywhere.' "

▨　　▨　　▨

Back in his suite on the twenty-first floor of the Americana, Carter had little to do except rehearse his speech for that night. For that he needed mostly privacy. Carter walked into the grand-scale living room, shut the large wooden double doors behind him, and then for good measure he slid some furniture over against the doors, building a barricade that would assure against unwanted interruption. There, in fortified privacy, Carter rehearsed a speech that had been put together through more than a month of painstaking drafting.

On July 2, Patrick Anderson had arrived in Plains with the first draft. Carter read the text that night and the next day, Saturday, he told his speechwriter he wanted to write a draft that would be his own. He asked Anderson to telephone people around the country and get them to make suggestions, offer ideas, even contribute a few paragraphs or an overall theme. Talk to some young people, Carter said. Talk to some bright people. Carter was torn between two concepts: since this was the most important speech of his life to date, he wanted it to be truly his; yet he also wanted a wide range of ideas to work with.

That afternoon, Anderson sat in the study of Carter's home and began working the telephone.

He called Washington and spoke to Henry Owen, who had been the head of planning in the State Department under Dean Rusk and was now at the Brookings Institution.

He called New York and spoke to Theodore Sorensen, who had been a speechwriter for John Kennedy and who has been credited with having written the inaugural address line: "Ask not what your country can do for you; ask what you can do for your country."

He called Vermont and spoke to Olin Robison, president of the Middlebury College.

He called Boston and spoke to Patrick Caddell, public opinion analyst and all-purpose adviser to Carter. And he spoke once more with Stuart Eizenstat, Carter's issues adviser.

Throughout the Fourth of July festivities, Anderson worked out of the study at Carter's house, set back among the trees at 1 Woodland Drive. From time to time, Anderson would type the suggested phrases, passages, and themes, and forward them to Carter.

The following Friday, several days after Anderson

handed Carter the last of the outside opinions, Carter
presented his speechwriter and Jody Powell with a draft
—twenty-five pages written by Carter in longhand on a
yellow legal pad. He had incorporated some of the suggestions and portions of the original Anderson draft, but
the work, several Carter aides later said, was now very
much a Jimmy Carter production. (The yellow legal pad.
It was the instrument on which Richard Nixon wrote his
speeches affirming Vietnam and denying Watergate. Said
one Carter adviser: "Not even Nixon can ruin the yellow
legal pad.")

Carter asked Powell and Anderson for their criticisms
of the work. The two men had some. Carter flew to the
convention in New York and Anderson began working
on a third draft, based on Carter's version plus talks with
Caddell, Eizenstat, and Adam Walinsky, who had written
for Robert Kennedy, and Ted VanDyk, who had written
for Hubert Humphrey. At 6:00 P.M. Sunday Carter asked
for the latest draft. At 9:00 P.M. Sunday, he got it.

Carter worked on the draft Monday night. Tuesday at
5:00 P.M. he met with Powell, Caddell, Rafshoon, Anderson, and a few others in his suite on the twenty-first
floor at the Americana Hotel. They went over a typewrit-
ten draft of the speech, line by line.

Carter and his men had carefully worked a number of
lines into the speech that would appeal to the Catholic
and ethnic voters. "Ours is the party that welcomed generations of immigrants—the Jews, the Irish, the Italians
[Carter pronounced it "eye-talians"], the Poles, and all the
others—enlisted them into its ranks, and fought the
political battles that helped bring them into the American
mainstream—and they have shaped the character of our
party."

Also: "We *can* have an America that encourages and
takes pride in our ethnic diversity, our religious diversity,
and our cultural diversity. . . ."

And there was a passage which hailed America's immigrants as "the best and the bravest." During a drafting
session, one Carter adviser took issue with the phrase. It
was not historically accurate, he insisted, "They just were
not often the best and the bravest."

Carter looked up and offered a crisp reply: "Well, *you* go tell Pete Rodino that his father was the worst."

The phrase stayed.

≡ ≡ ≡

The drafting process of this major political speech had itself been heavy on politics. Representatives and advocates of specific blocs and interest groups had been urging —even demanding—that Carter include words of praise for this group or that. Before it was over, drafts had been shown to people who had written for two generations of leading Democrats—writers for John Kennedy, Robert Kennedy, Lyndon Johnson, Hubert Humphrey. "They kept saying Jimmy's going to blow it, that there should be more of this and less of that," recalled one Carter man. "But they were looking for a JFK-type speech, and this was not JFK, it was Jimmy Carter."

The final speech wound up with one passage that was purely the product of Kennedy-man Theodore Sorensen. "It is time for America to move and to speak, not with boasting and belligerence, but with a quiet strength—to depend in world affairs not merely on the size of an arsenal but on the nobility of ideas—and to govern at home not by confusion and crisis, but with grace and imagination and common sense."

But the speech was, in the end, Jimmy Carter. Among the passages he penned in longhand and retained throughout the drafting process were these trademarks of his own populist appeal:

"We should make our major investments in people, not in buildings and weapons. The poor, the weak, the aged, the afflicted must be treated with respect and compassion and with love."

And a flat, no-frills statement on jail reform: "I see no reason why big-shot crooks should go free while the poor ones go to jail."

July 15. Night. This is a Democratic National Convention like none other in the party's modern history. A Democratic convention without warfare. Without bitterness. Without rancor. Without division. Without a liberal-conservative split or a North-South split. Without one side going home in bitterness determined to sit on its hands until after November.

This is the convention where the Deep South is welcomed back to the party. Welcomed back after it had captured it. But it is more. It is also the convention where the Democratic liberals and conservatives decided to stand together and cheer together, regardless of the ideology or sloganeering that had prompted the applause.

Nowhere was the new Democratic unity more obvious than in the first seat, right, of the Illinois delegation. This was the seat of the chairman of the Illinois delegation, the man who came back, Richard J. Daley, mayor and still boss.

It is 9:25 P.M. and the convention is awaiting the arrival of Jimmy Carter. A couple of Chicago toughs—bodyguards for the boss—lock arms around the mayor's aisle chair, so a reporter cannot get near to ask a question. Daley has asked for a glass of water and he is clearing his throat and wetting the dryness that has settled in his mouth. "Jesus, you picked a helluva rotten time to want to do an interview," says the bodyguard in the brown suit. "He's not going to do it. Not now."

Somebody has just passed word to the mayor that the first thing Jimmy Carter will do upon entering the Garden is walk up the aisle and shake Daley's hand. It will be a symbolic gesture that the past is buried and that the mayor who was unceremoniously thrown out of the Illinois delegation by the liberals who ran things in 1972 is back again in good graces and great power.

"It's a great satisfaction for the mayor to come back and prove he was right," says William Lee, president of the AFL-CIO in Chicago and probably Daley's oldest friend in the Illinois delegation.

"Mayor Daley never was gone really," says Adeline P. Keane, who has taken the delegate seat of her husband, Chicago Alderman Thomas Keane, the Daley ally who would be there himself except for the fact that he is now in jail on a conflict-of-interest charge.

"The Mayor's never been down," says Senator Richard J. Daley, Jr., who refers to his father by his father's title.

"He never looks back. He figures 'That's life.' He's been building toward his present position since 1928, when he went to his first convention."

A couple of other reporters have come over to the Illinois delegation. One is Dan Rather of CBS, who was reporting at the Chicago convention in 1968 when Daley's police rioted and smashed demonstrators—the hectic convention where television caught Daley making an obscene gesture at a speaker who was denouncing the police tactics. Now, from midway in the Illinois delegation, a man in a very white sportcoat says to a man in a very white suit, "that Rather's got a helluva lot of nerve showing up at the Illinois delegation. Let him go stand with the kookies."

Carter arrives at the hall. Daley clears his throat and straightens his jacket. But Carter, led by his security men, turns left instead of right and heads straight for the podium instead of straight for Daley. Daley leans over to his candidate for governor, Michael J. Howlett, and shrugs. "Life is full of surprises," Daley says, and he begins to applaud the party's nominee, pounding his hands so hard that the wattles beneath his jowls commence to quiver.

      ≋   ≋   ≋

As Carter made his way to the microphone, reporters in the press grandstand areas flanking the podium began rereading the advance text of the speech text provided to them by Carter aides. What they did not know was that there were a couple of passages that were in Carter's own text that were not included in the texts prepared for the reporters. These were the few light touches that had been submitted by two Hollywood comedy writers—Jack Kaplan (who used to work for Jerry Rafshoon's ad agency) and his associate, John Barrett—who had been flown in to bring a few smiles to the Carter epic. "We left them out of the press texts because it would look, well, too corny to have them in," a Carter assistant explained.

Kaplan and Barrett had presented their comedy offerings to Carter in short memos, hand printed in capital letters on a yellow legal pad. For all the drafting and consulting that went into the speech, for all the efforts of all the highly regarded political speechwriters, it was a memo by the two Hollywood writers that produced the most famous, most frequently quoted passage of Jimmy Carter's nomination speech of 1976. The memo, from Kaplan and Barrett to Carter, came complete with parenthetical cues and stage directions.

(AFTER THANK YOUs, JIMMY TURNS TO AUDIENCE AND SAYS:) HELLO, I'M JIMMY CARTER. (LAUGH) AND I'M RUNNING FOR PRESIDENT OF THE UNITED STATES. (APPLAUSE).

Appendix One

Memorandum

To: Jimmy Carter
From: Hamilton Jordan
August 4, 1974

Personal and Confidential

I think we have reached the stage in our efforts where we should pause to assess our progress to this point and take a hard and realistic look at the future. I have attempted in the following pages to review the major aspects of our effort and to set forth some realistic detailed plans for the next several months. . . .

Pre-announcement activities

We will need to develop a system of informing key individuals and certain groups either in advance of the actual announcement or simultaneous with it. For the purpose of discussion, I divide the individuals you should personally talk with and/or notify into several groups. First, there is that group of key individuals who are politically significant or who are potential entrepreneurs or friends of yours, and who will be flattered and possibly persuaded to support your candidacy because you have chosen to personally confide in them. . . .

The second group are politically significant people who you know and who are friendly to you but are **not** likely to respond to being told of your plans with a pledge of support. This includes leaders in major labor unions and politically active national organizations, certain newspaper and magazine publishers, certain Democratic members of Congress, some Democratic governors and key Democratic activists. . . . The people I am talking about in this group are Al Barkan, Mike Mansfield, Katherine Graham, Carl Albert, Joe Crangle, and others of this sort.

. . . The third group of people to be notified are the Democratic members of Congress, Democratic governors and mayors, state party chairmen, members of the Democratic National Committee, and key Democratic Party workers and activists. My suggestion here is that we send a high-quality, personalized mailing to these people that would arrive simultaneous with your announcement. The message would be positive . . . [concerning] your commitment to run anywhere against anybody and convincing in terms of analyzing your prospects for winning the party's nomination. This mailing would not ask for money, but would ask for their advice and/or their support. . . .

The fourth group are our Georgia friends and supporters. We have computer tapes with the names of 8,000 persons who have contributed to your campaign and/or the Democratic Party. . . .

The fifth group of people to be contacted are your key out-of-state friends who are not necessarily Democrats and not necessarily active in politics but have met you somewhere along the way and had a favorable contact or experience with you. This should be a personal mailing which asks for their help and financial support.

The last group of people to be contacted are the large number of out-of-state names that we have accumulated from the last four years. These range from a trooper who drove you several years ago in Ohio to a businessman who met you at a prayer breakfast in Oklahoma to a woman that met you at a Democratic meeting in New York. By late November, Steve and I estimate that you will have 13,000–15,000 names that fall into this broad and very general contact. They should receive a positive, friendly letter which asks for their help and money. . . .

Announcement statement

When you consider how jaded and cynical the members of the national press corps have become and think about all the cliches and doubletalk they are presently hearing from ambitious politicians, then possibly you can imagine the challenge you have to say something that is fresh, bold, and believable. I will not attempt to write your speech here—that is something that should evolve from you, Jody, Stu, and the issues group.

Outline pragmatic strategy for winning Democratic nomination

It is our hope that your being the first to announce will result in your receiving a disproportionate amount of press coverage initially. Your being covered on a continuing basis and being treated as a serious, viable candidate depends to a large extent on your being able to convince the working press that you can—in fact—win the Democratic nomination. Consequently . . . [emphasize that] you are totally committed to the race and will run against anyone anywhere. You will run against Wallace in the South, Kennedy in New England.

Time and place

I believe that we have generally agreed that you should announce your candidacy for the Presidency the week following the Charter Conference in Washington, D.C. It was tentatively agreed that we should pursue the possibility of the press club announcement at least to the point of determining if that is—in fact—one of our options. . . . On the same day or next day I believe that it is important that we have some function here in Georgia where you announce your plans to our friends in Georgia. It is terribly important that you "share" your announcement with the Georgia people to avoid [it] being said that Jimmy Carter has gone national and has forgotten his state and people. . . .

We should never forget that our early announcement is a tactical maneuver which will hopefully result in your receiving inordinate amounts of coverage and publicity.

Your schedule between now and December

. . . We would all do well to keep the primary schedule uppermost in our minds—particularly in terms of your schedule in out-of-state trips. It doesn't make sense to worry about West Virginia and Oregon if you haven't first [done] some work in Illinois and Pennsylvania. . . .

Relationship with Strauss and the DNC

We are laboring under one handicap at present that is not particularly significant now, but it will become more significant with the passage of time and increasingly difficult to correct or overcome. We lack having a strong Carter supporter on the inside of the Party apparatus to keep generally informed and [who] can effectively advocate a point of view on important matters that is favorable to you.

. . . Almost every potential Democratic candidate has someone on the executive committee who is close to them except us. . . . At an appropriate time—right up to the 1974 election—you need to discuss your plans with Strauss anyway. I think you can make the argument to Strauss that you are entitled to have representation on those committees which make the major decisions which will impact on the nomination process—particularly in view of the fact that most of the other potential candidates already have supporters on the executive committee in the DNC. . . .

Application of the targeting concept to a national campaign

In our national campaign to win the Democratic nomination for President, there are three major factors to be considered—the relative **size** of the state and the delegation to the Democratic National Convention, the **sequence** of the primaries and the **sequence** of the delegate selection process in the non-primary states, and our own campaign **strategy.** . . .

Sequence

Primary states: Sequence or chronological order of the

primaries are important for obvious reasons. Good or poor showings can have a profound and irrevocable impact on succeeding primaries and a campaign's ability to raise funds and recruit workers.

The press shows an exaggerated interest in the early primaries as they represent the first confrontation between candidates, their contrasting strategies and styles, which the press has been writing and speculating about for two years. We would do well to understand the very special and powerful role the press plays in interpreting the primary results for the rest of the nation. What is actually accomplished in [the] New Hampshire primary is less important than how the press interprets it for the nation. Handled properly, a defeat can be interpreted as a "holding action" and a victory as a mediocre showing. I remember the McCarthy–McGovern campaign in '72 and '68 as "victories" when in fact they ran second to Muskie and Johnson.

Non-primary states: The sequence of the selection of delegates in the non-primary states is important, but more as a test of organizational ability than as a test of the candidates and their campaigns. The initial delegate selections will generate some news stories and will be important, but in the long run they will take a back seat to the coverage of the primaries and will be significant in relation to the number of delegates being selected and its impact on the delegate totals of the various candidates. . . .

Strategy

. . . The strategy outlined below is general and tentative. The real value of this exercise is to develop a system for testing this and other strategies.

a. Early primaries. The prospect of a crowded field coupled with the new proportional representation rule does not permit much flexibility in the early primaries. No serious candidate will have the luxury of picking or choosing among the early primaries. To pursue such a strategy would cost that candidate delegate votes and increase the possibility of being lost in the crowd. I think that we have to assume that everybody will be running in the first five or six primaries.

A crowded field enhances the possibility of several inconclusive primaries with four or five candidates separated by only a few percentage points. Such a muddled picture will not continue for long as the press will begin to make "winners" of some and "losers" of others. The intense press coverage which naturally focuses on the early primaries plus the decent time intervals which separate the March and mid-April primaries dictates a serious effort in all of the first five primaries. Our "public" strategy would probably be that Florida was the first and real test of the Carter campaign and that New Hampshire would just be a warm-up. In fact, a strong, surprise showing in New Hampshire should be our goal which would have tremendous impact on successive primaries.

Our minimal goal in these early primaries would be to gain acceptance as a serious and viable candidate, demonstrate that Wallace is vulnerable and that Carter can appeal to the "Wallace" constituency, and show through our campaign a contrasting style and appeal. Our minimal goal would dictate at least a second-place showing in New Hampshire and Florida and respectable showings in Wisconsin, Rhode Island, and Illinois. Our national goals (which I think are highly attainable) would be to win New Hampshire and/or Florida outright, make strong showings in the other three early primary states and beat Wallace.

b. April and May primaries. The late April and early May primaries will dictate difficult and strategic deficiencies on the allocation of resources. Lack of funds in time will restrict us from running a personal campaign in every state. Hopefully, good press in the early primaries will have solved some of our name recognition and given Jimmy Carter some depth to his new national image. Nonetheless, there will still be ten primaries in two weeks. If, by this point, we have knocked Wallace off in left field in a primary or two, we will be in a strong position to raise funds and enter them all. The result of the first primaries are not likely to be conclusive, and we will be in a position of making some tough decisions that can win or lose a Democratic nomination.

Appendix Two

Remarks by Governor Carter at the
Martin Luther King, Jr. Hospital
Los Angeles, June 1, 1976

We are here today to honor a man with a dream.

We are here to honor a man who lived and died for the cause of human brotherhood.

Martin Luther King, Jr., was the conscience of his generation.

He was a doctor to a sick society.

He was a prophet of a new and better America.

He was a southerner, a black man, who in his too-short life stood with Presidents and kings, and was honored around the world, but who never forgot the poor people, the oppressed people, who were his brothers and sisters and from whom he drew his strength.

He was the man, more than any other of his generation, who gazed upon the great wall of segregation and saw that it could be destroyed by the power of love.

I sometimes think that a southerner of my generation can most fully understand the meaning and the impact of Martin Luther King's life.

He and I grew up in the same South, he the son of a clergyman, I the son of a farmer. We both knew, from opposite sides, the invisible wall of racial segregation.

The official rule then was "separate but equal," but in truth we were neither—not separate, not equal.

When I was a boy, almost all my playmates were black. We worked in the fields together, and hunted and fished and swam together, but when it was time for church or for school, we went our separate ways, without really understanding why.

Our lives were dominated by unspoken, unwritten, but powerful rules, rules that were almost never challenged.

A few people challenged them, not in politics, but in the way they lived their lives. My mother was one of those people. She was a nurse. She would work twelve hours a day and then come home and care for her family and minister to the people of our little community, both black and white.

My mother knew no color line. Her black friends were just as welcome in her home as her white friends, a fact that shocked some people, sometimes even my father, who was very conventional in his views on race.

I left Georgia in 1943 and went off to the navy and by the time I returned home ten years later, the South and the nation had begun to change.

The change was slow and painful. After the Supreme Court outlawed school segregation, the wrong kind of politicians stirred up angry resistance, and little towns like mine were torn apart by fear and resentment.

Yet the change was coming. Across the South, courageous young black students demanded service at segregated lunch counters. And in the end they prevailed.

In Montgomery, a woman named Rosa Parks refused to move to the back of the bus, a young clergyman named Martin Luther King joined the protest, and a movement had found its leader.

In 1961, we had a new President, John Kennedy, who responded to the demands of the civil rights movement, and who used the power of his office to enforce court orders at the University of Alabama and the University of Mississippi, and who by the last year of his life was giving moral leadership in the struggle for equal rights.

In August of 1963 Martin Luther King stood on the steps of the Lincoln Memorial in Washington and told a quarter of a million people of his dream for America.

"I have a dream," he said. "I have a dream that one day on the red hills of Georgia, sons of former slaves and sons of former slaveowners will be able to sit down together at the table of brotherhood."

"I have a dream", he said, "that my four little children will one day live in a nation where they will not be judged by the color of their skin but by the content of their character. I have a dream."

And so the dream was born. The challenge was made. The rest was up to America.

Three months after Dr. King's speech, President Kennedy was dead, and we had a new President, a Texan, a man whom many black people distrusted. But soon Lyndon Johnson stood before the Congress of the United States and promised, "We shall overcome!"

Lyndon Johnson carried forward the dream of equality. He used his political genius to pass the voting rights bill, a bill that was the best thing that happened to the South in my lifetime. The voting rights act did not just guarantee the vote for black people. It liberated the South, both black and white. It made it possible for the South to come out of the past and into the mainstream of American politics.

It made it possible for a southerner to stand before you this evening as a serious candidate for President of the United States.

But war came, and destroyed Lyndon Johnson's Great Society. Martin Luther King spoke out against the war. There were those who told him to keep silent, who told him he would undercut his prestige if he opposed the war, but he followed his conscience and spoke his mind.

Then in the spring of 1968 he went to Memphis to help the garbage workers get a decent wage, to help the men who did the dirtiest job for the lowest pay, and while he was there he was shot and killed.

But his dream lives on.

Perhaps some of you remember the night of Dr. King's death. Robert Kennedy was in Indianapolis, running for President, speaking before a black audience. At that point, on that awful night, Robert Kennedy was perhaps the only white politician in America who could have spoken to black people and been listened to.

Let me tell you what he said.

He said, "What we need in the United States is not division, what we need in the United States is not hatred, what we need in the United States is not violence and lawlessness, but love and wisdom and compassion toward one another, and a feeling of justice toward those who still suffer within our country, whether they be white or whether they be black."

Those words are still true today.

We lost Martin Luther King.

We lost Robert Kennedy.

We lost the election that year to men who governed without love or laughter, to men who promised law and order and gave us crime and oppression.

But the dream lived on.

It could be slowed, but never stopped.

In Atlanta, a young man named Andrew Young, who had been Martin Luther King's strong right hand, was elected to the Congress of the United States.

All over America, black men and women were carrying the dream forward into politics.

In Georgia, when I was governor, we appointed black people to jobs and judgeships they had never held before, and one day we hung a portrait of Martin Luther King, Jr., in our state capitol.

There were protests, but they didn't matter. Inside our state capitol, Coretta King and Daddy King and Andy Young and I and hundreds of others joined hands and sang "We Shall Overcome."

And we shall.

I stand before you, a candidate for President, a man whose life has been lifted, as yours have been, by the dream of Martin Luther King.

When I started to run for President, there were those who said I would fail, because I am from the South.

But I thought they were wrong. I thought the South was changing and America was changing, I thought the dream was taking hold.

And I ran for President throughout our nation.

We have won in the South, and we have won in the North, and now we come to the West and we ask your help.

For all our progress, we still live in a land held back by oppression and injustice.

The few who are rich and powerful still make the decisions, and the many who are poor and weak must suffer the consequences. If those in power make mistakes, it is not they or their families who lose their jobs or go on welfare or lack medical care or go to jail.

We still have poverty in the midst of plenty.

We still have far to go. We must give our government back to our people. The road will not be easy.

But we still have the dream, Martin Luther King's dream and your dream and my dream. The America we long for is still out there, somewhere ahead of us, waiting for us to find her.

I see an America poised not only at the brink of a new century, but at the dawn of a new era of honest, compassionate, responsive government.

I see an American government that has turned away from scandals and corruption and cynicism and finally become as decent as our people.

I see an America with a tax system that does not steal from the poor and give to the rich.

I see an America with a job for every man and woman who can work, and a decent standard of living for those who cannot.

I see an America in which my child and your child and every child receives an education second to none in the world.

I see an American government that does not spy on its citizens or harass its citizens, but respects your dignity and your privacy and your right to be let alone.

I see an American foreign policy that is firm and consistent and generous, and that once again is a beacon for the hopes of the world.

I see an American President who does not govern by vetoes and negativism, but with vigor and vision and affirmative leadership, a President who is not isolated from our people, but feels their pain and shares their dreams and takes his strength from them.

I see an America in which Martin Luther King's dream is our national dream.

I see an America on the move again, united, its wounds healed, its head high, a diverse and vital nation, moving into its third century with confidence and competence and compassion, an America that lives up to the majesty of its Constitution and the simple decency of its people.

This is the America that I see, and that I am committed to as I run for President.

I ask your help.

You will always have mine.

Thank you.

Index